The Unfinished Reformation

THE WILLIAM HENRY HOOVER LECTURESHIP

ON CHRISTIAN UNITY

The Disciples Divinity House of
The University of Chicago

The William Henry Hoover Lectureship on Christian Unity was established by the Disciples Divinity House at the University of Chicago in 1945. Resources for the Lectureship are a Trust Fund established in the amount of Fifty Thousand Dollars some years prior to his death by Mr. W. H. Hoover, of North Canton, Ohio. The purpose of the Fund was designated as the promotion of Christian unity, a cause for which Mr. Hoover demonstrated a life-long interest. In the past the Fund had been used for initiating publications, notably periodicals which have since become well established. With the successful launching of these enterprises it was decided that the cause of Christian unity could best be served by establishing at a major university center a lectureship on Christian unity, no such lectureship having yet come into existence. The Disciples Divinity House of the University of Chicago was asked to accept Mr. Hoover's Trust for the purpose of sponsoring a lectureship on Christian unity.

The intention of the Lectureship is that each lecturer shall be a distinguished Christian churchman of this or some other country, whose experience, research and knowledge eminently qualify him to discuss the problem of Christian unity and to make a positive contribution toward closer co-operation of the many Christian denominations and the ultimate unity of the Church of Christ.

The Hoover Lectures

THE UNFINISHED REFORMATION

by

Charles Clayton Morrison

HARPER & BROTHERS, PUBLISHERS, NEW YORK

Library of Congress Catalogue Card Number: 52-11079

DEDICATED

*To the Memory of
My Father and Mother
The Rev. Hugh Tucker Morrison
and
Anna Macdonald Morrison*

Contents

Contents

Foreword

THE NAMING OF this book has caused me some perplexity. I had assumed that its title would be, "The Idea of a United Church." This had the virtue of being an exact description of its purpose and its content. But that title seemed to please none of my friends, whose advice I asked. They felt that a less formal and more suggestive name could be chosen that would truthfully represent its content and perhaps distinguish it from the many important books now appearing which deal with the subject of Christian unity. Searching for another name, I asked myself this question: What distinctive idea in the book would I desire to stand out most prominently and which, at the same time, would suggest the thesis that runs through all its chapters? I came to believe that the conception of the ecumenical movement as the re-emergence in Protestantism of the unfinished task of the Reformation was such an idea. Hence, the book was christened with its present title.

Its scope is expressly delimited to American Protestantism. This does not imply unconcern for the Christendom-wide movement for Christian unity which came to a head in the organization of the World Council of Churches at Amsterdam in 1948. On the contrary, my profound sympathy with that larger and more inclusive undertaking is presupposed. But we should not allow the glamour of the more remote ideal to obscure the obligation which the near-by situation of American Protestantism lays upon us. The problem of achieving unity on a world scale will be solved more readily if many lesser units of world Christianity provide actual demonstrations of church union. The most convenient, natural and promising of these units is the church within a particular nation. Each national church is a distinct entity and will continue as a distinct entity even when it is ecclesiastically united in a world-wide church. When, therefore, we limit our consideration of the problem of church union to the American scene, we are doing so as full partners in the ecumenical movement as a whole.

In accepting this limitation upon our present outlook we shall have to ignore some of the fascinating drama which marks the gathering together of representatives of many Christian traditions hitherto not too well acquainted with one another. The novelty and color of such a gathering is likely to cause us to exaggerate the realism of its concrete achievements. This universal approach must be accompanied by parallel movements within the national units of the world church lest the total ecumenical movement may find itself arguing endlessly over academic points of theology and church order. American Protestantism is such a unit, and the movement for the union of its churches is actually more advanced here than in any other country. Thus in concentrating our attention upon a united Protestantism in our own country we are not only adopting a convenient simplification of the ecumenical problem but making a major contribution to its world-wide solution.

A further delimitation of our task might seem so obvious that it could go without saying. But it will not be amiss to say that in centering our attention upon Protestantism we must not be diverted by any attempt to include Roman Catholicism as a factor in our problem. This would only confuse and unprofitably complicate the main issues which concern us, and delay action. The differences between Roman Catholicism and Protestantism are crucial and insoluble short of the radical transformation of one or the other. Therefore, to be diverted from our search for Protestant unity by a sentimental consideration of reconciliation with Roman Catholicism would be like dropping the bone to seize the shadow.

In delimiting the scope of our undertaking we should recognize also a certain marginal indefiniteness in the word "Protestantism." In the United States, numerous religious cults and denominations have emerged on and beyond the periphery of historical Protestantism. Some of these have no appreciable points of contact with

Protestant ideas, aims or feeling. Others, though sincerely evangelical, emphasize idiosyncrasies of doctrine and practice which isolate them, not only from evangelical Protestantism, but from one another. They have not been touched with the spirit of the ecumenical movement and any participation in church union would in all probability not appeal to them. Their peculiarities should not be allowed to complicate the undertaking to achieve a united Protestantism.

It is not necessary to define the boundaries of Protestant territory, and we shall have no occasion to make distinctions among the evangelical denominations as to which ones are and which are not responsive to the ecumenical imperative. We shall be dealing with Protestantism in gross terms. The considerations that will occupy our attention will be addressed equally to those denominations which are ardently committed to this cause, those which are but mildly committed, and those which, though truly evangelical, seem as yet quite indifferent to any proposal of change in the prevailing sectarian system. Each denomination must decide for itself in which of these categories it should be included.

We have before us the whole body of historical Protestantism whose denominations freely acknowledge their affinity with one another in terms of the evangelical Christian faith. These denominations represent, roughly, 92 per cent of the membership of Protestant churches in the United States. Most of them have felt the impact of the ecumenical movement in greater or less degree. Even among those which have been more lightly touched there is an appreciable minority who share in the ecumenical awakening. By and large, we may say that the Protestant denominations which participate in the National Council of Churches of Christ represent that portion of Protestantism from which the ecumenical ideal may expect the most ready and positive response to a sound proposal for further development of Protestant unity.

Perhaps I should say something about my use of the word "ecumenical," a term whose recent rapid and widespread adoption in the vocabulary of Protestantism is little short of phenomenal. Prior to 1937, the word had been only casually used in the speech and literature of the movement for Christian unity. But it remained for the late Archbishop William Temple, chairman of the Edinburgh Conference of 1937, to give it a kind of "official" coinage as the titular term for the movement. It is an old and distinguished word, used from near the beginning of Christian history to express the universal character of Christianity and the Christian Church. Thus an ecumenical council was a council constituted of representatives of the world-wide church. The term "ecumenical" differs etymologically from "catholic" (with a small "c") in that the latter, while expressing the idea of universality, also expresses the idea of unity in faith and order.

The new movement for Christian unity needed a word that would express both the concept of universality and of unity in faith and order. The word "catholic" itself would have been perfectly suited to serve this need. But the presence of a great church that carried "Catholic" in its title caused ambiguity and confusion in its use by the non-Roman churches. Thus the term "ecumenical," for which, naturally, a divided Protestantism had had virtually no use, was brought forward with the idea that it would eventually, by actual usage as the title for the movement for Christian unity, take on the whole meaning of "catholic." This has proved to be the outcome, and "ecumenical" now has the identical meaning of "catholic" (in its generic sense). I have used the term with its enriched meaning.

Throughout these chapters the reader will sense not only a strong feeling of urgency but a spirit of confident hope. I believe that the union of American Protestantism is practicable, and that it is much nearer realization than many suppose. The book has been written to substantiate this belief by projecting a conceptual envisagement of the goal and by a candid analysis of the issues that must be resolved in its attainment. In appraising the prospect of such a union, one who stands too closely within his own denominational tradition is likely to exaggerate the differences and difficulties that must be surmounted in attaining it. His judgment will tend to be pessimistic. Just as one who has not deeply identified himself with any denomination is likely to minimize the problem; his judgment of the future tends to an irresponsible optimism.

But there is another position from which one may see the situation and appraise the future with realism. I might call it a position of "detached attachment," adopting a phrase used, I believe, by Aldous Huxley. Applied to the appraisal of the prospect of church union, this phrase means that the observer stands loyally within his own denomination, sharing all its sensitivities—ideological, historical and procedural; but at the same time, without dislodging these attachments, he is sufficiently detached to see them in relation with the ideological, historical and procedural sensitivities of other Christians. In this position of detached attachment he is able not only to see the differences among the denominations but to *see through them,* to discover similarities long hidden under opaque verbalisms, to distinguish real obstacles from illusory and trivial ones, to find common meanings in dissimilar practices, and therefore to discern possibilities of reconciliation and union which the completely detached or the completely attached observer is unable to see.

I wish I dared to claim that this book represents the realism of such a reconciler. I can only say that, more by instinct than by a deliberately chosen method, I find that my thought has actually moved in this dimension, with whatever shortcomings the reader must judge. I sincerely believe that the problem of a united Protestantism has been made far more difficult than the situation warrants. A realistic analysis of its difficulties, a broad conception of its goal and a penetrating exposure of the precise locus of the sin of our sectarianism, together with an honest recognition of the ecumenical spirit and practice which already pervade the churches, should, it seems to me, open the way to a confident hope for a not too distant consummation.

These chapters constitute the William Henry Hoover Lectures on Christian Unity for 1951. The first four, considerably condensed, were delivered at the University of Chicago where this lectureship is established by the Disciples Divinity House, an affiliate of the University. The other five chapters are a continuation of the theme only partially treated in the delivered lectures.

When I think of the eminence of my three predecessors in this lectureship—Bishop Dun, Professor Horton and Bishop Oxnam —I am fully aware of the honor of standing in such an "apostolic succession." But when I reflect upon the fact that the choice of the fourth lecturer fell upon one who has lived for many years within a five-minute walk of Mandel Hall where the lectures are delivered—well, I know that, in addition to whatever qualifications it was assumed that I possessed, the friendly feeling of my long-time neighbors, Dean Blakemore and his associates, must have played an appreciable part in their decision. I can only say that I accepted the task, not only as an honor, but as a most congenial obligation.

CHARLES CLAYTON MORRISON

Chicago
January 10, 1953

The Unfinished Reformation

I

The Ecumenical Awakening

IT IS NOT AN OVERSTATEMENT to say that the ecumenical movement is the most arresting and significant development in modern
Christianity. This movement is concerned with the general
problem presented by the multiplicity of separate and independent churches into which the historical Christian Church has
been differentiated. It has arisen from the widespread conviction
among Christians of many names that these divisions in the church
are unnecessary, unworthy, deplorable and actually sinful. The
ecumenical movement represents an awakening of Christian
intelligence and conscience to the truth that, in the will of God,
the Church of Christ should be one church. Under the solemn
sense of this divine imperative, the most distinguished and trusted
leaders of the non-Roman churches throughout the world—ecclesiastics, theologians, missionaries, parish ministers and enlightened laymen—have united in a concerted endeavor to find ways
and means to bring this united church into visible and empirical
realization. This is the ecumenical movement.

It came dramatically to a head at Amsterdam in 1948 when the
World Council of Churches was born. One hundred and fifty
different denominations or churches have taken membership in
this ecumenical fellowship. They still maintain their separate
identities and autonomies. But they are federally joined together
for co-operative work and Christian witness and in the pursuit of
the goal of a united church.

We shall be concerned with only one segment of this world-wide
ecumenical movement, that is, with the churches of Protestantism
in the United States. The problem of achieving a united Protes-

1

tantism in America is, admittedly, no simple one. But it is obviously less complex and more readily amenable to a solution than that envisaged on a world scale. We can therefore undertake to deal with it with more realistic promise of success in a proximate future. Besides, Protestantism in the United States has already made more progress toward the ecumenical goal than is true of the churches in any other major country. This movement in its contemporary phase really emerged first in the United States. And it has developed further in terms of interdenominational fellowship, and in actual commitment, than is the case elsewhere. This should lend encouragement to our present undertaking which is delimited to the scene of American Protestantism.

THE PROTESTANT SCENE IN THE UNITED STATES

Looking at the religious situation in the United States, the most striking feature which arrests the attention of the observer is the multiplicity of its separate and independent denominations or churches. No other country presents a comparable picture. The *Year Book of the American Churches* lists 256 religious bodies. But this includes many non-Protestant and non-Christian as well as Protestant bodies. In order to get a true picture of Protestantism we must undertake a series of subtractions from this inclusive list. The Roman Catholic Church, the largest single religious body in the United States, counts one in the list; the Jewish bodies count three; the Eastern Orthodox count ten; the Mormons count six. Subtract twenty. Then there are certain cults, more or less theosophical in character, which are definitely beyond the borders of evangelical Protestantism and unassimilable to it—perhaps 25 of these. Subtract 25. We have remaining 211 denominations which, in varying degrees, and with some charity, may be called Protestant. Someone has described the Protestant scene in this country as an "ecclesiastical zoo." This is a fitting characterization of a scene which exhibits all sorts of religious wild life, each specimen in its own separate sectarian cage.

But it gives an unfair picture of Protestantism and unnecessarily complicates the ecumenical problem to use this overall figure without further breakdown. For about 140 of these bodies are small, some of them tiny, all of them more or less peculiar and ineffective groups, with memberships below 25,000 and many with as few as 100 or 200 persons represented in two or three local congregations. Yet each counts as one in the statistics. Most of these groups exist in the backwaters of American culture and have become static. The total membership of these 140 bodies amounts to less than one-half of 1 per cent of the Protestant total. They do not and should not complicate the gross problem of uniting American Protestantism. Subtract 140, then, from 211. This leaves 71 denominations of more than 25,000 members each, which account for more than 99 per cent of the Protestant total. But the ecumenical problem can be further simplified.

The great bulk of American Protestantism is contained in 50 denominations whose memberships range from 50,000 to nearly nine million each. These represent 92 per cent of the 48 million members of our Protestant churches. It is with the denominations in this top bracket that the ecumenical movement is realistically concerned. This picture of Protestant divisions is bad enough, but it puts the problem in a more manageable light than the bare statistics would indicate. Thirty of these denominations are members of the National Council of Churches, and are therefore in some degree advanced in what might be called their ecumenical education. It is within this group of churches that the aspiration for a united church has emerged. As a realistic procedure, at the present stage, our consideration of the many problems involved in the achievement of a united church can, without prejudice to other bodies, be limited to this group of evangelical Protestant denominations. The fissiparous tendency which has characterized the whole of Protestantism has run riot in the United States.

Any judgment upon the variegated aspect which this picture presents must, however, take account of the historical fact that many of these denominations represent importations from other countries, especially from Europe. The immigrants who peopled the original thirteen colonies brought with them their distinctive types of church life and organization. As the population movement flowed westward the familiar forms of church organization were carried along and deposited at the ever-advancing frontier. This cross-country migration was predominantly Protestant until the middle of the nineteenth century when unrestricted immigration brought many millions of Roman Catholics and Jews to our shores. Our religious diversity is therefore not altogether indigenous, but in large measure is an importation from the Old World.

However, this is only half of the truth. For, while the ground plan of Protestant divisions was laid by immigration from European Protestantism, the picture as of today presents a far greater number of denominations that are indigenous to this country. They represent defections and subdivisions of the earlier denominations. We thus have in the United States twenty Methodist denominations, twenty-four Baptist, twenty Lutheran, ten Presbyterian. The Disciples of Christ have become two bodies, the defectionist group taking the name "Churches of Christ." The Quakers have divided into nine sects. Among the major bodies, the Episcopalians have no record of serious defection, nor have the Congregationalists since the Unitarian rupture of a century and a half ago.

Many denominations which sprang from existing churches have taken new names and are not included in the foregoing list of denominational families—such, for example, as the Seventh-day Adventists, various Pentecostal groups, the Assembly of God, the Church of God and an unpicturable network of many others. Making due allowance for any simplification of the overall statistics, the picture of our Protestant sectarianism remains solemnizing and challenging. Our American soil has seemed to provide an ideal spawning ground for the proliferation of sectarian churches beyond anything known elsewhere in Christendom. How shall we account for this unique phenomenon? I suggest three possible explanations.

1. The principle of religious liberty guaranteed by our Constitution tended to be carried over from the political sphere to the sphere of religion, that is, from the state to the church. This psychological transference was more or less unconscious. The neutrality and impartiality of the American state toward all forms of religion subtly predisposed Protestant people to assume that the creation of a new denomination was not only legally irreproachable but could be religiously approved. "This is a free

country, isn't it?" became the colloquial justification by which the withdrawal of a disaffected group to form a new denomination was appreciably relieved of any moral or religious reproach. James Madison who, more than any other statesman, was responsible for the First Amendment, had said, "The more independent religious bodies, the more secure would the government be in its freedom from church influence." The Protestant mind easily, though fallaciously, tended to assume that if this multiplication of denominations was good for the government it was also good for religion. Sectarian diversity was therefore accepted as an ecclesiastical virtue and any Christian inhibition on further division was not seriously felt.

2. A denomination from whose membership a disaffected group threatened to secede was in no position to present an effective religious reason why it should not do so. The parent denomination itself had originated in essentially the same kind of situation as that which it now confronted in the threatened secession of its own children. With what consistency, therefore, could the parent now chide her children for doing what she herself had done a century or two centuries or three centuries ago?

When we view the whole history of Protestant denominationalism, it appears as a long series of schismatic chain reactions— one schism producing other schisms and they in turn producing others, in a process which continued up to, let us say, the late nineteenth century. Prophets of church unity periodically appeared throughout this history who endeavored to arrest this chain reaction, but their valiant efforts were futile. The denominational system was generally regarded as established, as a normal expression of Protestantism.

The individualism of the time and of the country provided a favorable environment for the proliferation of denominations. It also provided an unfavorable environment for Protestantism to think in terms of the church catholic. The church, as church, had virtually passed out of the Protestant mind which was now preoccupied with the churches. The church catholic had become the church invisible, a transcendental or spiritual entity, not a historical and empirical entity. There was no conceivable limit to the number of denominational churches which could legitimately arise. The creation of one more denomination by secession from an existing denomination could hardly be conceived as violating any fundamental Christian principle. Indeed, it was implicitly assumed and often explicitly argued that the rivalries among the denominations would stimulate and intensify the spiritual life of all the churches, to the benefit of Christianity as a whole. This result would follow in much the same manner as *laissez-faire* competition in the economic order was supposed to produce a net result of harmony and the maximum welfare of all.

3. Another factor explaining the uninhibited spawning of so many denominations on American soil may be found in the psychology of the frontier. Until modern times, the American people have always lived on the frontier. Geographically, it was an ever-moving frontier, and behind its advancing border there was going on a progressive consolidation and stabilization of political, cultural and religious institutions. But even so, the frontier psychology remained after the frontier had passed on. This was the dominant characteristic of the American spirit, not only in the newer west but in the older east. It took the form of a lusty independence, a distinct feeling of having broken with the past. In this New World the people now confronted not only the opportunity but the necessity of fashioning new institutions with only a dim reference to the past and to the Old World. Thus the continuities of history were appreciably severed and the sense of loyalty to a heritage whose values should be conserved was dimmed. This spirit of self-sufficiency and independence pervaded the whole political, cultural and social life of the people. It also pervaded their religious life.

Naturally, the concept of the church catholic, the universal church of history, could hardly be assimilated by a mentality conditioned by such an environment. It would seem vague, unempirical and irrelevant. The church, as church, was indeed a reality, but hardly a historical reality. It was an invisible and transcendental reality. The denomination had taken its place. The denomination was the empirical ecclesiastical reality. The country was populated from the beginning by denominational dissenters who had broken with the historic church in the mother countries. In the New World their sense of denominational independence was reinforced and stimulated by their consciousness that a great ocean separated them from the milieu in which their ecclesiastical independence had been achieved. They were now on their own, completely detached from any disciplinary restraints. For them, the Bible completely supplanted history, tradition, heritage, catholicity. The right of private interpretation was the principle upon which they had won their independence. Over against this private right there was no adequate counterweight of discipline to inhibit defection and secession from an existing denomination. In the intense controversies over the meaning of Scripture, new denominations arose, all justified by their private interpretation of the Bible. Thus the soil and atmosphere of American freedom encouraged the anarchic proliferation of denominationalism.

But we have no grounds upon which to pronounce any harsh criticism or moral judgment upon the founders of our denominations. They were the children of a different age from that in which we live. They were caught in the denominational system of chain reactions and a just judgment demands that they be regarded and remembered with the charity of historical understanding.

A NEW SPIRIT IN PROTESTANTISM

We live in a different time and a new kind of world. Our Christian faith, in accordance with our Lord's own promise, has been discovering new meanings in his gospel and new imperatives in the mission of his church. Looking with fresh eyes upon the scene of American Protestantism with its forces separated in a multiplicity of walled-in ecclesiastical bodies, Christians began to say to one another, Surely, these divisions among Christ's followers are not the will of God! This they began hesitantly to say to one another in the late years of the nineteenth century. American society was settling down with a new sense of stability and permanent neighborhood after the long period of intensive pioneering at the edge of an ever-advancing frontier. These early expressions of disquiet over our sectarian divisions marked the humble beginning of what is now called the ecumenical movement.

We shall view the development of this ecumenical idea in two perspectives: first, in the shorter perspective of its emergence and growth in the United States; second, in the longer perspective of historical Protestantism.

First, then, let us trace the stages of growth of the ecumenical spirit in the United States. The beginning, as we have just said, was in the hesitant recognition of the anomalous character of sectarian divisions among Christ's followers. In the late nineteenth century, a new spirit had begun to manifest itself in the more settled communities of the country. There was a growing sense of neighborhood and community. Ministers remained longer in their parishes and thus had a better opportunity to become acquainted with one another. Fraternizing with their colleagues across denominational lines, they discovered common interests and responsibilities in the local community. Local ministerial associations were formed. Occasional union meetings of the local churches were held, especially on patriotic holidays. The churches even found ways of uniting in evangelistic meetings. Evangelists like D. L. Moody and others after him proved that the essential evangelical gospel could be preached in a manner that transcended denominational peculiarities and arrested the attention and response of the whole community as no single denominational effort could do. The sharp edges of sectarian sensitivities were appreciably worn down in an atmosphere of increasing mutual confidence and respect.

At the turn of the twentieth century, this more flexible spirit of local fraternization and co-operation had developed to the point where it gave rise to the suggestion that it be formalized on a national interdenominational scale. How this could be done was not difficult to discover. The principle for such a project was already at hand in the Constitution of the federal government with which everybody was familiar. It was proposed that the denominations form a federal union following, in a general way, the pattern on which the several states had joined together to form the national union, but without involving any legislative or legal principle. The purpose would be purely for co-operative action in those areas where the denominations shared a sense of common responsibility.

The Federal Council of the Churches of Christ, organized in 1908, was the outcome of a decade of deliberation and widespread discussion. It was difficult at first for the churches to believe that their denominational independence and autonomy—their "states' rights," so to speak—would not be encroached upon by the new federation. This suspicion kept a number of denominations from joining the federal union, and some never did join. But gradually the ranks of these self-conscious and overcautious denominations were decimated by one after another taking membership in the Federal Council. Parallel with this development on the national scale, the federal principle was carried to the churches in the several states and the local communities. Over 800 state and city Councils of Churches are now unitedly co-operating on this principle.

Another parallel movement has been the merger of various denominations two by two, and sometimes three. Since 1906 there have been fifteen such mergers. Among the more recent of these are: the union of the Congregational and Christian denominations, now known by the name Congregational Christian, with a membership well over a million; the reunion of three Methodist bodies—Northern, Southern and Methodist Protestant—to form the Methodist Church, with a membership of nearly nine million, the largest Protestant body in the United States; the merger of the Evangelical Synod of North America and the Reformed Church, with 708,000 members; the merger of the Evangelical Church and the Church of the United Brethren in Christ under the name of the United Evangelical Church, with 712,000 members. It is impossible to omit mention of the union of the Methodists, Presbyterians and Congregationalists of Canada in 1925, to form the United Church of Canada with over 800,000 members. The Canadian union has been both an inspiration and an example to the churches on the American side of the border.

To these actual unions that have taken place in recent years we should add the formally and officially completed preparations for the merger of the Congregational Christian and the Evangelical and Reformed churches (each representing an earlier union of two denominations) whose imminent consummation was estopped by the astonishing decree of a New York court. The case was appealed to a higher court where a sweeping reversal of the trial court's judgment was declared. It has now been appealed to the United States Supreme Court and it is confidently expected that the later judgment will be upheld.

However, the evidence for the existence of a deep yearning toward an ecumenical Protestantism is not limited to the mergers which have actually been consummated. It also appears in conversations and negotiations between two or more denominations now actively under way. There is a strong movement among the twenty Lutheran bodies toward some form of intra-Lutheran solidarity. Conversations between the Northern Baptists and Disciples of Christ have been encouraged by formal action of the general conventions of the two bodies. For several years the Presbyterian and Episcopal churches carried on officially approved negotiations looking toward a union of these two communions. This came to a temporary standstill in 1947, chiefly because of the intransigent opposition of the Anglo-catholic minority in the Episcopal Church. Current negotiations between the Presbyterian Church, U.S.A. (Northern), the Presbyterian Church, U.S. (Southern) and the United Presbyterian Church, for organic union, give every promise of ultimate success. Two of the less numerically strong denominations—the United Presbyterian and the Reformed Church in America, each with a membership of about 200,000—recently voted down a merger proposal submitted to their respective presbyteries. But the fact that a union effort got so far in these two conservative denominations is not without significance and encouragement.

The most significant of all these negotiations for union is that in which nine denominations, representing a total membership of 17 million, or 35 per cent of American Protestantism, are involved. This is commonly called the Greenwich movement, a name derived from the city in Connecticut in which its first plenary session was held.

Many less formal evidences of the loosening of sectarian restraints under the influence of the ecumenical ideal deserve our attention. It must suffice to mention (1) the Community Church movement whose more than 2,000 local churches are either independently undenominational or only unecclesiastically affiliated with some denomination, and (2) the numerous mergers of two or more parish churches in innumerable local communities. Local churches of these two types pay an appreciable price by accepting a somewhat nondescript or orphanlike status for what may seem to others a premature attempt to realize, even partially, the ecumenical imperative in their immediate communities. But they will be the first to give ecclesiastical allegiance to an ecumenical Protestantism when it emerges.

Several omens of a nonecclesiastical nature should be mentioned. One of these is the growing undenominational character of the leading theological seminaries of the country which still retain their denominational connection. At the University of Chicago, four denominational seminaries are united in a Federated Theological Faculty. Another encouraging omen is the establishment of the William Henry Hoover Lectureship on Christian Unity by the Disciples Divinity House at the University of Chicago. Still another sign of the times is the growing indifference of the laity to denominational considerations when choosing a church affiliation on moving from one community to another. Closely related to this interflow of members among all denominations is the increasingly frequent transfer of ministers from the pulpit of one denomination to that of another.

All the evidence to which we have drawn attention up to this point seems clearly to indicate that the walls of our sectarian isolationism are in a process of crumbling. The denomination appears to be losing much of its earlier significance.

Let us return now to the Federal Council and to the most recent development of the federal principle on the national scale. So wisely was the Federal Council administered for forty years, and so fruitful were its operations, that the denominations determined to broaden its functions so as to include seven other interdenominational agencies under the federal principle. The plan adopted at

Cleveland, Ohio, in December, 1950, was for these eight agencies, including the Federal Council, to unite in creating a new federation, called the National Council of Churches of Christ in the United States. Like the Federal Council, the new National Council was created by the official action of the denominations adhering to it. Structurally, it follows the same lines and, functionally, it absorbs all the activities of its predecessor, while taking on the activities of the seven other agencies.

It is worth special note, however, that three of these agencies bring into the federal union certain activities which, forty years ago, the denominations would hardly have allowed any but their own denominational hand to touch. These are home missions, foreign missions and Christian education. Their inclusion in the National Council marks an appreciable deepening of the feeling of Protestant unity. For these three functions come nearer being ecclesiastical functions than any which the denominations had ever committed to a federated responsibility. The Federal Council had been constituted in a manner that limited its operation to strictly nonecclesiastical fields. So also, in theory, is the new National Council. Its constitution provides especially meticulous safeguards of denominational autonomy in the functioning of its missionary and religious education divisions. There is no suggestion here that these restrictions could ever be disregarded. What is suggested is that the denominations themselves, having taken this cautious and timid step in recognition of the ecumenical nature of foreign missions, home missions and religious education, will gradually find the way to emancipate them completely from the scandal of sectarian control and administration.

Plainly, American Protestantism is experiencing an ecumenical awakening. For the past three-quarters of a century its feeling and its conscience have been gradually evolving out of their enthrallment in the denominational system. We have seen how this awakening began in simple, natural fraternization of church leaders across denominational lines; how this fraternal spirit prompted the undertaking of informal projects of co-operation in the common life of the local community and in united evangelistic efforts; how this informal local co-operation gave rise to a formalized co-operation on a national scale under the name of the Federal Council of Churches, and how this federal idea has been extended to every state and more than 700 local communities; how it has recently been expanded in the new National Council of Churches to include seven additional functions, some of them bordering on the ecclesiastical area hitherto jealously reserved to inviolable denominational autonomy. And parallel with this evolution of federal union, we have seen the phenomenon of particular denominations merging in organic unions, and other similar unions now in process of negotiation.

All this seems clearly to add up to this conclusion: that American Protestantism is becoming aware that its denominational system is a decadent survival of an era that is past. Few and apologetic are those who now defend it. The occasions and controversies out of which these denominations arose are now being viewed in their historical context. In this view it is clear that the historical situation has profoundly changed. The issues that once divided the churches have largely lost their vitality in an age of greater enlightenment, of less brittle temper, and of a more tolerant and flexible feeling for co-operation, fellowship and unity. The achievements which we have just reviewed could hardly have been imagined a century ago. Nevertheless, there are few among us today who regard these achievements as the ultimate goal. Rather, they are the promise of something much better, more majestic, more heart-whole, to which our striving and God's providence are leading American Protestantism.

WHENCE COMES THE ECUMENICAL AWAKENING?

Let us now ask and endeavor to answer the following questions: How shall we explain this ecumenical awakening, this yearning for the emergence of the true Church of Christ so long hidden by our man-made denominational system? From what source has it come? Has it come from some source outside of Protestantism and therefore requiring a fundamental change in our conception of Protestantism? Or has it sprung from the genius of Protestantism itself? To answer these questions we shall have to shift our perspective from the American scene to a longer perspective that will include the Reformation of the sixteenth century.

Roman Catholic critics and opponents of Protestantism assert that the sectarian principle was inherent in the Reformation. They regard the contemporary movement for Protestant unity as a futile and illusory ideal. Such unity, it is said, can be achieved only by a return to the bosom of "Mother Church" which the Reformation and its sectarian progeny left behind in the sixteenth century. Many Protestants allow this reproach to go unchallenged. Independent historians also have too easily assumed that the differentiation of Protestantism into innumerable sectarian churches is proof that this development has been an expression both of the complete indifference of the Reformers to the unity of the church, and of an inherently defective principle in the nature of Protestantism. By and large, we may say that historians have tended to read back into the Reformation the spirit and attitude of the modern sectarian bodies, and especially of modern German Lutheranism.

Within the second quarter of the present century, however, there has been a genuine revival of historical research in the field of the Reformation, especially among German scholars. Much data hitherto unknown or disregarded has been brought to light. On our side of the ocean, our American scholars have conspicuously participated in this research and in the interpretation of the total body of material which it has produced. Outstanding in this work are Professors Wilhelm Pauck, of the University of Chicago, John T. McNeill, of Union Theological Seminary, and Roland A. Bainton, of Yale Divinity School.

Over twenty years ago, Professor McNeill published a book entitled *Unitive Protestantism*,[1] which is now out of print. There should be such a wide demand for it from the ranks of thoughtful churchmen as to insure its republication. This work should take its place as the indispensable handbook of the modern movement for an ecumenical Protestantism. It was the first scholarly attempt to

---

[1] Abingdon-Cokesbury Press, 1930.

enter the field of historical Protestantism from the particular angle of its ccumcnical implications.

Professor McNeill set himself the task which we now confront, namely, to inquire whether the present ecumenical movement is an exotic phenomenon in Protestantism, or whether it springs from the genius of Protestantism itself. This same inquiry can be stated conversely in the form in which our present discussion has led up to it: whether the denominational system is really indigenous and integral to Protestantism or an alien growth upon it, like the barnacles that impede the movement and imperil the vogage of a great ship.

It has long been known and often referred to that, throughout Protestant history, prophetic voices have been raised calling for Christian unity. The names of Dury, Calixtus, Comeñius, Ussher, Stillingfleet, Grotius, Baxter, Leibnitz and many others adorn the record of post-Reformation attempts to arouse the Protestant mind to a concern for a united church. But their prophetic labors ended in pathetic futility. Because their voices were unheeded by their contemporaries, it has been too hastily concluded that their own inspiration must have come from outside of Protestantism; and from the lack of any substantial response it was also inferred that Protestantism was traditionally and, one might say, congenitally, committed to the sectarian system.

Professor McNeill was far from satisfied with this hasty interpretation. He insisted upon looking deeper into the historical situation in which these prophets appeared. He declared that "Protestantism never was content with its divided state," and that if we look more carefully into the historical situation in which these inspired idealists appeared and into the particular proposals which they made, we would find other and more adequate explanations of the failure of their efforts. Thus his inquiry led him into the Reformation itself to discover whether the very fountain of historical Protestantism gave forth the bitter waters of sectarian division. His inquiry disclosed abundant proof that the spirit and intention of the Reformers was explicitly, actively and gravely concerned for the union of Protestantism, and that their concept of the Church of Christ was unqualifiedly ecumenical.

Stating the case, from this point on, in our own way, while acknowledging our indebtedness to the scholarly authorities mentioned, as well as others, we can now positively affirm that the ecumenical awakening which we are now experiencing is the resurgence under fairer conditions of the same ecumenical faith that informed the Reformation from the beginning.

We cannot understand the historical situation unless we keep in mind the fact that the Reformation emerged almost simultaneously in three different places—in Germany, Switzerland and England. There were, in reality, three independent movements of reform. Their separateness was not due to schism within a single movement; it was a geographical separation. The problem of union was not one of re-union, but of bringing together these unacquainted parts of a common movement. In this effort, the conflicting political interests of the three countries inevitably complicated the work of the Reformers. But all the leaders of these separate movements cherished a profound concern for such a union and carried on extended correspondence and numerous formal conferences in the hope of achieving it.

Luther and Melanchthoñ, Zwingli and Bullinger, Calvin and Bucer, Archbishop Cranmer and virtually all those whose names adorn the record of this heroic period shared earnestly and persistently in this attempt. Plans for union were prolifically produced and discussed on all sides until near the end of the sixteenth century. With the passing from the scene of the great pioneers of the Reformation, these attempts at rapprochement gradually waned and classic Protestantism settled down in the historical molds of Lutheranism, Presbyterianism and Anglicanism in which its multiple origin had cast it. Then began the long process of schismatic defections in each of these tributaries, a process which the ecumenical movement in our time is striving to overcome.

Why did these earnest and vigorous attempts to unite the separate streams of the Reformation meet with repeated disappointment and ultimate defeat? Obviously, in view of the attitude of the Reformers themselves, it was not because the principle of sectarianism was inherent in the Reformation. We must look more closely into the actual but futile negotiations and into the circumstantial situations in which they took place. As one reads this history, two explanations stand out above many incidental ones as the prime causes of the abortive result of the long and persistent efforts to unite Reformation Protestantism in an ecumenical body. One explanation was the unchallenged acceptance of the interdependence of church and state. The other was the inherent impossibility, then, or now, or ever, of achieving unity on the basis of theological agreement. Let us examine these two explanations.

1. The church had been tied in with the political state for a thousand years, and the great Reformers could not bring themselves to challenge this interdependent relation. They accepted uncritically and as a matter of course the long established Roman Catholic theory that the welfare and unity of society required such a union of church and state. At all three of its geographical sources, the Reformation followed the logical leading of this theory. How closely the origin and early development of Protestantism was bound up with the political interests of princes, kings and the emperor has always been recognized by historians, and need not be denied by Protestants. Hostile critics of Protestantism like to point out that, had it not been for the protection given Luther by the Elector Frederick whose favor toward the Reformation was heavily mixed with political interests, the German Reformation might have been hardly more than a tempest in a teapot. The intention of these critics is to cast a shadow upon the religious character of the Reformation.

But this puristic way of appraising historical events is a betrayal of history itself. Is it not true that all great creative ideas and events enter the stream of history in close association with, and even dependence upon, some irrelevancy or some incongruity? Does not truth often come leaning upon the crutch of some error before it finds strength to walk alone? Certainly this was the way Christianity itself originally emerged. Christ came in "the fullness of time," which means, in one of its aspects, that historical conditions, including many irrelevancies and incongruities, co-operatively aided the spread of his gospel. It is no reflection on the Reformation to admit that it came closely intertwined with the interests of rulers and classes some of whose motives were quite irrelevant to, and often incongruous with, the religious passion that motivated the Reformers.

What concerns us here is the fact that the Reformers, in their effort to unite the three tributaries of the Reformation, were unable to strip from their problem its political associations and confront it as a strictly religious and ecclesiastical undertaking. Notoriously was this true of Archbishop Cranmer who intensely desired to effect a union of the Anglican Reformation with its continental counterparts. We can understand his failure if we simply remember that he was Archbishop of Canterbury under Henry VIII, who, having broken with the papacy, had made himself the head of the Church of England.

As for Calvin, it should be noted that the church at Geneva was less involved in European politics than the German and English churches. This was because Geneva had established its own state which, in effect, it ruled as a Protestant theocracy. This fact probably accounts in part for the greater amenability and initiative which Calvin and his associates displayed in the pursuit of the union ideal.

But in Germany we find Luther, great ecumenical churchman that he was in his ecclesiological theory, so sensitive to the political interests and policies of the princes and the emperor that these interests played an inevitable subconscious role in determining his attitude to the various plans for union. A single illustration will reveal the inhibitory effect of the involvement of the Reformation with the political situation of Europe.

That famous episode, the colloquy at Marburg between Luther and Zwingli, designed to unite the Swiss and German Reformations, gives us an insight into the whole pattern of proceedings in which all negotiations for union were carried on. For forty years, these efforts were frustrated by the religiously irrelevant orientation of the Reformation in political affairs. The story of Luther's final refusal to take the hand of Zwingli with the querulous explanation, "You are of another spirit than we," has been often told as if it were a clear case of difference of biblical interpretation that separated them. The words, "This is my body," Luther declared meant literally the objective presence of Christ in some form in or with the elements of the Eucharist. To Zwingli, these words were a rhetorical way of saying, "This signifies my body."

But their final deadlock on the proposed union cannot be explained simply as due to their different interpretation of these words of Scripture. In the background of their theological discussion, there was a conflict of political interests which haunted the entire colloquy. Zwingli was at that time engaged in forming his Swiss Protestant cantons in a league with Austria against the Swiss Roman Catholic cantons. The union of German and Swiss Protestantism would greatly strengthen this project. But Luther was opposed to such a league. He saw it as rebellion against the emperor upon whom he was at that moment working to bring religious unity into the empire by means of an ecumenical council which he hoped the emperor would call. Not until the late years of his life did Luther abandon the hope of precipitating a sweeping reformation of the Roman church itself. This he knew could be accomplished only by an ecumenical council entirely free from the control of the papacy. Only in a council called by the emperor could it be expected that its members would be free from papal pressure.

This project was in the mind of Luther throughout the sessions of the Marburg colloquy. There can be no doubt that it explains his disinclination to enter the conference with Zwingli in the first place. And his querulous behavior during the conference can be explained in considerable degree by the political consequences which he foresaw in case a union with Zwingli should be consummated. Thus the entanglement and interdependence of church and state, illustrated at Marburg and reproduced in the many later attempts to achieve union, affords one explanation of the frustration of the ecumenical ideal which all the Reformers cherished as fundamental in their conception of the Church of Christ.

2. The other explanation we have stated as the inherent impossibility of achieving, then, now, or ever, any viable and permanent union on any plan requiring theological agreement. All the plans proposed for union represented the attempt to formulate a body of theological doctrine upon which the three separate

Reformation movements could agree. The range of theological agreement among them was amazingly wide and deep, considering their separate origins. Nevertheless, there existed certain doctrinal peculiarities belonging to one and not to the others. These, it was assumed, must be fully reconciled before union could take place.

It is unnecessary here to consider these specific points of difference. Our sole interest lies in the general question whether uniformity of belief, even if it could be attained, is the true and necessary basis of union in the Church of Christ. Without arguing the matter, we shall have to be content to affirm that the whole course of church history, and especially Protestant history, demonstrates that the attempt to provide a rigid and static creed, deviation from which constitutes heresy, leads to and encourages schism rather than unity.

The attempts at union in the Reformation period failed because no complete theological consensus could be achieved. From our modern point of vantage, we are able with confidence to affirm that, even if such a consensus could have been achieved, it would not have provided the union with stability and permanence. Near the beginning of his reforming career, Luther seemed to take a more liberal view. He then conceived the unity of the Reformation to rest upon the simple basis of "the forgiving love of God in Jesus Christ."

But, as the late Professor A. C. McGiffert has shown, the mind of the great Reformer changed with the years. The change was due largely in reaction to the sectarian radicals who hung on the flanks of the Reformation and caused the Reformers no end of annoyance. Neither Luther nor Zwingli nor Calvin could tolerate the libertarianism of the Anabaptists and other sectaries. In reaction against their too simple application of the twin principles of "justification by faith" and the "priesthood of all believers," Luther appreciably modified his earlier enthusiasm for the "liberty of the Christian man" and felt the necessity of creedal formulations as the basis of unity both in the German churches and in any ecumenical union of Protestantism.

In addition to his determination to keep the Reformation unsullied by association with the Anabaptists, Luther, as we have

said, cherished for two decades the hope for a sweeping reformation of the Roman church. This is a fact not generally recognized by Protestants. Such a reformation, he believed, would
abolish the papacy and the sacerdotal hierarchy and reunite the
Protestant Reformation with the existing church. Thus Luther's
earlier liberalism, if we may so designate it, was tempered into a
theological conservatism by his attitude to the Anabaptists on
one hand and his hope for a thoroughgoing internal reform of
Rome on the other. Beset by these two contrary influences, between which he felt it necessary to steer a middle course, Luther
grew more and more intemperately dogmatic and could envisage
no form of union except on a creedal basis which fully embodied
his own theological ideas.

All the proposals for union, whether they originated in Germany, Switzerland or England, rested on a creedal basis. It was
assumed, with no hint of dissent, that an ecumenical union required theological uniformity. No doubt Luther's retention of the
Mass with only the slight deviation from transubstantiation was
motivated in large part by his desire to depart from the doctrine
and liturgy of the medieval church as little as conscience could
allow. To the Lutheran conception of the Lord's Supper, however,
Geneva was as irreconcilable under Calvin as Zurich had been
under Zwingli, though certain plans of union originating at
Geneva and Strassburg provided for some diversity of opinion on
this point. But Wittenberg would accept none but unqualified
uniformity of belief.

Thus the independent geographical units of the Reformation
were, before the end of the sixteenth century, frozen into permanent sectarian divisions. Lutheranism, Presbyterianism and
Anglicanism, separated from one another, became the proliferating sources of historical Protestant sectarianism.

Our analysis of the failure of the ardent and persistent efforts
for a union of classic Protestantism reveals no inherent sectarian
principle in the Reformation. On the contrary, the evidence
clearly shows that the spirit and principle of unity were distinctly
manifested in the long-continued effort to attain it. This effort was
defeated by two factors, both of them external to the genius of

Protestantism. One was the historical interlocking of the church with the state; the other was the misplaced emphasis of the Reformers upon the necessity of theological uniformity as the basis of union.

THE RESURGENCE OF THE REFORMATION SPIRIT

Let us now shift our perspective from historical Protestantism back to the shorter perspective of the American scene. Our purpose in examining classic Protestantism was to find an answer to the question whether the ecumenical awakening in modern Protestantism is an exotic phenomenon, an importation from outside of Protestantism, or whether it represents an indigenous movement springing naturally from the genius of the Reformation. Does our modern ecumenical movement have historical rootage in the essential nature of Protestantism? This is the vital question with which we are here concerned. The answer will have practical consequences. It will affect our appraisal of the ecumenical movement and our hopes for it. Moreover, it will affect our judgment of the denominational system in which Protestantism is today totally involved. If the ecumenical principle is indigenous to Protestantism we shall have a standard by which to judge our denominationalism as nothing short of an alien corruption, not only of the Church of Christ, but of Protestantism itself.

We have seen that the Reformation was itself an ecumenical awakening. It was an awakening to the real, but hidden, existence of the ecumenical church. Too easily do Protestant interpreters fall in with the Roman Catholic charge that the Reformers broke the historical continuity of the church catholic and set up a new church. While this charge may be justified in the light of the later developments of denominationalism, it does not lie justly against the Reformation. We misinterpret the Reformers when we take the doctrines of "justification by faith" and the "priesthood of all believers" as their primary insights. Profound and powerful as were these doctrines in the propaganda of the Reformation, they were embraced in a still profounder insight—their discernment of the nature of the church itself. The Reformers had no intention of breaking with the historic church. They were out to rescue the historic church from the clutch of an alien regime which had fastened itself upon it and kept it unconscious of its true nature for a thousand years.

Many Protestant ministers, with unenlightened eloquence, like to say that the Reformers "leaped across the centuries" to find the true church in the first century. This is not true history. The Reformers found the Church of Christ already here, but it was bound in what Luther called a "Babylonian captivity." It was the high task of the Reformation to emancipate this ecumenical church from its bondage to a sacerdotal authoritarian hierarchy which had stripped the church catholic of the very organs and functions by which it could manifest its true nature as the Church of Christ. This is also, word for word, a precise description of the modern ecumenical movement. Modern Protestantism is in bondage to the denominational system which has stripped the church catholic of the organs and functions by which it could manifest its true nature as the Church of Christ. The analogy between the Roman Catholic hierarchical system and the Protestant denominational system is startlingly exact in relation to the true church. In the third chapter, we shall develop and interpret this analogy in more detail.

The ecumenical awakening in our time is, thus, not an experience alien to Protestantism. It is the resurgence in Protestantism of the ecumenical awakening of the sixteenth century. As the Reformers discovered the true church behind the façade of the hierarchical institution, we are discovering it behind the façade of the denominational system. This discovery is opening our eyes to the true character of our denominationalism, and, as we shall see in succeeding chapters, is the primary cause of widespread discontent with our sectarian divisions. This discontent is developing into the conviction that our denominations represent an actual corruption of the Christian Church and that, by clinging to them, the destiny of Protestantism is precariously involved.

But this insight into the true nature of our denominations would not have emerged were it not accompanied by the deeper insight that the true church, the Church of Christ, actually exists in our midst, but is hidden from our eyes by our man-made churches. By a similar insight the great Reformers were inspired. Luther, Calvin, Zwingli, Cranmer and all the heroes and fathers of classic Protestantism were engaged in rescuing the hidden Church of Christ from a sectarian corruption. They saw that the Roman Catholic Church, despite its outward form of unity, carried within itself a scandalous schism in the body of Christ—a schism which divided the church into two parts, with Christ's people on one side and a professional class, the priestly hierarchy, on the other. The functions and responsibilities that belong only to the community of Christ's people had been taken away from them and lodged in a segment of the church, namely, the professional priesthood with the pope at its head. Thus the ecumenical church, of which alone Christ is the head, was smothered under the hierarchical system. The primary motivation of the Reformers was their determination to release the ecumenical church from its captivity to this alien regime by restoring to the community of Christ's people the responsibilities and the organs and functions of which the hierarchy had robbed it.

The ecumenical movement in our time is thus an awakening of Protestantism to the fact that it is the inheritor of an unfinished Reformation. It is motivated by the same insight which inspired the Reformers, but directed, now, not to the Roman church, but to Protestantism itself. It is an awakening to the fact that Protestantism is totally involved in a system which hides the true church and renders it empirically incapable of functioning in the world which Christ died to save.

We are not speaking cryptically, or in riddles, but in plain truth. The denominational system has superimposed its man-made sectarian structures upon the ecumenical church, thus not only dividing the true church, but rendering it invisible and empirically impotent. Our separate denominations have assumed that they could bear witness to the whole gospel of Christ. But now our eyes are being opened to the truth that only the whole church, acting as a united whole, can bear witness to the whole gospel. The world will not believe the gospel which our sectarian churches proclaim. Our Lord himself discerned this when he prayed for the unity of his church "that the world might believe."

The ecumenical awakening is a prayer arising from the heart of the hidden church as well as from the heart of Christ for the visible emergence of the ecumenical church which alone is his body. The denominational system blocks the way to the realization of this prayer. As the true church emerges from its long eclipse behind our man-made churches, our denominational walls must crumble. They are already in the process of crumbling. Strong forces both inside and outside the denominations are making breaches in the walls that separate Christians from one another. Our differences are falling into the background. Our unities are coming to the fore.

II

A Critique of Denominationalism

WE ARE HERE OPENING UP an inquiry into a phase of the problem of Christian unity which, strange to say, has not received serious attention in the literature of the ecumenical movement. What we have in mind is an inquiry into the nature of the denominational system. By directing attention to the denomination as the very nub of the problem of Christian unity, we may hope that others may be challenged to carry further the inquiry which we shall be able only to begin. In the present chapter we shall be thinking of the denomination in pragmatic terms; in the next, we shall be thinking in ecclesiological terms; and in the fourth chapter we shall be thinking in terms of the religious life. Under these three headings the denominational system will be subjected to a critical examination to discover, first, whether it is working well or ill; second, whether it is compatible with or alien to the nature of the Church of Christ; and third, whether, under the denominational system, Protestantism is able to realize and bear witness to the full values that belong to the Christian life.

Let us now address ourselves to the pragmatic question: Is the denominational system a success? Is Protestantism flourishing under it? A European visitor would call this a typically American question. The answer usually given could also be called typically American: "Of course it is a success; look at the growth of Protestant churches in numbers, in membership, in church buildings, in financial resources and in its far-flung missionary and benevolent activities." Our denominational cheer leaders assure us with statistical evidence that Protestantism, operating under the denominational system, is growing stronger with each passing

26

decade. There is no reason to challenge these statistical facts. But there is reason to challenge the cheerful inference drawn from them. Statistics provide a legitimate but not the only factor by which to measure Protestant success. Nor do they provide the most important or decisive criterion. It is quite possible that this statistical growth actually conceals from our eyes various elements of weakness and frustration.

Moreover, before drawing optimistic or complacent conclusions from the statistics of Protestant growth, we must also take into account the growth of certain other forces existing alongside of Protestantism and competing with it on the religious level. The rate of their parallel growth may actually exceed that of Protestantism. Two such forces are, obviously, secularism and Roman Catholicism—one the avowed opposite of all religion, the other a competitor of Protestantism for the soul of America. Protestant progress must therefore be measured, not merely in terms of its own absolute statistics, but in terms that are relative to the growing or declining strength of these other forces operating in the same field. Their growth or decline certainly affects the *relative* position of Protestantism. Applying this criterion of relativity, it appears indisputable that Protestantism, during the past two or three generations, has been actually and startlingly declining from its long ascendant position in American life.

Facing this disillusionizing fact, the Protestant mind cannot help asking for an explanation. It will not be satisfied with an explanation which relieves its Christian conscience of responsibility. From the very beginning of our country's history, Protestantism has been far and away the ascendant religious faith. Something must be wrong in Protestantism itself, something which explains its weakness in the presence of opposition and competition more formidable than any it has encountered in the past three centuries. We cannot concede that the Christian faith itself is unequal to the demands of a new age. Christianity can never rest content with an alibi. The Protestant conscience is aware that the church stands always under the divine judgment and is perennially in need of reformation. Instinctively, it subjects to a searching examination the form in which it conceives and presents the gospel and the manner in which its faith is ecclesiastically implemented, to find in one or the other, or in both, the explantion of its insufficiencies. The ecumenical movement has awakened Protestantism to the need of such a searching re-examination. And it finds that a fundamental cause of the insufficiency lies in its divided denominationalism. This system is not only an ineffective implementation of the Christian faith but it also obscures and misrepresents the gospel.

In the previous chapter we found that denominationalism was alien to the spirit and intention of the Reformation and that the ecumenical ideal was indigenous in Protestantism from the beginning. We shall now examine the denominational system directly. We shall find that in its actual workings it is an encumbrance and a handicap on Protestantism; that it obscures and, in an appreciable degree, falsifies the Protestant witness to the truth of the gospel; that it thwarts the Protestant impact upon its social and cultural environment; and we shall find grounds to believe that its unchallenged persistence in the kind of world our world has come to be, will surely forfeit for Protestantism its long-held ascendant position in American society and leave the field to other religious forces or to secularism. Unless a way is found to transcend its denominationalism and achieve some form of ecclesiastical solidarity, Protestantism is destined, in any realistic view, to be thrust out to the margins of our cultural and social order where it will exist as a dim and reminiscent survival of a light that failed.

There is no reason to obscure or mitigate the drastic nature of this indictment or this prophecy. But we must emphasize that it is pronounced, not against Protestantism, but in the name of Protestantism, and in loyalty to the ecumenical intention, albeit an unrealized intention, of the fathers of the Protestant Reformation. We shall examine the denomintional system from nine points of view stated in the form of nine propositions.

1. Denominationalism is exceedingly and scandalously wasteful of the resources of Protestantism.

2. It is a shameful embarrassment to the missionary expansion of Christianity.

3. It frustrates the efforts of Protestantism to discharge the

responsibility which the social gospel lays upon the Christian Church.

4. It robs Protestantism of its inherent strength in its inescapable competition with a formidable and aggressive Roman Catholicism.

5. It provincializes Protestant mentality by erecting barriers against the free flow of Christian thought.

6. It breeds a subtle and corrosive moral insincerity among Protestant Christians.

7. It denies to the local church the Christian status, the breadth of outlook, the spiritual inspiration, and the richness of fellowship which is its birthright as a part of the ecumenical church.

8. It condemns the parish minister to adopt methods and appeals which appreciably stultify his ministerial self-respect as well as the Christian dignity of his high vocation.

9. Glorying in its false freedom, denominationalism denies the freedom that is in Christ.

The last three—concerning the local church, the parish minister, and Christian freedom—will be held over for discussion in the fourth chapter.

It is obvious that these nine counts in our critique of the denominational system take us into a wholly different dimension from that in which numerical and material statistics are used as the measure of Protestant strength. Our criterion of strength has shifted from a quantitative to a qualitative standard. Let us now consider these items one by one. It is plain that our discussion of each must be brief.

1. *Denominationalism is scandalously wasteful of Protestant resources.* This has long been recognized and a brief treatment will be sufficient to remind the reader of the evidence of which he is already depressingly aware. This prodigal waste applies to the support of local churches and to the overhead expense of their many denominations. Protestantism supports far too many local churches. We are concerned with the fifty denominations which, as we pointed out in the previous chapter, contain 92 per cent of the total Protestant membership in the United States. These denominations support 220,000 local or parish churches. This would

be occasion for satisfaction if these local churches were distributed over 220,000 parish communities. But this is notoriously not the case. Nearly all of them exist side by side and in competition with other Protestant churches in small and large communities.

There is scarcely a town or village in the United States that is not scandalously overchurched. Six to ten churches in little villages and towns of less than 1,000 inhabitants. Often more than twenty churches in the typical county seat small town. Forty and fifty churches in small cities of 20,000 to 50,000 inhabitants. One hundred churches in cities with a population of 100,000 and 200,000, and so on up to the largest cities. The economic waste of this overlapping of churches has been recognized for more than a half century. But it has continued to the present day, and will continue as long as the denominational system lasts.

To the enormous waste of so many overlapping local churches, we must add the waste involved in the support of their overhead denominational organizations. Every denomination, no matter how small, has its own overhead organization. We venture to assert that a united Protestantism could administer the present activities of our fifty leading denominations with an overhead budget not much larger than that which the nation-wide Methodist Church alone requires. If this statement seems too extreme, we could throw in the overhead budget of the Presbyterian Church with that of the Methodist and safely say that a united Protestantism could save the whole amount now spent on the overhead of all the other denominations.

The mere saving of money is, of course, not an adequate motive for the achievement of a united Protestantism. On the contrary, we may well believe that a united church would receive and expend more money than all our denominational churches taken together are able to secure. But it would not be spent in competition with other churches, but directly to the great enterprises of the Kingdom of God. Denominationalism is a scandalous and unchristian waste of Protestant resources.

2. *The missionary expansion of the Christian faith is seriously handicapped and misrepresented by our sectarianism.* The

missionary impulse springs straight from the heart of the Christian Church. Nothing is more sacredly central in Christianity than the commission of our Lord to preach his gospel to every creature. During the past century and a half our missionaries have planted the Christian Church in nearly every country of the globe. In this magnificent achievement, each of our denominations has proceeded on its own initiative and its independent responsibility. The result is that, in addition to carrying the gospel, the missionaries have had to carry our sectarianism to China, India, Japan and the rest of the non-Christian lands.

The Christian churches established in these countries are grateful for the missionaries who have brought Christ to them, but they are restive and even resentful that they have had to accept the treasure of the gospel in the earthen vessels of our Protestant sectarianism. Our denominations mean nothing to them. Christ means all. The missionaries themselves are embarrassed and poignantly frustrated by the necessity of carrying a sectarian Christianity and planting sectarian churches. They are hobbled by denominational constraints and the necessity of operating in our denominational framework. On every occasion, our missionaries speak almost as one voice, pleading for an ecumenical Protestantism at home so that they may carry an ecumenical gospel and establish only an ecumenical church abroad.

The ecumenical movement in its global expression really originated in this missionary context. It was at the historic missionary conference at Edinburgh, Scotland, in 1910, that the plea for a united church was first heard in a setting that commanded attention throughout the whole of Protestantism. It was my unforgettable privilege to be a delegate at that epoch-making gathering. Bear in mind that it was called as a conference to consider the far-flung missoinary enterprise of the Protestant churches. Presided over by Dr. John R. Mott and the Archbishop of Canterbury, it drew many missionaries and some national representatives from the mission churches. They came pleading to be relieved of the incubus of denominationalism and set free to carry only the ecumenical gospel to the foreign field. This plea so impressed the assembly that, when the conference was only a few days old, it was, in effect, transformed into a conference on Christian unity. Its eyes were turned from the mission field to the home base where the existence of our denominational divisions presented the chief problem of the missionary enterprise. Out of that first world-wide conference in the history of Protestantism came the long line of ecumenical conferences on church union— Lausanne, Stockholm, Jerusalem, Oxford, Edinburgh 1937, Utrecht, Madras, and finally Amsterdam where the World Council of Churches was born. It is no exaggeration to say that the ecumenical movement had one of its chief sources in an awakening of the churches to the fact that a divided church at home must inevitably, in a high degree, misrepresent the gospel to the people of non-Christian lands.

The situation created by our denominationalism in non-Christian lands has been graphically described by Professor Walter Horton as follows:

When Christians in mission lands leave father and mother, caste and tribe, and the whole social order that has been home to them, for the sake of Christ, it is grievous and shocking to them to find the Christian community divided against itself. Sometimes the very places where Christianity has had the strongest influence are the most badly divided. In the strong Christian center of Kottayam in South India, I was scandalized to see the main sectarian divisions of Christendom, from Rome through Orthodoxy and Anglicanism to Protestantism, rearing rival edifices that seemed to "high hat" one another, and competing to annex the most members of the ancient Syrian community to their various and separate communions. It is particularly offensive when purely foreign divisions, which have no reality for the new convert, are artificially imported. What can it possibly mean but confusion and distress of mind when a Northern Chinese joins the American Southern Baptists, thus adding the divisive heritage of the American Civil War to a country already cursed with its own civil wars! Every experienced missionary knows that this is scandalous, and every young missionary church feels passionately that this is scandalous! . . . Where the younger churches have become articulate, they have spoken of the sin of disunity with a kind of savage intensity. They have seen this sin—they see it every day—slamming the gates of the kingdom of heaven in the faces of young believers and wistful inquirers; and they cannot speak mildly about it.[1]

Having looked upon this picture, it is inconceivable that any Christian can ever again look upon the denominational system with complacency. Only a united church at home can send the whole gospel abroad.

3. *Denominationalism frustrates the efforts of Protestantism to discharge the unique responsibility which the social gospel lays upon the Christian Church.* Protestantism has always laid primary emphasis upon the salvation of individual souls. There has never been any serious disposition to abandon or weaken this emphasis on personal regeneration. But at the turn of the present century a new note began to be heard in Protestant preaching. It was the note of *social* regeneration—the redemption of the social order itself. The Christian faith, it began to be affirmed, must hold itself responsible for the character of civilization—the moral ideals, the ethos, of the secular community. The mission of the church is not completed within the church. The Lordship of Christ who pervades the church with his life-giving Spirit, does not stop at the church's borders. His sovereignty extends to the whole range of human life, including the temporal good of mankind as well as the eternal good of human souls. This new note came to be called the social gospel. "The kingdoms of this world," quoted the social gospelers, "must become the Kingdom of our Lord and of his Christ."

Thus the churches were led into a new area of their Christian responsibility. This social gospel swept through American Protestantism and was received and proclaimed with ardor and optimism hardly matched in any period since the Reformation itself. It was a fresh discovery of unsuspected meaning in the gospel. But this movement, despite its Christian ardor, has been largely frustrated because Protestantism was unable to implement it. The social gospel soon discovered that the denominational system provided an utterly inadequate instrumentality through which the Chris-

---

[1] *Toward a Reborn Church.* The Hoover Lectures for 1948 (New York: Harper & Brothers, 1949), p. 24.

tian social responsibility could effectively be discharged. Protestant labors in the social field have been discouragingly formal, verbal, sentimental, undynamic and, in a discouraging degree, unfruitful. This, we may add parenthetically, was largely due to the lack of a sound theological basis. The social gospel movement was too intimately allied with the cultural liberalism of the period and found its motivation in an idealistic but superficial moralism. In our time, however, there is emerging in theological circles a more profoundly Christian undergirding of the social gospel. But this, we may be sure, is fated to remain a merely academic achievement so long as the social gospel has no other instrumentality than a divided Protestantism.

A disunited church is no match for the tremendous power of the social collectivities that have emerged in modern America. This is the lesson that we should learn from our half-century's abortive attempt to implement the social gospel. Our American society has completely changed its form as compared with the simplicities of the age of individualism. Great magnitudes of social organization have emerged, over against which our denominational churches present a picture of limp futility. Protestantism has not learned to live in the modern world. It has carried over from the era of individualism its atomistic and autonomous sectarian organizations and the simple procedures which seemed appropriate in that era, but are so no longer. Everything has changed—the whole structure and psychology of society—but Protestantism is compelled by its denominationalism to proceed as if it were living in the middle eighties of the nineteenth century.

The American mind is now predominantly collectivist in its structure. It is molded by a relatively few massive blocs of secular interest, each under the control of its own center of propaganda and power. The contacts of Protestantism with government, the labor unions, the tycoons of the radio, the movies and television, the press, industrial management, the educational system, the scientific enterprise, even the family, are tenuous and unimpressive. These blocs of collectivist power have ample reason to be respectfully conscious of Roman Catholicism. But they are unimpressed by the statistical difference between a Catholic membership of 27 million and a Protestant membership of 48 million. These tremendous magnitudes of social and psychological control of individual men and women have displaced the simple individualism of the "horse and buggy days." The individuality of man is steadily being absorbed in these multifarious collectivities.

Surely our Protestantism cannot longer cherish the illusion that its divided churches can penetrate these magnitudes of collectivist psychology with either the evangelistic or the social gospel. The federal union of some thirty denominations in the new National Council of Churches marks an appreciable advance over the futility of past isolationism. But the federal principle with its jealous reservations of denominational independence and autonomy cannot utter the potent voice of Protestantism nor mobilize its potentially mighty strength. A federal union of churches is, at best, an artifact. It lacks the strength of genuine solidarity. Nothing less than an ecclesiastically united Protestantism can match the systems of collectivist power into which the individuality of modern man is being engulfed.

4. *The denominational system robs Protestantism of its inherent strength in its inescapable competition with a formidable and aggressive Roman Catholicism.* No apology need be made for the use of the word "competition" in this connection. Three major forces are now engaged in a competitive spiritual struggle for the soul of America. They are Protestantism, Roman Catholicism and Secularism. Secularism is the common competitor of the other two. It so regards itself and is so regarded by both Protestants and Catholics. The term "secularism" implies something more than dumb indifference to religion. It implies a more or less conscious intellectual disillusionment with respect to the claims of religion, and the adoption over wide areas of modern culture of a "philosophy of life" from which religion is explicitly ruled out.

In the past century, secularism has made deep inroads into the cultural and spiritual life of America. Its success is accounted for by multiple factors. We shall name only four without discussing any of them: (1) The Protestant neglect of religious education, resulting from the total abandonment of the five-day school week to the control of the political state. (2) The overawing effect of the brilliant achievements of science and the wide acceptance of the messianic conception of the scientific enterprise. (3) The disintegrating effect of commercialized entertainment upon not only the morality but, what is even worse, the mentality of the people. (4) The too intimate identification of Christian liberalism with the liberalism of secular culture. We shall not be able, in the present connection to elaborate these factors, nor is it necessary to do so. We are concerned at the moment chiefly with the formidable emergence of Roman Catholicism in American life.

Protestantism and Catholicism are equally engaged in resistance to the secularization of Americn life and culture. This common purpose has led many Protestants to adopt the fallacious notion that Protestantism and Catholicism are therefore allies in a common endeavor. This notion, however, is not for a moment shared by Catholicism. The Catholic Church knows that itself and Protestantism represent two profoundly different kinds of religion, and it draws the line sharply between them. In the past, Protestants have also been as clearheaded on this matter as Rome has always been. It is only in our generation, under the influence of a sentimental and false conception of tolerance, that a considerable portion of the Protestant mind has been beguiled into the delusion that Protestantism and Catholicism are allies. No doubt this unrealistic sort of tolerance can be accounted for in considerable degree as a compensatory substitute for the loss of positive religious convictions due to the increasing sense of the irrelevance and unreality of Protestant denominationalism.

But these two religions, facing secularism as a common foe, are not allies, but competitors in the spiritual dimension for the soul of America whose culture is now dominated by a more or less reasoned secularistic philosophy. In this spiritual competition, Catholicism has been rapidly overtaking Protestantism. Though still a minority, being only half as strong numerically, the Roman Church exercises more influence over American life than is exercised by all Protestant churches combined. As Professor James Hastings Nichols, in his recent illuminating book, *Democ-*

A CRITIQUE OF DENOMINATIONALISM 37

racy and the Churches, says: "The United States is in many respects the greatest Catholic country, as well as the greatest Protestant country. And it has all happened in one lifetime."

The phenomenal growth of Catholicism has been due chiefly to immigration from Catholic countries during the seventy-five years preceding our restriction upon immigration in 1924, and to an exceptionally high birth rate. But Protestant eyes should now be opened to the truth that the Roman church no longer accepts a marginal or secondary position in our national life. In the great cities of the northern section of the United States it is steadily crowding Protestantism out of its long acknowledged pre-eminent position. In the city of New York the Roman church membership outnumbers that of Protestantism by 5 to 1—2,225,000 Catholics to 478,000 Protestants. In Chicago, the ratio is 3 to 2. In Buffalo, Pittsburgh, St. Louis, Philadelphia, Cleveland, San Francisco, Washington, Cincinnati, the ratio is roughly 50—50 with an edge in every one of these cities in favor of the Roman church. Boston, from Plymouth Rock to the beginning of the twentieth century the proud capital of New England Protestantism, is now overwhelmingly Roman Catholic.

These are only samples of the metropolitan concentration of Catholic power. When these facts are presented to an audience in the southern portion of the United States an objection is always raised to the assumption that this phenomenon is peculiar to the north. The same development is taking place in their cities also. And, similarly, if these facts are presented to the citizens of a smaller city anywhere in the nation as if they were peculiar to the great cities, this assumption, too, is promptly challenged with contrary evidence.

In Chapter V we shall be comparing Protestantism and Catholicism in terms of their religious differences. In the present context we are concerned with the growth of Catholic power and the forms in which it is manifested in American society.

It is unfortunate that the differences between these two faiths cannot be kept strictly within the area of religion. If this could be done, the principle of relgious liberty would enable these radically different churches to live together within the bounds of neighborly good will and the democratic amenities. But this ideal is subjected to serious strain by the Roman church which refuses to recognize the principle of religious liberty in the terms in which the Constitution and the long American tradition have defined and prescribed it. Having achieved its present status of power in the United States, the Roman church now feels itself able to challenge this principle and assert its own historical claim for a privileged relation to the state. It makes a direct attack upon the principle of separation of church and state by which religious liberty is implemented and guaranteed. Protestantism is determined that this principle shall be maintained. Thus the ideal democratic relation of all faiths as equally free churches in a free society is being vitiated by the emergence of a political issue which can be settled only in the political arena.

This political issue has arisen chiefly in two specific fields—one the field of education, the other the field of diplomacy. In respect to education, the most conspicuous issue is connected with a repeatedly proposed bill in Congress appropriating federal funds to lift the standard of public education in the less economically resourceful states of the Union. The merits of this proposal are not relevant to our present interest. What concerns us is the fact that for a whole generation the Catholic hierarchy has been able by political pressure to keep the proposal from coming to a vote unless its parochial schools would share in the distribution of the funds. Naturally, Protestant and other churches oppose this attempt of a church to secure public money for its schools as a violation of the separation of church and state. In the political contest that has had to be waged much bitter feeling has been engendered. It was such political struggles of organized religion that the separation of church and state, among other considerations, was designed to prevent, and has largely prevented for a century and a half.

Less conspicuous, but no less ominous, instances of actual encroachment upon the separation principle in the field of education have been discovered to exist in innumerable local communities in nearly all the states. These violations take a variety of forms but are alike in that they involve the use of public money or public property or public school authority for parochial school education. Some of these instances have become notorious. In some, even Protestants have been unwittingly involved by their eagerness to secure a paltry fragment of public school time for religious educaton. In some states where there was no opposition, there has been an actual invasion of the public school by church-sponsored teachers of religious subjects. Protestant offenders, however, represent local unawarenese of the principle which their action violates, while the Catholic encroachments represent the deliberate and avowed policy to break down the principle of church-state separation.

In the field of official diplomacy the Roman church was able to secure the appointment of an ambassador to the Pope under the disguise of a "personal representative" of the President of the United States. This plainly was a union of the diplomatic processes of the American government with the diplomatic processes of the Vatican. The arrangement lasted for a decade. It was expected, under authoritative promise, that with its lapse no further attempt would be made to renew it. President Truman, however, throwing off the "personal representative" disguise, startled the nation with the appointment of a "minister plenipotentiary and ambassador extraordinary" to the Vatican. When the appointee declined the post as the result of the bitter controversy it aroused, the President announced that he intended to appoint someone else. At the time of this writing, no further appointment has been made, though the threat of it keeps the issue alive in public feeling.

This is not the place to discuss in any detail the constitutional question involved in either the educational or the diplomatic violations of church-state separation. It must suffice to make the following statements. (1) The use of public money or public authority in support of religious instruction conducted or sponsored by a church is a clear case of the intermingling of the legal powers of the state with the official processes of organized religion. This is a violation of the First Amendment which forbids the government to use its legal power in any manner "respecting an establishment of religion." (2) The appointment of an ambassador to the head of the Roman Catholic Church similarly involves an intermingling or interlocking of the diplomatic processes of our government with the diplomatic processes of the Roman church. This is not separation of church and state; it is a union of church and state in the only manner in which church and state can be united. It is not, of course, a complete union, but it involves the principle of a complete union; that is, it is an action of the government *respecting* an establishment of religion, and this the Constitution forbids.

Such a union of our government with the Roman church would give that church a secret and privileged access to the ear of our government and an influence over its policies in a relation which no other church enjoys or would accept. It would place all non-Roman churches in an appreciably subordinate position in American society. Protestant and all other churches would be compelled to operate in the shadow of an embryonically established church, officially recognized as enjoying a unique relation with and the special favor of our government, and in a position steadily to increase its intergration with our government. With the coming of an exchange ambassador or nuncio, from the Vatican, its psychological effect would be to say to the American people: This is the really important religion; this is the religion of the United States.

Should such an appointment eventually be made, and confirmed by the Senate, it is unthinkable that Protestantism would ever yield to it as an accomplished fact. The issue would permanently exacerbate the relation between Catholics and Protestants and would be resisted until it should be decisively annulled. The principle of religious liberty and equality before the law, guaranteed and implemented by the separation of church and state, is too precious a heritage for Protestantism to allow it to be flouted under pressure of the political power of a church whose historic principles commit it to the identical system which the fathers of our Constitution were determined to exclude forever from our national life.

What does all this mean for Protestantism? I offer three answers. First, it ought thoroughly to dispel from the Protestant mind the illusion that its long ascendant position in American society is secure. Second, it should dispel the illusion of Protestant strength derived merely from the statistics of its own growth. Third, it should release Protestant leadership from the squeamish timidity which hesitates frankly and without apology to give instruction concerning the profound differences between Protestantism and Catholicism. This can be done without justly raising the cry of bigotry if it is kept clearly in mind that Protestantism is not anti-Catholic except in the same sense that Catholicism is anti-Protestant. That is to say, they are competitors in the realm of truth and faith for the soul of America.

Finally, and most important, the present formidable and aggressive emergence of Catholicism should be a ringing challenge to Protestantism to be itself. It can be itself only by drawing together its divided forces into an ecclesiastical integration competent to deal with the entrenched secularism of American society—the same secularism which Catholicism is aggressively out to win.

5. *Denominationalism provincializes Protestant mentality by erecting barriers against the free flow of Christian thought.* No denomination can think in categories that are large enough to express the full range and majesty of the Christian faith. The denominational mind is necessarily narrow, provincial, short-sighted. It lives in detachment from the total reality of Christian experience. It cannot rise to the eminence from which alone the whole of the Christian enterprise can be envisaged. Because the denomination is but a fragment of the church, its feeling and vision of the whole gospel is necessarily truncated. The full witness to the Christian faith finds no adequate expression in the "broken lights" of the denominational system. The truth of Christianity is not exhausted by the uniformities to which it is reduced by our sectarian creeds and ideologies. It will be found, rather, in the very diversities of apprehension on the part of all those who approach Jesus Christ in love, in loyalty and in obedience.

It is an insult to Christian truth to build a sectarian wall around it. Our denominations have been under the delusion that, in order to conserve and propagate the special truth which they cherished, it was necessary to maintain a separate church. But the whole history of sectarianism disproves this assumption. The effect is precisely the contrary. To build a sectarian wall around a Christian truth puts that truth out of circulation. If it is a genuine truth, it would fare better were it maintained on its merits within an ecumenical fellowship. Once a truth is sectarianized in a fragment of the church, it raises barriers of prejudice and pride against its acceptance by others. There is no surer guarantee that such a truth will not be accepted by others than to brand it with the copyright of a walled-in sect.

A sectarian church not only shuts its own faithful in and other Christians equally faithful out; it also shuts its own truth in and other truth out. Its own truth cannot get out to win its way on its merits, and the truth held by others cannot get in to enrich the truth and perhaps correct the errors of those who hold it. The Christian faith and the democratic principle alike require a free circulation of truth and error. Denominationalism isolates truth and coddles error.

Protestantism today stands in need of an ecumenical theology. Our scholars are increasingly becoming aware of this need and working at the task of developing such a theology. It will not be the replica of any sectarian theology. Of that we may be assured. But this aim of Christian scholarship cannot be achieved in academic isolation. It must wait for its fuller development until there is an ecumenical church. An ecumenical theology can arise only within the actual experience of an ecumenical fellowship, where thought is free, and where diversities are welcomed as the condition of creative growth. As compared with our sectarian theologies, an ecumenical theology will have a new power and dignity, and will command respect in our science-minded world which now treats our sectarianized creeds with levity.

In the free untrammeled exercise of Christian intelligence, under Christ, in the spiritual democracy of an ecumenical fellowship, the Holy Spirit will, no doubt, confirm much that is old— much more, we may well believe, than the latitudinarians imagine. And the same Spirit will guide the mind of the Christian fellowship in the perennial discovery of those things which Christ withheld from his disciples until the Spirit should reveal them.

6. *Denominationalism breeds a subtle and perilous moral insincerity among Protestant Christians*. This is a serious observation, and will require delicate exposition if we are to avoid a

reaction of resentment. But if any enlightened churchman will search his own heart, I believe he will find a conflict there between his sense of the hollowness and unreality of the claims of his denomination, on the one hand, and on the other hand, the practical necessity of supporting these claims in the interest of denominational morale. Whatever distinctive meaning our denominations once had has largely disappeared in the profound change that has taken place in modern Christian thought and feeling. Our denominations, as such, are hardly more than survivals of an era that is well on its way out. The issues upon which they were founded are losing their vitality. Yet the structure, the shell, of the denomination persists, and both the parish minister and the denominational ecclesiastic feel compelled on occasion to galvanize these obsolete issues into a semblance of reality in order to inspire and maintain denominational loyalty. This procedure is more or less vaguely felt to be insincere by any churchman whose mind has been even partially enlightened by the ecumenical ideal.

Such action, however, can be easily rationalized, because it is necessitated by the denominational system within whose framework the churchman is compelled to labor. He is a victim of this system. He is caught in it and cannot extricate himself from it. Protestantism provides him with no opportunity for a Christian ministry except one that is identified with and results in the strengthening and greatening of his denomination. However sincerely he would desire his ministry to strengthen and greaten only the ecumenical Church of Christ, his denominational involvement can find no way out of his moral dilemma. There is no way in which church work can be carried on except within the denominational system which the ecumenically minded churchman knows to be the antithesis and the usurper of the ecumenical church. Therefore, though we may not condone insincerity, a fair judgment requires that the major responsibility for it, in this instance, must be placed in larger measure upon the system than upon the churchman who is more victim than free agent.

The point we are making can perhaps be sharpened if we look closely at our denominations to see just how much importance they actually attach to those features which were the historical bases of their distinctiveness. We shall find that a great change has taken place in their actual practice and feeling. It is a change in the direction of hospitality toward deviations from the historic norm of the denomination. All our denominations now make room for diversity and disagreement in the very matters that historically occasioned their founding as separate churches. In all our churches there are conservatives and liberals, conformists and dissenters, strict constructionists of the creed and latitudinarians, literalistic fundamentalists and a more profound kind of fundamentalists who read their Bibles with a free and flexible mind. The uniform patterns of thought and belief which once characterized all our denominations are plainly disintegrating under the influence of the ecumenical spirit.

Do all Episcopalians see alike on apostolic succession, or the sacraments, or the ministry? Manifestly, no. The standardized conception of these matters is challenged in the utmost candor by large sections of the Episcopal communion, including some of its most outstanding scholars and ecclesiastics, among them not a few bishops. Do all Presbyterians see alike on the Westminster Confession? By no means. There is wide divergence of doctrinal views, ranging from the strictest conformity to a strong belief that this classic standard requires radical revision, while many Presbyterians believe that the ancient creed should be laid on the shelf as a historical symbol, rather than used as a witness to the things modern Presbyterians should emphasize. Do all Baptists and Disciples see alike on immersion baptism? Far from it. Their traditional arguments in support of it have undergone radical revision in the minds of large sections of both denominations. Do all Congregationalists and all Disciples and all Baptists see alike on the absolute autonomy of the local congregation—a doctrine that has historically characterized these three bodies? Definitely, no. Some still adhere to the traditional view, but others in increasing number hold the view that the local church should recognize its organic integration with its sister churches and that this recognition should be manifested in some orderly relationship—something like a presbyterial or diocesan connexionalism.

Many of the features formerly claimed by our denominations as distinctive are losing their significance within the denomination itself. A dim but appreciable ecumenical consciousness is emerging in all our churches. The sectarian test for church membership has almost universally been abandoned. Even in the ordination of ministers the historic creedal standards are evaded with ingenious rationalizations and are almost wholly disregarded. The test to which a candidate is subjected has less to do with his doctrinal soundness than with his personal devotion to Jesus Christ. Ministers pass with increasing facility from one denomination to another. And church members moving into a new community find their church home with little concern for their past denominational affiliation.

How shall we account for this enlarging hospitality by the denominations themselves to wide diversities of doctrinal and ecclesiastical conviction, or this indifference to the historical standards of the denomination? One answer lies in the fact that all our churches are more or less pervaded by the spirit of modern scholarship which has brought about a deeper understanding of the Bible, of the church and of the Christian revelation. But this is only half of the answer. The other and the greater half is that, along with modern enlightenment, Protestantism is experiencing an ecumenical awakening. It is becoming conscious of a church greater than any of the churches. There is a growing discontent with the limitation of the Christian fellowship to the denomination. This discontent is accompanied with a deep yearning to belong to the ecumenical church. Yet we cannot belong to it in any empirical sense, for it does not exist in actuality, but only in vision and desire —and in the mind of Christ. The denominational system prevents the emergence of the ecumenical church into empirical reality. But though we cannot belong to the ecumenical church, we can, and increasingly do, extend the hand of Christian fellowship across the dividing barriers of the denominational system. This is the real meaning of the widespread disregard of historical denominational standards and the enlarging hospitality to Christians of other traditions.

Let us keep our bearings in this discussion. We are now thinking under the heading of the subtle moral insincerity which denominationalism breeds among Christians. We have previously directed attention to the way in which the parish minister and the denominational ecclesiastic are confronted with this unavoidable peril of insincerity. We must now say that each denomination as a self-conscious body is beset by this same peril of insincerity. As the ecumenical spirit reaches into a denomination, it creates a tension between the denomination and the ideal of the ecumenical church. It is more than a tension; it is sensed as an outright contradiction. A denomination cannot consistently devote itself to the ecumenical ideal and to the defense of the denominational system at the same time. To try to do so is to fall into the pit of insincerity.

This peril did not exist prior to the ecumenical awakening. So long as our sectarian divisions were unchallenged by an ecumenical conscience, the denomination could be innocently taken for granted or even sincerely defended. But the ecumenical ideal has now taken such hold upon the heart and conscience of the churches, and such hostages have already been given to it in both profession and action, that the denominational system cannot go unchallenged much longer without pervading the psychology of the churches with a corrosive insincerity. This double-mindedness often unwittingly betrays itself. When certain peculiarities of a denomination are referred to in conversation and even in public address, the reference is often accompanied with an indulgent smile, a half-veiled apology or even by a wisecrack. But when a high-pressure campaign is on, the slogans of the past are likely to be dusted off and brightened up to provide motivation for denominational morale and loyalty. This subtle temptation to insincerity cannot be easily resisted so long as the denominational system continues to exist in an age in which it has lost any realistic meaning.

It is difficult to formulate this ethical consideration without seeming to say that the Christian activities of our denominations should be summarily relaxed. This we are far from saying. On the contrary, it is every Christian's duty to aid in supporting every truly Christian undertaking of his denomination in order that the denomination may contribute its maximum strength to the united church in the day when the denominational system is dissolved. This can be done with the minimum of insincerity provided the temptation is resisted to galvanize the sectarian issues that were once distinctive, and may have been important, but are so no longer. Our argument offers no encouragement to that nondescript advocate of Christian unity who, in his disillusionment with denominationalism, withdraws his participation from the work of his denomination. Such an advocate of unity puts himself out of touch with the very movement he professes to espouse. A united Protestantism will not be achieved by weakening our denominations, but by strenghtening their indisputably Christian endeavors and fostering the ecumenical spirit within them.

Let us look beyond Protestantism at the world in which we find ourselves. Our civilization is in a state of collapse. The old stabilities are dissolving before our eyes. The old world of America and of historical Protestantism is passing away. Whether a new world will rise from the chaos of the present, and whether, if it does, it will be better or worse than the world we have known, no man can tell. Only faith in the God of history can enable us to ride the tempestuous waves of this universal unrest and uncertainty.

Under the shadow of an impenetrable and portentous future, how can Protestants think small thoughts and emphasize trivial differences? If the end of our era proves to be like the end of other great eras in history, it may fall out, as Arnold Toynbee suggests, that all that is left of civilization will be found in the keeping of the Christian Church. The responsibility that will then rest upon Christianity will be staggeringly greater than any it has borne in any period since its earliest beginnings. The thought of carrying our impotent sectarianism into such a scene as that toward which the forces of history may be taking us, should awaken us to realize that in this world convulsion the destiny of Protestantism itself is involved. Either it will decay with the decaying significance of its sectarian churches, as some believe it will, or a new Protestantism will emerge, emancipated from its anarchic sectarianism and competent, under Christ, to gather up the fragments of a shattered civilization and build a new world.

III

The Churchism of the Denomination

As one recalls the proceedings of the many ecumenical conferences, from the first at Edinburgh in 1910 to Amsterdam in 1948, and reads the literature of the ecumenical movement, one is impressed by a strange and serious omission. It is the absence of any systematic and penetrating analysis of the nature of the denominational system. Indeed, it seems that the denomination, as the outstanding feature of Protestantism, has not even been carefully defined. This is a strange omission because the existence of the denominational system is the occasion of the emergence of the ecumenical movement itself.

How can we speak about the ecumenical church without speaking also about our denominations? And how can we speak intelligently about our denominations without having a clear conception of what a denomination is? In the literature of the ecumenical movement the denomination is referred to in euphemistic and sentimental terms. Our divisions are deplored. They are even made the subject of repentance. But the repentance seems to apply only to the fact that we are divided into denominations, and hardly comes to grips with the denomination itself as a concrete phenomenon. The literature seems to reflect a conscious obligation to deal tenderly with the denomination and to forbid a too close examination of its essential nature.

How shall we account for this silence on a subject that so obviously belongs in the context of ecumenical consideration? Two explanations may be suggested. Perhaps there exists a fear that the values and treasures which every denomination carries may be jeopardized by a too candid examination of its nature. Such an undertaking would imply a certain challenge. This might evoke the pride and loyalty of the members of the denomination and particularly of those who are officially responsible for its vested interests. But this sensitive restraint is without justification. None of the Christian values that belong to our divided fellowships will be imperiled by a critical examination, and none will be sacrificed by the achievement of a united church. On the contrary, these treasures would be enhanced in an ecumenical fellowship far beyond their present value.

The other explanation might be stated as a tactical one. It is perhaps felt in the circles of those who are chiefly responsible for the guidance of the ecumenical movement, that it would be unwise to bring the denomination, as such, under the light of critical investigation, lest certain bodies now participating in the ecumenical movement might be alienated. There are, it is true, some denominations whose commitment to this movement is highly tenuous, cautious and accompanied with misgivings as to the direction in which the movement may be going. If they were assured that it was going no futher than a federal union such as the World Council of Churches or our National Council of Churches, they would not be too much disturbed. But if the denomination, as such, is brought under examination to inquire what its relation to the ecumenical church may be, the leaders of these hesitant denominations shrink from the consequences. Naturally, therefore, those who guide the movement hesitate frankly to suggest that its goal would necessarily involve some adjustment, if not radical abandonment, of the denominational system.

In whatever degree these considerations have operated as a counsel of silence in the past, it would seem that the time had now come for the denominational system to be subjected to a thorough analysis designed to reveal its essential nature. The ecumenical movement is sufficiently mature for such a realistic inquiry to be undertaken. Indeed, it would seem that the movement has gone as far as it can until its own mind is clarified as to the nature of the denominational order. Without a realistic understanding of what the denominational order is, the movement for Christian unity is in danger of bogging down in obscurantism and sterile generalities.

An honest and objective facing of the denomination would vitalize the ecumenical movement by bringing its appeal home to the Christian conscience. Its appeal has not yet reached the Christian conscience. It has been largely confined to the realm of sentiment and idealism. It has therefore lacked a profoundly moral dynamic. An ideal is sterile unless it is mated with a vivid sense of discontent with the real. Until the Protestant conscience is profoundly disturbed by the unchristian character of its denominational system, the ecumenical movement will be unable even to envisage its goal, to say nothing of attaining it.

So far in these chapters, we have been using the word "denomination" without defining it. But we must now undertake to do this. It is necessary because the denomination lies at the very center of the ecumenical problem. In our critique of the denominational system we have described it in radical terms as an encumbrance and a handicap upon Protestantism and as a misrepresentation of Protestant Christianity. We have also shown that it is alien to the genius and intention of the Reformation of the sixteenth century.

It may be that some readers have reacted to these strictures with the feeling that they have been one-sided and even unfair. It is felt that there is a good side to the denomination which has been ignored. And one cannot quite give his full assent to our indictment of the denominational system because of the values which are felt to inhere in it. That there are such values cannot be denied. It is necessary, then, to define a denomination in language that will carefully distinguish its values from its disvalues and its evil effects. We shall try to get at the inmost meaning of a denomination by first noting some of the ways a denomination is conceived by those who emphasize its values.

In the first place, a denomination is said to represent a particular fellowship within the wider fellowship of the Christian community. This is obviously true. Certainly there can be nothing unchristian or wrong in the existence of such a fellowship. The fellowship which all Christians enjoy in Jesus Christ is bound to differentiate itself into many groups with particular affinities. These affinities may be based upon common beliefs or tastes or social backgrounds or even racial or national origins. This is a common human phenomenon and should operate to strengthen and enrich the total fellowship of the Christian Church. Such particular fellowships already exist within all our denominations. This being so, we can hardly accept the concept of a particular fellowship as a definition of the denomination, as such. It is rather a description of a certain value which the denomination carries.

Second, it is frequently emphasized that a denomination is the inheritor of a particular tradition which is precious to those who belong within it. This tradition is appropriated by successive generations and kept alive in the corporate consciousness of the group by the perennial remembrance of the great men who inaugurated the tradition. Obviously there can be nothing unchristian or wrong in treasuring a noble tradition. If this were a true definition of a denomination, no case could be made against the divided state of Protestantism.

A third, and the most frequent, way of describing the denomination is to point out the convenient manner in which it provides for the diversity of beliefs and tastes in matters of doctrine and worship. Those who think substantially alike are, it is said, naturally drawn together; those whose taste in worship calls for more formal expression can conveniently find a denomination that satisfies their taste; while those who prefer more spontaneous and free expression in worship are provided for in another denomination. This diversity of beliefs and forms of worship which the unlikeness of men's minds and tastes seems to require, is not in itself subject to criticism. It is not necessarily schismatic. On the contrary, such variety should enrich and deepen the fellowship of the whole church, rather than divide it or subtract from it. Any plan for a united church that makes no room for these diversities which the denominations carry would not only be futile but would be less than Christian.

In Search of a Definition

None of these three features of the denomination provides us with a definition. They are, rather, by-products of the denomination or, as the scholastics used to say, accidents, while the substance must be found by further inquiry. We have to ask, What are the characteristic functions which the denomination exercises and what kind of corporate body is it which maintains this special fellowship and this treasured tradition and provides so neatly for these kindred convictions and tastes? It will not be difficult to answer these questions. All we need to do is to observe what the denomination is actually doing.

We find that all the denominations receive members into their fellowship by the sacrament of baptism. They celebrate the sacrament of the Lord's Supper. They educate, appoint and ordain their own ministers. They project their own separate and independent programs of missionary expansion at home and abroad. They provide Christian education for their own children and youth. They have their own liturgical forms of worship. They determine for themselves a creed or an ideology appropriate to their special fellowship. And, finally, these and all subsidiary activities are co-ordinated in an orderly polity either by a formal constitution or by generally accepted precedent and custom. Each denomination is thus a self-constituted, self-contained, independent and autonomous ecclesiastical body.

Now, it is plain that in a denomination we have something more than a particular fellowship, a treasured tradition or a group of like-minded Christians. What we have is nothing less than a church; an ecclesiastical body organized and functioning as a church, exercising all the prerogatives that belong to the Church of Christ. The great majority of our denominations so conceive themselves. They call themselves churches—Methodist Church, Lutheran Church, Episcopal Church, Presbyterian Church, and so forth. Certain denominations disclaim this churchly status. These are the so-called congregational denominations, such as the Baptists, the Congregationalists and the Disciples of Christ. But their disclaimer is illusory. In their connexional organization they operate in essentially the same manner as do the denominations which frankly accept the status of churches. The only difference between these two classes of denominations is that in one class the churchly organization is more integrated and orderly; in the other class, less so. Functionally, however, they all exercise the same ecclesiastical prerogatives. Each receives members by baptism, celebrates the Lord's Supper, ordains its own ministers, carries on its own missionary work, educates its youth, constructs its liturgy, and determines its normative ideology—all this it does as a corporate body, whether closely or loosely integrated, by which it is identifiable as a distinct entity, ecclesiastically separate from all other denominational churches.

That the denomination is a church is, of course, no new discovery. It is the frank and open claim of most of our denominations. Indeed, many if not most of them are incorporated under the civil law as "churches." And, as we have previously said, those denominations which disavow the appellation of "churches" do, nevertheless, exercise the same churchly functions as do those which accept this designation. The ecumenical movement itself refers to the denominations as "churches"—31 of them in our National Council of *Churches,* 151 of them in the World Council of *Churches.* In the churchism of the denomination, we find its substantive and essential characteristic.

It might seem, then, in our emphasis upon the churchly character of the denomination, that we have been only laboring the obvious. This would be true if we should stop here. We would have learned little nor advanced far toward the definition that we seek. But in sharply distinguishing the churchism of the denomination from its fellowship affinities, we have found at least a starting point from which we can go on to a definition.

What should primarily concern the ecumenical movement is, therefore, the churchism of the denomination. Its concern arises from its commitment to the achievement of a united church. The existence of denominations creates the problem of Christian unity. Therefore the ecumenical goal cannot be envisaged unless we clearly conceive what a denomination is. Without such a clear and precise conception our ecumenical talk will be going round and round in circles. One feels bound to say that the ecumenical movement has too long postponed a forthright and radical attack upon this central citadel of its problem.

The master problem which the movement has set itself to resolve can be stated therefore in terms of the relation between two churches—the ecumenical church, on one hand, and the denominational church, on the other. These two churches are mutually exculsive. If we have denominational churches, we cannot have the ecumenical church. And, *vice versa,* if we are to have the ecumenical church, we cannot have denominational churches. Our denominations, in the sense of special fellowships and affinities, may continue to exist indefinitely in the ecumenical church, but they cannot exist as churches. In order to clarify this situation it is necessary to think further about the ecumenical church itself.

Let us remind ourselves of the conception of the ecumenical church which is accepted and, we might say, standardized in the ecumenical movement. All the literature of this movement defines the ecumenical church as the community of all those whom Christ has received into fellowship with himself. This conception was given repeated formulation, in varying but equivalent terms, by the conferences at Oxford and Edinburgh and at Amsterdam where the World Council of Churches was oganized.

But the ecumenical church, so conceived, is an amorphous thing. We cannot see it. We cannot lay hold of it. It eludes our grasp. Nor can it lay hold of us to draw us into itself. The Church of Christ is, we might say, a phantom church. Yet we know that it exists, and not merely as a platonic idea, but as potentially an empirical entity. We know this because the ecumenical church does exist in the mind of Christ. It is this amorphous character of the Church of Christ, its formlessness, its intangibleness, its invisibility and its empirical impotence that the ecumenical movement is out to overcome. In a word, the whole aspiration and purpose of this world-wide movement among Christians is to bring the Church of Christ into an empirical existence so that we *can* see it, *can* lay hold of it and so that it *can* lay hold of us and draw us into itself. The goal of the ecumenical movement cannot be envisaged in any terms short of the actual embodiment of the now unembodied Church of Christ.

Why, we now ask, does the Church of Christ, the ecumenical church, exist in impotent invisibility? The answer is: Because it has no organs by which to manifest itself in the actual world of human observation and experience. And why has it no organs? The answer should now be so clear as to be inevitable. The Church of Christ has no organs because its own organs have all been stripped away from it by our man-made denominational churches. This is the tragic plight of our Protestant Christianity. Protestantism has no church; it has only churches. These churches have bodies and they have organs by which their bodies function as churches. But the Church of Christ, which is the body of Christ, cannot function because its functions have been usurped by a multitude of churches which exercise them in separate, independent, self-contained and autonomous ecclesiastical denominations.

In contrast to the amorphous and invisible character of the Church of Christ, these denominational churches are visible, empirical entities. We can see them, and join them, for they have organization and meeting times and meeting places where they manifest their empirical existence. They perform corporate or collective acts which they have taken over from the Church of Christ—acts which, because they have thus been taken over by separate, self-contained and autonomous churches, can no longer be performed by the Church of Christ itself. Therefore, though we would be Christians, we cannot join the Church of Christ, but can join only a part of it. Nor can we participate in those functions of the church which are the characteristic marks or evidence of the presence of the Church of Christ, but only in the performance of these acts by a part of the church.

What are these functions which are the characteristic marks of the Church of Christ? They are precisely the same functions which we have previously listed as the functions of our denominations: baptism, the Lord's Supper, ordination, missionary expansion, Christian education, corporate worship, creedal ideology, and all these functions exercised within a distinct structure or polity which separates it from all other Christians save those of its own denomination. These marks of the churchism of the denomination are also the essential marks of the ecumenical church. Not only do they belong to the whole church, but they belong to the *unity* of the whole church. By this is meant that if any of these functions—baptism, the Eucharist, ordination, and the others—is performed by a part of the church, without the participation of the whole church, it reflects an existing schism or tends to create one. Not only so, but their exercise by any body less than the whole church robs the action itself of its full significance. This usurpation of the organs and functions of the Church of Christ by the denominations prevents the whole church, the united church, the ecumenical church, from exercising them and thus emerging from its amorphous invisibility and manifesting itself as an empirical entity.

We are now ready to reduce all this to a definition of the denomination. *A denomination is a part of the Church of Christ existing in a structure of its own and exercising by itself and for itself those functions which belong to the unity of the whole Church of Christ.*

Our ecclesiastical nomenclature has been seriously confused by the current adoption of the misleading distinction between the so-called "sect type" and "church type" of denomination. This distinciton was first used by Ernst Troeltsch in his monumental work interpreting the social teachings of the various denominations. As a practical device, it was well suited to his particular purpose as a sociological historian. But it has misled many writers to take it as an essential ecclesiological distinction.[1] In ecclesiological theory, however, no such distinction between church and sect in our denominational system can be maintained. All our denominations are sects, including those which have come down from the classic period of the Reformation—Episcopal, Lutheran and Presbyterian—no less than those which have historically stemmed from them—Baptists, Congregationalists, Methodists, Disciples of Christ and all the rest. All are sects, because each is a part of the Church of Christ which exercises by itself and for itself those functions that belong to the ecumenical church.

It is generally taken as an affront to apply the term "sect" to the more venerable and respectable denominations. They prefer to be called "churches," imagining that to be a church is a more reputable designation than to be a sect. But being a church does not relieve them of the stigma of being a sect. *They are sects just because they are churches*. It is their churchism that makes them sects. Of the two terms, we could say that to claim the status of a

[1] For further comment on Troeltsch's "types," see p. 135.

"church" carries with it not only all the implications of being a sect, but adds thereto a touch of arrogance which the humbler term does not imply. No denomination can escape the stigma of being a sect so long as the denominational system continues. As the late Archbishop William Temple declared: "So long as any of us are in schism, all are in schism." The notable statement issued by an officially appointed commission on the doctrine of the Church of England, frankly said, "All our churches are in schism."

THE MARKS OF A DENOMINATION

Let us now return to our list of those eight churchly practices of the denomination and examine them one by one in the light of our definition of a denomination. We shall find that in taking over these practices from the ecumenical church and exercising them by and for an independent and autonomous part of the church, these practices are shorn of their inherently ecumenical or catholic character.

1. The first on our list is baptism. It is the sacramental act of the corporate body of Christ by which it receives new members into itself. This, in its true meaning, is an act of the whole church, performed in the name of Christ as the head of the church, and should be so conceived and administered that the one baptized becomes a member of the whole church which is the body of Christ. Baptism is administered by a local church which in its true character is the ecumenical church made manifest in a particular place. But when, as in our denominational system, the local church is the manifestation of a denomination, a separate and autonomous fragment of the church, its baptismal act is, in principle, vitiated. The effect of the baptismal act cannot extend beyond the borders of the denomination. The one baptized is not thereby made a member of the whole church. This is true, in the first place, because the whole church into which he could be received has no empirical existence.

But neither does his baptism induct him into the whole church considered as the sum of its separate denominational fragments. As a matter of fact, he is not universally accepted as a true member of the Church of Christ by all these denominations. If he should apply for membership in a local church of some denominations, he would have to submit to rebaptism.

Those churches which accept the baptism of other churches do so as a manifestation of that emerging Christian spirit which transcends the boundaries of our denominational churches. The acceptance of a baptized Methodist into a Presbyterian local church without rebaptism is a wholly illogical, albeit a highly Christian, procedure. And a Baptist or Disciples church which would demand the rebaptism of such a Methodist applicant for membership would be acting strictly within the logic of sectarianism, though other Christians would surely hold that the practice is arrogantly unchristian. The sacrament of baptism can be released from its anomalous plight only by restoring it to its true place as a sacrament of the ecumenical church.

2. Consider now the matter of ordination to the Christian ministry. Much that has been said about baptism applies in principle to ordination. It is a fact, of course, that the ministry of many denominations is acceptable to many others, without reordination. One of the signs that our denominational walls are crumbling is found in the frequency and facility with which ministers are crossing over the lines of separation and are being received as true ministers without reordination. As in the analogous case of baptism, this generous practice must not blind us to the sinful implications of the denominational system which are to that degree transcended by the Christian spirit. A ministry accepted by and responsible to the whole church can be provided only by restoring to the church as a whole the prerogative of ordination. For a part of the church to take upon itself the responsibility of ordaining a ministry is to usurp a function that belongs only to the ecumenical church itself. This is one of the most stubborn problems confronting the ecumenical movement, and we shall return to its consideration in another chapter.

3. The third ecumenical function which the denominational church has usurped is that of the expansion of the church into new fields. This we call Christian missions. The Christian Church, concerned as it is with the maintenance of its unity and integrity, can-

not, under Christ, tolerate the exercise of its missionary function by a part of itself acting autonomously and without responsibility to the church as a whole. For a part of the church so to act divides the church, as we see it divided on the mission field, and perpetuates and sharpens the divisions that already exist at the home base. The most vigorous demand for a united church at the home base comes from our missionaries and from the younger churches in faraway lands. This subject was discussed at greater length in our second chapter.

4. Christian Education. This is a double function of the church. It includes the education of the church's youth in the convictions and ideals and the lore of the Christian tradition, including preeminently the Bible. It also includes the training of a ministry for the church. Both are ecumenical functions now exercised by denominational churches. The Christian education of the church's youth is in a parlous state in American Protestantism. It is not relevant to discuss its shortcomings in the present context. The one thing that concerns us here is to recognize that this educational task is one of the most vital of the functions of the whole church. The denomination cannot provide a Christian education that will equip the membership of the church with the intelligent understanding of the Christian faith which our fundamental Protestant convictions assume and require.

The doctrine of the priesthood of all believers carries educational implications that have not been taken seriously. Protestantism cannot, like Roman Catholicism, be content with merely an educated clergy; it requires that the laity also shall be, in its degree, intelligent concerning the biblical, historical, doctrinal, hymnodic and literary content of the Christian faith. The denomination cannot provide this. It cannot be itself and at the same time inculcate an ecumenical Christianity. Unless the function of Christian education which the denominational churches have usurped is restored to the church as a whole, and reprojected on an ecumenically adequate scale, the religious literacy of Protestants is destined to fall to the level of the Roman Catholic laity.

Moreover, the denomination cannot train a ministry for the whole church. And there can be no united church without a ministry that is ecumenically minded and ecumenically accepted. The maintenance of denominational theological schools for the training of a denominationally minded ministry obviously has the effect of perpetuating division in the Church of Christ. The ecumenical ideal requires the abandonment of this organ of denominationalism and the transformation of its theological seminaries into ecumenical institutions.

5. The Church's Worship. In the united church, we shall have ample room for diversity in modes of worship—a diversity as wide as that which is now represented by our separate denominations. The broad distinction in Protestant worship is that between the more formal and the more spontaneous types of liturgy. Each of these has its own special value and justification. Each also is beset with its special temptation: the formal type, with the temptation to make the form do service for the lack of spiritual wholeheartedness; the spontaneous type, with the temptation to adopt an indecent irreverance before the altar of God. In the united church our diversities of taste and culture and habit will find expression in local churches, not in separate autonomous denominations. In the denominational system these two types of worship have no opportunity to be brought into contact with each other and thus to influence and enrich each other. On the contrary, each type of worship, maintained in sectarian isolation, tends to breed its own defects. But in the united church, this variety represented in the local churches would be interpenetrative, resulting in the enrichment of worship throughout the whole church.

Nothing is more admirable—or more pathetic—in contemporary Protestantism than the widespread yearning on the part of local churches for adequate liturgical forms of worship. This has resulted in a colorful imitation of certain traditional forms and procedures. But our processionals and gownings and liturgical prayers and litanies and candles and an altar, pathetically lack the feel of reality. It is pathetic because its noble objective is unattainable within the denominational system. These nobler forms of worship are religiously ineffective because they lack depth and background. The denomination cannot provide its parish churches with a background that is congruous or commensurate with the nobility of worship which modern Christians long for. Their worship lacks transcendent implications—it begins here and it ends here.

Great worship requires a great church—not merely great in numbers, but great in its wholeness. Only the ecumenical church, manifesting itself in the worshiping congregation, can supply the background and depth of meaning which will invest the noblest worship with Christian realism. Even so, at its noblest, it will be felt to be still unworthy of the majesty of the God whose gift to man the church is. In denying to the worshiping congregation its most holy inspiration of worshipfully participating in the whole body of Christ, the denominational system impoverishes and cheapens the church's worship.

6. The Lord's Supper. What has just been said about worship in general applies pointedly to the holy communion, and need not be repeated. Is there in the whole range of divided Protestantism anything so sad, aye, and so sinful, as that this most precious symbol of the body and blood of him who is the head of the whole church which is his body should be celebrated in schismatic isolation? Instead of symbolizing the unity of his followers, it cannot be celebrated by separate, independent and autonomous denominational churches without symbolizing the dismemberment and disunity of his body. The inherent meaning of this sacramental action of the eucharist is corporate. It is not an action of the individual as such, but a corporate action of the whole church manifested in the local congregation in which each individual Christian participates. Our sectarian celebration of the Lord's Supper within the framework of a separate, independent, self-contained and autonomous man-made church is little short of unwitting, though necessitated, sacrilege.

7. The Creed. The term "creed" is ambiguous. In one of its meanings it connotes a formalized statement of belief which is officially used as a basis and often as a test of fellowship in a church. There are some denominations which claim that they have no creed. They do, however, have a clearly recognized ideology which pervades the collective mind of the denomination and operates with substantially the same effectiveness as if it were

officially standardized in a formal instrument. A creed in either of these meanings of the word is used by the denomination to maintain and justify its separate existence. A creed, that is to say, is a function of the churchism of the denomination. Without such a creed it would be difficult, if not impossible, for a denomination to exist as a church. Even those denominations which profess to have no creed cannot avoid making a creed of their alleged creedlessness.

Our present concern is not with the merits or demerits of any creed, as such. What concerns us is the fact that every denominational creed used as a basis of Christian fellowship is a violation of the unity of the ecumenical church. All our denominations fall under this indictment. Regardless of the diversity of their creeds or ideologies, the entire membership of all our evangelical denominations is embraced in the hidden ecumenical church. This is the definition of the Church of Christ which the ecumenical movement itself has explicitly adopted as the goal of its endeavor. It is the community of all those whom Christ has received into his fellowship. This means that our creedal differences are irrelevant to the constitution of his church. It does not mean that our creeds are matters of indifference to us who hold them or to the ecumenical church. What it means is that in the ecumenical church, if and when its actualization is achieved, we shall find ourselves in a common fellowship bringing with us the creedal diversities which have so long separated us into divided and divisive denominational churches. We shall return to this subject for a more extended treatment in the eighth chapter.

Meantime, it must be confessed that it is difficult to discuss the creedal question in terms that are felt to be realistic in our time. A century or even a half-century ago this issue would have been at the top of the list of the ecumenical problems. But today, the denominations have largely abandoned the rigidity of their creeds. A new conception has taken form in the churches—the conception that all these creeds are but "broken lights" of the ecumenical Christian faith. This is a mark of the ecumenical awakening in whose light the churches are becoming more and more aware of the illusion of their former claims to possess the fullness and richness of the Christian faith.

8. Polity or Organization. Finally, each denomination not only exercises by itself and for itself alone, the ecumenical functions previously enumerated, but it embraces its local churches in an integrated organic unity of structure which completely separates it, ecclesiastically, from all other Christians. This structure of organization is called its polity. Some denominations are more closely knitted in their polity, others less so. But the polity of every denomination is sufficiently integrated to enable it to exercise its churchly functions as a united body, acting independently as a self-contained, autonomous and full-panoplied church. There is no essential feature belonging to the true and only Church of Christ which has not been taken over by every one of our denominational churches.

Certain denominations, such as the Baptists, the Disciples of Christ and the Congregationalists, imagine that they have escaped the presumption of being churches because they reserve the idea of "church" for the local church only. They, therefore, disclaim the appelation of "church" for their denomination and use such terms as "association" or "brotherhood" or "fellowship" or "communion" of local churches. The Disciples have been historically squeamish about being called even a denomination. But by whatever name these distinctly separate and autonomous entities are called, they cannot conceal the fact of their churchism.

These denominations like to believe that their local churches are in some manner directly related to the invisible ecumenical church without any denominational intermediary. But this is impossible, for the ecumenical church is not an empirical actuality with which they could be related. To claim that they transcend the churchism of the denominational system is to be under the illusion of a platonic abstraction or to mistake ecumenical sentimentalism for the reality. Their own denomination stands as a barrier between these local churches and their ideal ecumenical church. It assumes to exercise all the churchly functions and organs that belong to the ecumenical church. The churchism of

these so-called congregationally organized denominations differs
from the churchism of their more corporately organized neighbors
only in being less integrated and orderly in their polity.

DENOMINATIONALISM AS SIN

Our analysis of the churchism of the denomination has thus
brought us to the point where we must now say, sweepingly, that
the denominational system commands the field—the whole field
—of Protestantism. No body of Christians and no individual
Christian can transcend it. This is the tragic plight of Protestantism—it has no church, but only churches. Under the eye of
Christ, these churches are not true churches, for he knows but one
church, the ecumenical church, whose functions these man-made
denominational churches have usurped, leaving the Church of
Christ impotent to bear its witness in the world.

The radical and comprehensive problem of the ecumenical
movement is therefore to restore to the Church of Christ those
organs and functions which our denominational churches now
exercise as schismatic sects. This means nothing less than the
dissolution of all our denominations as churches. It need not
mean the dissolution of their special fellowships; it means the
abandonment of their churchism. This churchism of the denominations must be perceived as sin against Christ—a sin which
only the Christian conscience can recognize. A non-Christian
will be unable to see any meaning in such a confession of sin. This
is because he conceives sin only as a violation of the Ten Com-
mandments. Our denominational churchism may not be a violation of the moral law; but it is a violation of the law of Christ. It
may not be a moral sin; but it is surely a Christian sin, a sin against
Christ who is the head, not of any of our denominations, but of the
Church which is his body.

To awaken the conscience of the churches to the fact that their
churchism is sinful and that in penitence they must cease being
churches—this is the radical, primary and imperative task of the
ecumenical movement.

The great ecumenical conferences, from Lausanne and Stockholm to Oxford, Edinburgh and Amsterdam, have more or less

clearly recognized the Christian anomaly of denominationalism. This recognition has found expression in all the studies that have been made of the nature of the Christian Church. It found its most impressive recognition in the liturgies used in the services of worship at these historic gatherings. In the earlier conferences the prayers of confession used the language of the Prayer Book in deploring "our unhappy divisions." But at Oxford and Edinburgh in 1937, and most consistently at Amsterdam in 1948, it was evident that a more profound conviction had taken hold of the ecumenical mind. The liturgical rubrics were not content to refer to our divisions as merely "unhappy"; they were openly and penitently avowed as sin. Day after day at Amsterdam the World Council of Churches opened its every session with solemn prayers of deep repentance for the *sin* of our divisions. Pleading for divine forgiveness, the World Council looked forward in prayerful hope to the visible manifestation of the one church, the Church of Christ. These seasons of worship, carrying the unfailing note of repentance for the sin of our sectarianism, remain with those who were present as the most significant and memorable features of their historic experience.

But there was a hidden contradiction between the prayers and some of the pronouncements of Amsterdam. Certain pronouncements seemed to take away or to condone the thing of which the prayers repented. Perhaps it would be more accurate to say that the prayers were not too clear as to the specific sin that was being repented of. And the pronouncements failed to make it clear. On the one hand, our denominational divisions were branded as sin. On the other hand, these divisions seemed to be condoned, if not justified, on the ground that the beliefs represented by them were held in all good conscience by each separate church. Now, we must ask, if each separate church holds its distinctive convictions in all good conscience, where is the sin, and what need have we for repentance? Can we repent of matters concerning which our conscience is clear?

Perhaps the sin of which Amsterdam repented was mystically felt, though not specifically discerned. And there is no doubt that God hears such prayers and answers them in his own way. Perhaps he will answer these prayers by further enlightenment of the ecumenical leadership as to just what it is they are repentant of. But the repentance, that is, the turning away from the sin, cannot be realistic unless the sin to be turned away from is clearly perceived, and perceived as sin.

We must avoid any semblance of being hypercritical of the ecumenical movement, for it is a marvelous answer to so many of our prayers. But it seems necessary to say that, in our judgment, the movement has not yet found the bedrock upon which the structure of the ecumenical church can come into empirical existence. It is apparently proceeding on the assumption that, because the distinctive doctrines which mark off one church from the others are held in good conscience, therefore unity must wait until doctrinal agreement has been achieved. Thus the sin of sectarianism remains obscure.

Where, then, is the sin of sectarianism of which we are called upon to repent? The locus of the sin cannot conceivably be in the realm of theological or other differences conscientiously held. Is it not clear from all that we have said that *the sin consists in establishing and maintaining separate churches based upon these conscientious differences?* It is the churchism of the denominations that is sin.

Christ has not left us in doubt as to his condemnation of our sectarian churchism. True, he gave us no commandment. But he did more. He *prayed* for his followers that they might be one. And his prayer plainly implied a visible unity, for he added, "that the world might believe that thou hast sent me." This, then, is our sin, that our disunion into separated churches stands in the way of God's answer to the prayer of our Lord.

In the proceedings at Amsterdam there occurred a momentary but illuminating episode which has entirely escaped mention in the reports and the literature of that inaugural meeting of the World Council. But there was a fateful moment when that assembly came very near saying what we have been saying throughout this chapter. The final draft of the statement on "The Nature of the Church" was being read by the chairman of the commission to the plenary session. Advance copies had been distributed and I had mine in my hand. Having finished the reading of the document, the chairman called attention to three sentences in the final paragraph and moved that they be deleted. The sentences were as follows:

The very name, "World Council of *Churches*" implies a situation that ought not to be, because we acquiesce in calling our denominations "churches" in a way which the New Testament will never allow. There is but one Lord and one Body. Because we know this, we cannot rest content with "churches."

The chairman of the commission gave his reason for asking that this passage be stricken out. It was, he said in effect, tactically unwise to call attention to an embarrassing implication in the title of the World Council. There was no discussion of his motion. My seat on the platform was within five feet of the speaker. I had some doubt that the import of his motion to delete these words was fully understood. The presiding officer put the motion and the passage was stricken out without dissent.

Here was a clear statement of the specific sin upon which the whole liturgy of repentance should have been focused. For one brief moment, the eyes of the assembly rested upon it, and then, as I believe, unaware of the implications of their action, turned away. Thus Amsterdam was put in the regrettable position of refusing to face the sin for which it had been fervently praying to be forgiven.

The ecumenical movement, having reached a clear understanding of the nature of the ecumenical church, cannot longer evade the responsibility of attaining an equally clear conception of the nature of the denomination. Its formal pronouncements and the utterances of its spokesmen should no longer be satisfied to speak of the denomination merely in terms of the precious treasures of fellowship and tradition which each denomination carries, as if these were the substantive elements of the denomination. To continue thus to evade the churchism of the denominational system and its implications for the ecumenical ideal is to miss contact with the concrete reality with which the ecumenical ideal is primarily concerned. The ecumenical movement has not yet

captured the unreserved commitment even of its ardent sup-
porters. Many of its friends support it in hope mixed, however,
with an inarticulate feeling that its undertaking is vague and unrealistic. Inevitably, this feeling that the movement is operating
in an idealistic vacuum will be increasingly confirmed if the
implications of the churchism of the denominations continue to
be glossed over or ignored. The result will be that present enthusiasm will pass into widespread disillusionment.

Our denominations are waiting to be challenged by the ecumenical ideal at the point of their churchism. They do not know
that they are waiting for such a challenge. They are like the man
of Macedonia who called to St. Paul in a vision: "Come over and
help us!" He did not know, or knew only vaguely, that he needed
help, or that Paul could bring it to him. Indeed he had never even
heard of Paul. But Paul knew and went and preached the gospel
to him. So, our denominations do not know that they are bound
in a system that falsifies the Church of Christ and denies to it the
possibility of an empirical existence. Under the sentimentalism
of the hymn, "We are not divided, all one body we," our conscience has been soothed into accepting the wish for the fact. The
ecumenical movement is the call of God to awaken the conscience
of the churches to the sin of their churchism and bring them the
enlightenment and liberation of the ecumenical gospel.

PROTESTANT COUNTERPART OF THE ROMAN HIERARCHY

It will help us to understand the nature of the churchism of our
denominations if we consider the striking analogy between the
denominational system and the hierarchical system of the Roman
Catholic Church. This analogy, mentioned in Chapter I, needs
further amplification. The denominational system is the Protestant counterpart of the Roman hierarchy. It stands in the same relation to the true church as the hierarchy stands in relation to
Catholicism. It will require careful statement to make this clear,
and also careful thinking to discern precisely wherein the analogy
consists. The form of the sacerdotal hierarchy and the form of the
denomination do not at once suggest any analogy between them.
In outward appearance they do not look alike, and the denomi-

nation cannot be charged with the monstrous pretension of the hierarchy to be the sole carrier of divine grace and salvation. On what grounds, then, can any comparison be made between them?

Certainly, no one would assert that the denomination is a hierarchy. But if the statement is turned around, one is bound to affirm that the hierarchy is a denomination. It answers precisely to our definition of a denomination. The Roman hierarchy is a part of the church, self-constituted, self-contained, independent and autonomous, which has usurped the functions that belong only to the whole church, and is exercising them by itself apart from any responsible participation by the church as a whole. These are, point by point, the precise terms in which we have defined a Protestant denomination. It is not in their external form that the analogy between them appears, but in their identical relation to and effect upon the ecumenical church. What we have been saying about the churchism of the denomination is precisely what the Reformers of the sixteenth century said about the Roman hierarchy. They said that the hierarchy, with the pope at its head, had usurped the functions that belong only to the church itself, just as we have said that the Protestant denomination has usurped the functions of the ecumenical church. Let us look into this matter carefully.

The most fundamental and controlling insight of the Reformation, as we saw in the first chapter, was its discovery of the true nature of the church. The church, said the Reformers—long before our ecumenical movement said the same thing—is the living community of believers. The Christian people—the laity—those whom Christ has received into fellowship with himself—these constitute the true Church of Christ—they *are* the church. The most radical charge which the Reformers brought against Roman Catholicism was that it had divided the church into two absolutely separate parts—the hierarchical priesthood and the laity. The hierarchy, they said, was an alien structure which had been built up within the church and superimposed upon it. The true church, which consists of Christ's people, had been led into spiritual bondage to a professional priestly caste, a hierarchical order, which dispossessed the church of the organs and functions that belong to it, and is exercising them in absolute independence and autonomy. The effect of this usurpation, said the Reformers, was to degrade the church into an irresponsible multitude of docile subjects and followers, instead of the corporate body of the faithful which is directly responsible only to Christ its living head.

But the insight of the Reformers was even more penetrating. They saw that the usurpation by the hierarchy of the prerogatives that belong only to the church of Christ's people, had the effect of reducing the church to invisibility. The hierarchy itself had become the visible ecclesiastical entity. Where it was not present there was no church. The Christian people did not constitute the church. There could be no church where there was no priest, and "where the bishop was, there was the church." The blessings of the gospel could not be received by Christ's people without the presence and the action of the priesthood. Through it alone could the grace of God be conveyed to the faithful.

The sacraments which belonged by right to the whole church were now in the absolute control of the hierarchy. These sacraments, by which the church could manifest itself as the empirical body of Christ, had been taken out of its hands and lodged as a monopoly in the hands of the priesthood. The governance of the church had been withdrawn from the people and concentrated with absolute authority in the hierarchy. The faith of the church was no longer an expression of the faith of the Christian people, but was held by the hierarchy as a divine deposit and imposed upon the people by infallible decree. The mission of the church was not planned by the people, nor had they the slightest part in it; it was planned, projected and carried out by this self-constituted and absolutely autonomous organization of privileged men who, with infinite presumption, claimed to receive their illicit power directly from Christ himself.

Our recital of these features of the hierarchical system is not conceived as a polemic against Catholicism, but solely to refresh Protestant memory concerning the fundamental insight of the Reformation. It was a new insight into the nature of the church as consisting of Christ's people, and an insight into the effect upon the church of the hierarchy's usurpation of the organs and functions that belong to the very nature of the church as the body of Christ's people. The Reformers clearly discerned that, by divesting the church of its corporate responsibilities, under Christ, the hierarchy had reduced it to impotence and rendered it invisible. Having lost its organs and functions—that is, its sacraments, its self-governance, its right to its own faith, and, under Christ, the control of its mission—the real church of Christ's people had lost the implementation by which alone it could manifest itself as an empirical corporate entity.

But the church itself had not thereby been destroyed. Though hidden, it still existed. It had been led captive by the false and unholy churchism of the hierarchy. From this captivity the Reformers sought to set it free. Their procedure was to cast off the alien habiliments of the apostate hierarchical system and reclothe the church of Christ's people with the shining garments which had been divinely designed for it, and of which the hierarchy had robbed it. Thus the church would again be the visible church, the truly church catholic, manifesting itself in its true nature as an experienceable entity.

We are affirming, now, that the denominational system is the Protestant counterpart of the Roman hierarchy. Allowing for the obvious dissimilarities between them in structure, mode of operation, and in pretension, they are nevertheless alike in that each consigns the church of Christ's people to impotence and invisibility. From what we have said up to this point, the analogy between them is clear in four respects:

1. The denomination, like the hierarchy, has usurped the organs and functions of the ecumenical church and is exercising them in absolute self-sufficiency and autonomy, even as the hierarchy does.

2. The denominational system, like the hierarchical system, is an alien, man-made structure superimposed upon the true Church of Christ.

3. The multiple schisms in Protestantism which create an impassable cleavage between the denominations and the ecumenical church, correspond to the internal schism existing in the Roman

church which sets the hierarchy apart from the true church of Christ's people by an impassable cleavage.

4. The absolute independence and autonomy of the denomination in carrying out the mission of the church as if it represented the whole church and the whole gospel, is analogous to the exclusive and autonomous administration of the church's mission by the hierarchy with no participation of the laity in planning and projecting it.

We have previously listed and discussed eight of these ecumenical features of which the denomination has dispossessed the ecumenical church. We here need only to generalize them. They are the church's sacraments, its faith, its governance and its mission. These all are in the control of a fragment of the church— in one case, the hierarchy, in the other, the denomination. The effect in each case is to consign the true church of Christ's people to impotence and invisibility.

Let us look again at the Reformation. It was against the arrogant usurpation of these functions by the hierarchy that the Reformers of the sixteenth century leveled their most vehement attack. Precisely and fundamentally, it was at this point that they called upon the existing church for radical reform. The nature of the reform for which they uncompromisingly appealed was nothing less than the complete abrogation of the hierarchical system. This they demanded in order that the true church of Christ's people, long held in a "Babylonian captivity" by the churchism of the hierarchy, might be set free and made manifest as itself the true Church of Christ.

The aim of the ecumenical movement in our time can be described in essentially the same manner as that of the Reformation itself. The ultimate goal of this modern movement in Protestantism is the realization and implementation of the ecumenical church as alone the true Church of Christ. Like the Reformation, it finds this church of Christ's people in a "Babylonian captivity" to the churchism of the denomionational system. The ecumenical movement, therefore, like the Reformation, confronts a task of radical reform—a reform of Protestantism itself. It can accomplish its reform only by uncompromisingly calling for the complete dissoluton of the churchism of the denominations in order that the ecumenical church of Christ's people may stand forth in strength and in empirical objectivity as the true Church of Christ.

We, the inheritors of the Reformation, have received the blessings of its epochal achievement. But we are also the heirs of its unrealized intention. The Reformers longed for unity. But the time was unready for it. Luther and Calvin and Zwingli and Cranmer, working under historical conditions unfavorable to the maximum fulfillment of their common hope, could only bequeath to us an unfinished Reformation. Ours is the challenging mission, in a fairer time, with the advantage of historical experience, aye, and under pressure of the precarious position of Protestant ascendancy in American life—ours is the mission to complete the labors of the great Reformers, that their faith, by our faithfulness, under God, might be made perfect.

IV

The Christian Life in a United Church

WE HAVE NOW EXAMINED the denominational system from three points of view: historical, pragmatic and ecclesiological. We have reached three conclusions. First, that denominationalism is alien to the historical genius of Protestantism and a denial of it. Second, that the denominational system is not, pragmatically, a success, but is an encumbrance and a handicap upon Protestantism in its striving to discharge the responsibilities which the Christian faith lays upon the Christian Church. Third, that the denominational system is the Protestant counterpart of the Roman Catholic hierarchy in that it, too, has usurped the functions of the true church, thus denying to the true church the power to manifest itself in its essential nature as the living, empirical and ecumenical Church of Christ.

In the present chapter we shall shift to a distinctly different point of view. Without abandoning our critique of denominationalism, let us turn our eyes toward the goal of the ecumenical movement, namely, the united church itself, and compare the spiritual values we may expect to find in the united church with the spiritual life of our denominations. This will require some exercise of our imagination, for we shall try to envisage the united church as already in existence and ourselves as members of it. In our attempt to perform this feat of imagination, we need not be troubled about the realistic difficulties and problems involved in the actual attainment of the united church, nor need we try to conceive what its structure may be like. These are serious problems and we have no intention of evading them. Some of them will be considered in the following chapters.

Let us, then, leap over all the problems and difficulties that must be resolved before a united church is achieved, and imagine ourselves in the common fellowship of the ecumenical Church of Christ. Our denominations will have ceased to exist as churches. Whether they continue to exist as special fellowships in the united church will be entirely optional. We can imagine that some of them will continue to exist for some time as kindred fellowships. But they will not be churches. Their functons as churches will have been restored to the true church from which they were taken away. The sectarian ecclesiastical walls between these denominations will therefore have vanished. With all our diversities of theology, of opinion and of tradition, we shall awake to find ourselves one flock under one Shepherd.

Looking thus imaginatively toward the united church, we may expect to find the Christian life of Protestantism profoundly changed in depth of feeling, in range of outlook, in the significance of our belonging, and in the quality and dignity of our spiritual satisfactions. If this expectation proves to be well-founded, it should provide strong motivation for the attainment of the ecumenical goal.

This word "spiritual" requires some attention before we proceed. It is used in two senses. In one sense it applies to the particular experience which the individual Christian enjoys in his private devotional relationship with God. This, of course, is the very heart of the Christian life and it must be included in our use of the term. But we shall not confine our use of the word "spiritual" to this central Christian experience. Its meaning spreads out to include many other aspects of the Christian life which, because they are imponderable and intangible, are only spiritually apprehended. This broad meaning of the word is, of course, not peculiar to the church nor to religion. We speak of the spirit of a nation, a city, a college, a club, a civilization, a culture, because each is characterized by a certain intangible quality which is more or less distinctive of itself. Our usual term for it is *esprit de corps*

—the spirit of a group or a society, by which we mean its morale, its significance for itself and the quality of allegiance which it evokes in its members. It is in this broad and more flexible sense of the word "spiritual" that we shall be thinking as we consider the spiritual values of a united church.

In passing, we might well point out that it is in this broad area of spirit that the Holy Spirit is manifested in the life of the church. The doctrine of the Holy Spirit has been the subject of much controversy. But whatever theological doctrine one may hold as to the *nature* of the Holy Spirit, the *manner* in which the Spirit becomes manifest in the church is clear. The Holy Spirit is manifested not only in the personal experience of the individual Christian, nor primarily in the individual, but primarily and supremely as the *esprit de corps* of the Church of Christ. All the spiritual values which inhere in the Christian fellowship are nothing less than the gifts of the Spirit to the church. It is interesting to note that Christian liberalism which for a long time seemed to ignore the Holy Spirit is finding its way back to a more evangelical position under a distinct prompting from sociology.

Also in passing, we ought to note that a united church would restore to the Holy Spirit the field and condition necessary for its complete and most fruitful manifestation. Our sectarian fragmentation of the Christian fellowship denies to the Spirit the essential condition upon which its exercise chiefly depends. The Holy Spirit is the Spirit of the whole body of Christ; it is the Spirit of the whole and not of a part. Its manifestation is necessarily partial and curbed by our denominational separatism. What the Spirit of God could do with a united church is beyond our power to imagine.

A New Birth of Freedom

Let us gather into a single sentence all that is to be said in this chapter. When the walls of our denominational churchism have crumbled and the united church appears, we may expect to experience nothing less than *a new birth of freedom*.

The simple statement of this expectation will at once encounter a resistant surprise. Our Protestant minds have been taught to believe that freedom is the pride and glory of the denominational system. As Methodists, Presbyterians, Episcopalians, Baptists— to name no others—do we not enjoy freedom in the highest degree? And is not our system of separate denominations little short of a providential arrangement for securing and insuring our freedom? Were not all our denominations founded in the pursuit and love of freedom? Are they not independent and self-governing bodies, each going its own way, living its own life in accordance with purposes and rules of its own devising, without let or hindrance from any outside sources? How can we expect in a united church more freedom than we enjoy in the convenient arrangement provided by our denominational system?

To these questions the answer is that Protestant sectarianism has historically mistaken independence and autonomy as the equivalent of freedom. From the Christian point of view this equation is false. It may be taken to represent with fair accuracy the general political concept of freedom, but it does not represent Christian freedom. In a subtle and unconscious manner the political concept of independence and autonomy has been taken over into the thinking of Protestantism as if this concept of freedom as self-determination were also the measure and meaning of Christian freedom. And this error has vitiated the conception of the church in many Protestant minds.

If we would understand the Christian concept of freedom we shall find it in a wholly different dimension from that of the political order. We are familiar with the Christian conception when we think in terms of the freedom of the individual Christian man. He finds his freedom in being what he really is. And Christianity defines what he really is. He is a child of God, created in the image of God who made him for fellowship and co-operation with himself in the pursuit of ends which the Creator himself, not man, has determined. Man's true freedom is found, then, not in the consciousness of his independence, but of his dependence, not in terms of autonomy but of theonomy—the sovereignty of the will of God. In the surrender of his will—his independence and autonomy—to the will of God he finds his freedom. This is the Christian conception. "Make me a captive, Lord," so prayed George Matheson, "and then I shall be free."

It should not be too difficult, now, to discern the freedom of the church in the same terms in which Christian faith conceives the freedom of the Christian man. For the church is also a divine creation. It conceives itself sacramentally as the creative gift of God, a holy thing. Its freedom, therefore, is found in being what it really is. And what it really is, is determined by the mind of Christ who prayed for its unity that the world might believe. The freedom of our denominations is a delusion. They are not really free; they have been lured into bondage by an egoistic conception of freedom which boasts of its independence and autonomy. Of the one church which God gave us, man has made many churches. These churches all embody human self-will and each exists in contravention of the will of Christ.

Let us quote here a few sentences from the recent fine book, *God Makes the Difference,* by Edwin McNeill Poteat. He says:

As to the divisions among the Free [Protestant] churches it must be said that they, no less than Rome, are the victims of the historic secularistic perversion of freedom into independence and autonomy. . . . We of the Free [Protestant] churches are independent and autonomous. How we love to describe ourselves with these orotund syllables! Yet are we free in being what we truly are? No. We have not only missed the essence of freedom, but we have institutionalized our errors in the ever-mounting proliferations of sectarianism. The whole meaning of the ecumenical movement . . . is to be understood properly as a creative effort to correct an error and recapture freedom.[1]

We should find special satisfaction in reading these words on church union from the pen of a distinguished Baptist writer, and a Southern Baptist at that! We can well believe that Elijah's seven thousand who have not bowed the knee before the idol of sectarianism are found even in those denominatons which are commonly thought to be less responsive than others to the ecumenical ideal.

Our sectarian churchism thus involves our denominations in

[1] New York: Harper & Brothers, 1951, p. 127.

an inescapable position perilously akin to idolatry. Estranged from the freedom of the true church, the independent and autonomous denomination is in captivity to its own self-sufficiency and self-righteousness. This man-made church accepts, and conceives itself worthy to receive, the allegiance of its members, an allegiance which, under Christ, may be rightly given only to the Church of Christ. The true church is free because its allegiance is given to Christ who is its head. But the denomination is not free, because, in its apostasy from the true church, it is not under Christ. This is instinctively recognized by our evangelical denominations not one of which would claim that Christ is the head of its denomination. Ecclesiastically speaking, the independence and autonomy of the denomination are absolute. A Protestant denomination recognizes no empirical responsibility beyond itself. It is completely independent of every other part of the divided church. Nor is it empirically responsible to the true church, for the existence of the denominational churches has robbed the Church of Christ of its empirical existence. The denominational system commands the whole field and has forced the true church into invisibility.

Here again we confront the sin of which the ecumenical movement penitently confesses that we stand in need of divine forgiveness. It is the sin of absolutizing the independence and autonomy of a fragment of the church over against the true Church of Christ. It is a sin so long established and so universal that familiarity blinds us to its true nature. We may try to hide the scandal of it under the increasing volume of good will across denominational lines which is happily displacing the older animosities, but we shall fail. We may try to conceal the sin of our denominational autonomy by a federation of the denominations. But one has only to read the constitution of the National Council of Churches to discern with what meticulous care the independence and autonomy of each participating denomination is jealously safeguarded. Behind the façade of co-operative federation there hides the stubborn fact that the denominations hug their independence and autonomy to their sectarian breasts with an idolatrous absolutism. They refuse to let the Church of Christ be what it really is.

The attainment of a united church must not be conceived as a mere correction of a theoretical or formal irregularity in organization. On the contrary, it will bring with it profound changes in the spiritual life of the entire Christian community. The all-inclusive change, we are now saying, will be a new birth of freedom. This freedom will be registered in the actual experience of the whole Christian community as a transfiguration of its spiritual life. It will be felt as a release from the absolutism and self-sufficiency of our man-made churches into the liberty of the church of which Christ is the head. The knowledge that the united church has become, under Christ, what the church really is, that it is not a man-made church, but that its existence transcends our human contriving—this knowledge will invest it with a depth and range of meaning and a spiritual enrichment unknown in the churches of our denominational independence and autonomy.

Before going further, we must be assured against the possibility of a grave misunderstanding. We are striving to envisage the great difference in the quality and depth of the spiritual life in a united church as compared with that which we experience in our denominations. We must avoid giving the impression that the argument invalidates the authentic Christian character of our present religious experience in our denominational churches. Let it then be explicitly affirmed that, even as members of denominational churches, we are living the authentic Christian life. The sin of our sectarian system is not in our hearts, but in the system. It can become our sin only if, when our eyes are opened to perceive it as sin, we remain undisturbed and complacent. Our Christian experience is impoverished, but it is not vitiated by the historical necessity of living the Christian life in the isolation of these autonomous fragments of a dismembered church.

As we reflect on the problem which occupies us in this chapter, we must recognize that the churchism of all our denominations is sublimated by an ideology which orients its members toward Christ and directs our denominational allegiance consciously toward him and the world-wide mission of his true church. Thus, in spirit and in feeling we transcend in some degree the denomination and, also in spirit, we share, though not in full empirical reality, in the ecumenical fellowship of the hidden church. This idealistic and subjective transcendence of the autonomous church-ism of the denomination invests our Christian life with authentic reality, despite the faulty medium to which, for the lack of an ecumenical medium, we are compelled to give our churchly allegiance.

The freedom of the united church will be experienced as a release from many forms of limitation which our man-made churches could not transcend. We shall consider four respects in which the united church may be expected to experience a new birth of freedom.

1. We may expect in the united church *a release from the static uniformity of the denomination into the inspiring diversity that belongs to the Church of Christ.*

This should be one of the most alluring of our expectations. And yet, strange to say, most people who contemplate the prospect of a united church think of it in terms of a dead level of uniformity. It is assumed that, before we can have a united church, all our theological and many of our other differences must be ironed out to a smooth surface of complete concord. It is further assumed that these differences must be so permanently settled that the spiritual life of the united church would have easy sailing on quiet seas with no controversial winds to buffet and no waves of diversity to surmount.

This is a great mistake. If Christian unity means that the Christian fellowship in a united church would no longer be disturbed by such differences as those which have existed between our de-nominations and across denominational lines, one would have to say that our striving for the ecumenical goal is not only futile but foolish. Such uniformity, if it could be attained, would spell decadence and the stagnation of the spiritual life. Our evangelical diversities are essential to spiritual vitality and growth. They play into and determine the quality of our spiritual experience. The Christian life cannot be divorced from the intellectual problems inherent in it and presupposed by it. Numerous attempts have been made to effect such a divorce. Both pietism and modern liberalism have been infected with this fallacy.

Pietism assumes that the subjective aspect of the Christian life can be maintained by transcending and disregarding theological conceptions. The devotional life of the Christian, in this view, has no stake in theological controversy. Similarly, moralistic liberalism has maintained that the objective, activistic aspect of the Christian life can be sustained in disregard of theology. It tends impatiently to waive all considerations of theological clarity and calls us to "get down to business" in the many forms of service which the social gospel has, in our lifetime, brought urgently to the attention of the Christian conscience. It is pertinent here to say that the failure of the social gospel to command an adequate response from the general church has been due, among other things, to its lack of a sufficient theological undergirding.

The actual experience of the ecumenical movement itself confirms this. In the early days of this movement, it projected a historic conference at Stockholm on the theory that Christian unity could be achieved by activistic co-operation in Life and Work. After nearly two decades in pursuit of its goal along these "practical" lines, the undertaking was merged at Amsterdam in 1948 with the parallel movement on Faith and Order. This was done because it had been discovered that the issues involved in uniting the churches on the basis of life and work could not be resolved except in the context of faith and order.

We are thus led directly into the question: What, in a united church, shall we do with our differences? There can be only one answer. They must be welcomed and embraced as essential to the fulfillment of the Christian life. Our diversities are not a spiritual liability, but a spiritual asset, of the Christian life. They do not derogate from our unity; they contribute to it. Embraced in the ecumenical church, these diversities, freely intermingling and interacting, would stimulate, guide and enhance its spiritual life beyond anything we have known in our sectarian separation.

Those who shrink from giving assent to the ecumenical movement under the misapprehension that it seeks uniformity should look again at the denominational system. They will discover that the ideal of the denomination is nothing less than uniformity. Those who shrink from uniformity should be the first to welcome a release from the denominational system. Most of our denominations were founded in order to escape diversity and to establish a single pattern of thought and practice. And every denomination strives with jealous consistency to maintain this uniform pattern. It is from this constrictive bondage to uniformity that the achievement of the ecumenical goal will deliver the Christian Church.

The movement for a united church turns its back upon uniformity and its face toward diversity. It sees the static conformity of the denominations as an impoverishment of the spiritual life. And it recognizes variety and difference as the condition, not only for a growing understanding of the Christian faith, but also for the highest fulfillment of the Christian fellowship. It does not ask, How can we compose our differences and so have a united church? It asks, rather, How can we attain a united church which welcomes and embraces our differences?

It is not yet clear that the ecumenical movement itself has reached the point where it is willing boldly to affirm this. In spending so much time upon the attempt to find a theological consensus, one cannot help wondering whether this aspect of the ecumenical problem is not being unduly magnified. This remark is not made in a mood of criticism. For we have to remember that the World Council of Churches, in which the ecumenical movement comes to a head, includes churches of such divergent traditions and ideologies that great patience is necessary in dealing with so comprehensive an undertaking. But the problem of uniting American evangelical Protestantism to which we have delimited the chapters of this book, and to which all our statements refer, presents a sufficiently homogeneous ideology, despite its shades of diversity, to justify the strong statements we have made.

2. We may expect that in a united church *the Christian spirit will be released from its bondage to the unchristian class distinctions which characterize the denominational system and will find fulfillment in the inspiring fellowship of a classless church.*

The true Church of Christ is a classless church, a classless society. This statement is not a paraphrase of Karl Marx. It is borrowed from the New Testament, from the whole ethic of the Christian faith and from Christ himself. The unity of all sorts and conditions of men in a common brotherhood is a fundamental insight of Christianity. And this ideal finds its realization within the Christian Church when the church is allowed to be what it really is. It is unnecessary to quote many passages of Scripture in support of this conception of the church, for the whole New Testament—in the Gospels and the Epistles—breathes this spirit of unity in a classless community. One great passage will suffice. Writing to the church in Colossae, St. Paul declares that "in Christ there is neither Jew nor Greek, circumcised nor uncircumcised, barbarian, Scythian, slave nor freeman, but Christ is all and in you all."

Our sectarian churches are a standing denial of this principle. Our denominations are, in one aspect or another, class churches. This is a form of spiritual bondage reflecting the self-righteousness of the denomination and its rejection of the freedom that is in Christ. The classism of our denominations is the direct effect of their churchism, which creates and tends to perpetuate a membership based upon class affinities. Almost automatically (and in charity we may say, unconsciously) the denomination rejects those who do not share its particular affinities. Thus pride and a complacent smugness are stimulated in one type of denomination and an often articulate resentment is stimulated in another type.

Under all the amenities of present-day interdenominational fraternization and federation, this class discrimination among Christ's followers is hardly concealed. No more serious error infects our ecumenical conversations than the assumption that the denominations are held apart solely, or even chiefly, by their theological differences.

If the apologists for the continuing separate existence of their particular denomination would search their own hearts with "the candle of the Lord," they would find, one is bound to say, though in all kindness, that theological considerations are utilized in an appreciable degree to rationalize their unwillingness to let their particular class fellowship merge into the fellowship of the whole Church of Christ.

In his book on the *Social Sources of the Denominations,* Professor Richard Niebuhr made it clear that the cultural ethos of each denomination is a fundamental factor in binding its members together and keeping them separate from other Christians. It is this cultural ethos which we are now calling the classism of our denominations. In our class pride we shrink from taking potluck in the democratic fellowship of the Church of Christ. This means the impoverishment of our Christian life. Our unwillingness to abandon the churchism which provides the semblance of a divine sanction for the classism of our churches is a hidden explanation of our sectarian intransigency.

Let us be as specific as we can without pretending to identify particular denominations. What are the class lines along which our denominations divide? We shall name eight. First, they divide along a socioeconomic line. The local churches of one denomination tend to operate on the right side of the tracks, those of another on the wrong side. One denomination attracts particularly the well-to-do, another the economic and social middle class, another works among still humbler folk. (It should be noted in passing that American Protestantism has only the most tenuous contact with the industrial workers of the nation.) Second, these class divisons are also cultural. One type of denomination attracts the intellectual class, another the moderately educated, while another exploits the undiscriminating emotions of the ignorant. Third, we are also divided on aesthetic lines. One type of denomination elevates form and beauty into a place beside holiness and virtue, another type, scorning all this as formalism, magnifies spontaneity, while still another carries this spontaneity to an ecstatic extreme, on the one hand, and to a crude slapdash rotarianism on the other.

Fourth, we are divided by the separate historical traditions which each denomination justly cherishes but unfairly magnifies out of reasonable or Christian proportions, largely through ignorance of other traditions. This provincialism generates an unjustifiable class feeling of superiority. Fifth, one type of denomination centers its spiritual life in the experience of corporate worship, another in a moralistic activism, another in some form of pietism. Sixth, one type of denomination attracts people of conservative mentality, another those of more flexible or liberal mind, while still others provide a home for those who are just chronically heretical. Seventh, there is the classism of immigrant populations who are drawn into separate churches by the ties of a national heritage brought with them from overseas. Eighth, and finally, there remains the broad class distinction between white and colored races; a few denominations have succeeded in crossing this line, as the Roman Catholic Church has done, by erasing the distinction at the ecclesiastical level without modifying segregation in the parishes.

It is obvious that the class distinctions in this rough catalogue cannot be applied indiscriminately to every denomination. To some, a particular distinction may not apply at all. In some, they are more evident than in others. These class lines cut across the whole denominational system and appear sharply or vaguely in one body or another. Each denomination may look into this catalogue as in a mirror and identify for itself those class characteristics which belong to it.

Moreover, it must be emphasized that these eight types of class affinities have not been catalogued in order to condemn them. Some of them represent natural and fruitful associations. Most of them represent inevitable diversities which, or the like of which, will always exist in the Christian Church. What then, it will be asked, is the point in bringing them to our attention? The point is that, when these class affinities are segregated in a sectarian autonomous denomination, they are inevitably intensified and vitiated by the churchism of the denomination which obscures their radically unchristian character.

One further comment. Our strictures on the classism of the denomination cannot be applied wholesale to the local churches. A parish church will necessarily partake of the class characteristics of its local community. A local church in a fine residence community, or an industrial or a suburban or a rural or a university community, or in a down-town center, will inevitably reflect the class constituency of its locality. But in a united church this local church will not be ecclesiastically integrated in a class-conscious denomination; its ecclesiastical fellowship will be ecumenical. We shall have more to say about the local church in this connection further on.

We are striving imaginatively to anticipate certain spiritual values which will be released in the freedom of a united church. In this true Church of Christ, our denominations will have ceased to be churches. They may continue to exist indefinitely as particular fellowships, if they desire, but they will perform no ecclesiastical functions, and their former local churches will have transferred their ecclesiastical connection from the denomination to the united church. With the disappearance of the churchism of the denomination the bulwark of its classism will have been removed. Christians of "whatever name or sign" will find themselves together in one undivided ecumenical fellowship. Their ecclesiastical allegiance will be given, under Christ, to the one church of which, alone, he is the head.

It is unrealistic and unnecessary to assume that the natural and legitimate class distinctions which have long been nursed behind denominational walls would suddenly disappear in the united church. Our social affinities, our cultural, theological and traditional affinities, our colonial and racial affinities, even our temperamental affinities, would inevitably have a place in the united church. This is only a way of saying that the gregarious characteristic of our human nature, instead of being suppressed, would be released by its emancipation from the restrictive walls of our sectarian churchism and find a higher fulfillment in the open intermingling fellowship of the ecumenical church.

It is also unrealistic and unnecessary to assume that the fellowships with which we have long been familiar in our denominations would have to be obliterated. Instead, most of them would be welcomed and embraced in the united church. It would not be incompatible with the ecumenical fellowship for our denominations—Methodist, Presbyterian, Episcopal, Congregational, Lutheran, and all the rest—to continue in the united church as unecclesiastical groups as long as memory and momentum kept them alive. But these denominations would no longer be churches. They would be particular fellowships within the one church, just as we now have particular fellowships in all our denominational churches.

We may therefore expect to find in the united church the very spiritual values whose conservation we have erroneously imagined required their embodiment in a separate denominational church. Freed from the sanctimonious smugness of their churchism, these familiar affinities now isolated in our denominations would be enriched and ennobled by contact and fellowship with other affinities in a united church. It is the fear of losing these familiarities which offers the most stubborn resistance to the ecumenical appeal. And, unfortunately, the ecumenical appeal has not yet been formulated by its spokesmen with sufficient clarity to enable the members of our denominations to differentiate sharply between these familiar values of their denominations and their churchism.

Let us, then, state the matter, this time, sharply and sweepingly. There is no value now enjoyed by the denomination which must be given up in response to the ecumenical appeal save only the false and unchristian value of its churchism. The churchism of the denomination must give way; it is in absolute conflict with the freedom that is in Christ. But every true and legitimate value now treasured in the fellowship of the denomination will be conserved in the richer fellowship of the united church. And not only conserved, but enhanced and heightened. A minister, speaking at a funeral service, once expressed this tender thought: When we wake up in heaven, he said, we shall be surprised to discover how familiar it is! A united church will not be heaven, but when we find ourselves in it we shall be surprised to discover that all our legitimate familiarites have been not only kept inviolate, but renewed, enriched and ennobled in the larger fellowship from which the sin of sectarianism has been cast out.

3. In the united church we may expect to find that *the local or parish church has been emancipated from its anomalous and invidious position as a unit in a mere fraction of the church and invested with the Christian dignity and self-respect which are its birthright as an integral part of the whole Church of Christ.*

The local church of Protestantism is the most obvious sufferer from the denominational system. It partakes necessarily of the artificial and alien character of the denomination, and this precludes its conception of itself in terms of its more profound religious character. The result is that the local church is exposed to the temptation (or the necessity) of supplementing its religious appeal with a disproportionate recourse to motives and attractions that are irrelevant, or only adventitiously relevant, to the serious religious purpose for which it exists. In a word, the denominational system denies to the local church the right to be what it really is. We cannot understand its predicament unless we have a clear conception of what the local church really is. The denomination hides its reals nature. In all the literature of Christian scholarship dealing with the nature of the Christian Church, it is doubtful that there exists a single page that gives any legitimate place at all to the denomination. Theological scholarship, like the New Testament itself, knows the Christian Church only in two aspects, namely, the ecumenical church and the local church. The denomination is plainly regarded as an alien entity which has no legitimate place in ecclesiological interpretation. We have all heard a sermon now and then, or an address by a headquarters representative of his denomination, or have read an article or editorial in a denominational journal, designed to give the denomination a legitimate status in the Christian system. But theological scholarship gives the denomination no such status. It sees only the church ecumenical and the church local.

Let us, then, define a local church in its true Christian character: *A local church is the ecumenical church manifested in a particular locality*. The denominational system is a denial of this conception. The denomination is an interloper between the ecumenical church and the local or parish church. The parish churches of Protestantism are not the ecumenical church made manifest in particular localities; they are local manifestations of their several denominations.

The local churches of Protestantism were not founded by the ecumenical church, they are not dependent upon it, they are not integrated in it, their support is not given to the ecumenical church—all this because the ecumenical church has no empirical existence. Their sense of belonging, their loyalty, their outlook and all the practicalities of their churchly devotion are inevitably oriented within the narrow framework of the denomination. The denomination thus stands between the local church and the ecumenical church, obstructing its communication and communion with the ecumenical church of which it should be the manifestation in its particular locality.

There is, of course, in the denominational local churches some awareness of the ecumenical significance of its churchly devotion, but this consciousness is necessarily a surplusage, an overflow beyond the primary loyalty inherent in the claims of the denomination. This is because the denomination is itself a church, and though it does not, in theory, claim to be *the* church, it works out in practice that the local church inevitably thinks of the denomination as *its* church. It cannot be otherwise when every local church has been founded by a denomination, is dependent upon its denomination and responsible to it for the support of all the general Christian enterprises. The local church has no other integration than with the denomination. It cannot have, because Protestantism provides no other church with which it could be integrated. It is envitable, therefore, that local churches, operating in the ecclesiastical context of only a fragment of the Church of Christ, will lack the consciousness of their own dignity and significance which they would find in an ecclesiastical integration with the church as a whole. To put the matter still more sharply: The denomination cheats the local church of something precious which belongs to its very nature.

But this is not the whole account of the spiritual injury which the denominational system works upon the local church. In addition to severing its connection with the church ecumenical, the denomination, by its very nature as a mere fragment of the church, is unable to command the profoundly religious allegiance which the Christian faith requires of every Christian and every parish church. The local churches of Protestantism do not enjoy the sense of having the full sky over them—they have only patches of sky. Lacking the inspiring consciousness of belonging to the whole Church of Christ, they are exposed to the temptation to become merely local churches—with the emphasis upon "local." Yielding to this temptation, the parish church removes itself still further from its own norm of being what it really is. It inevitably becomes

parochial-minded, short-visioned and concerned with innumerable irrelevancies and trivialities which demean the church and
the Christian faith.

Severed from their true ecclesiastical mother, the parish
churches of American Protestantism are driven to all sorts of
superficial and secular appeals to keep themselves going. One
shrinks from itemizing too specifically the activities and concerns
which fall into these categories. Every enlightened and sensitive
parish minister is well aware of them. The denominational system
which produces the scandalous overlapping of local churches in
American communities, subjects them to an unholy competitive
struggle to maintain their own existence. In this rivalry it is humanly inevitable that such churches will appeal to superficial or
irrelevant motives in gaining new members. By this is meant
motives that fall short of a profound religious response. The act of
uniting with the church carries with it hardly more than local
implications. It is but little above the level of the act of uniting
with the Rotary Club, the Masonic lodge, the Parent-Teacher
Association or any of the numerous social or uplift organizations
of the community. One unites with *this* church, and the act is
accompanied with only the minimum of consciousness that one is
uniting with *the* church.

A membership recruited in this way has to be held together by
the same motives which recruited it. Great numbers of Protestant
Christians, when they have moved their residence into a new community, wait inertly to be coddled into a church home. They lack
religious spontaneity, because their past relation to the church has
been based, not upon genuine religious feeling and conviction, but
mainly upon local attractions.

Let any denominational pastor examine his own routine with
the purpose of appraising the quality and significance of his daily
labors in keeping his church going and building it up with new
accessions to its membership. He will find that, in addition to the
true shepherding of his flock, he has been engaged in making
approaches and appeals that are dishearteningly superficial and
trivial. He has not done this of his own accord or because he is
unaware of the lack of religious seriousness in his procedure. In-

deed, he inwardly recoils from this cheapening of his high vocation. And he would reproach himself for engaging in it, but for one consideration: he *has* to do it! He is driven to it by the practical necessity that is forced upon him by the denominational system which multiplies competitive churches in his community, and condemns these local churches to an inferior quality of Christian allegiance.

It should be unnecessary to explain that what we have said is no narrow-minded or pietistic criticism of the sociabilities of local church life. The point of this discussion will be completely missed if it is so interpreted. From its earliest beginnings the Christian faith has found a positive expression of its fellowship on the common level of social intercourse. Nor are we uttering a petulant criticism of the local church or its parish minister. Both church and minister are victims of a system that is ecclesiastically unchristian —the denominational system that spawns perhaps twice if not three times as many local churches as American Protestantism needs, and denies them the religious inspiration, the Christian dignity and spiritual self-respect which can be possessed only in their consciousness of belonging to the whole body of Christ. Not until the denomination, as church, disappears in the united church can the local church become, in truth, the manifestation of the ecumenical church in its particular place.

A strange argument is often used to inhibit action toward the realization of this ecumenical ideal. It is the pious argument that church union must wait for a profound change in the spiritual life of Protestant church members; then we could take up the matter of a united church. One fears that those who reason this way are only rationalizing their unwillingness to act. It is safe to say that there never will be any more spiritual vitality in our denominational churches than we now have. These churches have already passed their zenith in spiritual vigor.

Our attempts to galvanize the spiritual life into a revival heat within the sectarian churches are proving more futile with every fresh outburst of the revival spirit. Conventional evangelism in the medium of our sectarian system has long since worn itself out. Where it still continues, its apparent successes, gained under methods of high-pressure emotionalism, are illusory, ephemeral and barren. Our churches are losing as many members as they are gaining—losing them, not necessarily from the roll, but by indifference and inattendance. The reasons for this are numerous, but the fundamental explanation is that our denominationalism does not provide a church that is either competent or worthy to conserve the fruits of its evangelism. The gospel preached is so much greater than the church which preaches it, that the harvesting of the fruits of the revival leads to disillusionment and, too often, ends in indifference and virtual falling away.

So also with our programs intended to deepen the spiritual life of the members of our churches. These programs are destined in advance to virtual futility. The quality of spiritual life we now have is the maximum that can be attained in our sectarian fragments of the Church of Christ. Those who long for a revival of grace and spiritual depth in contemporary Protestantism—and who does not long for it?—will have their prayer answered by helping to remove the walls of sectarian division, thus restoring to the Holy Spirit the true medium in which the fruits of the Spirit may be made manifest.

We have now envisaged three inestimable spiritual values which we may expect the united church to enjoy in the freedom of being what the Church of Christ really is. Let us recapitulate:

First, the static and dreary uniformity of the segregated denomination would be superceded by the stimulating spiritual dynamic of a fellowship embracing our diversities.

Second, the classism of our denominations would be dissolved in a classless ecclesiastical fellowship.

Third, the local church in a united church would take on a dignity, a vitality and a sense of its religious depth with which the denomination is unable to invest it.

One more spiritual value which we may expect to find in a united church must now be considered. It concerns the individual Christian.

4. *In the united church we may expect to find that the individual Christian himself will experience a new birth of freedom— the freedom to be what he really is.* Released from the artificial

man-made system of denominationalism, we may expect that, in his consciousness of belonging to the whole church, he will actually become *a new kind of Christian*. Every individual member of the church will participate in the inspiring freedoms which we have previously discussed. The simple fact of his membership in the true Church of Christ will act upon his spirit to invest his consciousness of *belonging* with a significance he could not derive from his membership in a sectarian part of the church. This access of spiritual significance will be due, not to the fact that the united church is merely bigger than the denomination, but because, under Christ, it is intentionally complete. The completeness of the church will register itself in the potential completeness of the spiritual life of every member of the body.

The freedom of the church's unity will be his freedom. His fellowship within the classless ecclesiastical structure of the ecumenical church will tend to dissolve whatever kind of unchristian classism his denomination has nourished in his own heart. His participation in the diversities embraced in a common fellowship under Christ will ennoble his understanding of Christian truth when he finds it no longer prejudiced by a sectarian monopoly. And, finally, the individual Christian will undergo a profound change by virtue of his membership in a parish church which is nothing less than the ecumenical church itself manifested in his particular locality, in contrast to the parish church which he formerly knew as the manifestation of the denomination in his locality.

All the spiritual values of the united church at every level of its functioning will be concentrated in the experience of the individual Christian. The ecumenical church to which he will then belong will have become the visible church by the dissolution of the denominational system. As a member of the whole church, he will look back upon his membership in a fragment of the church and measure the gulf that he has crossed. He will see that the sectarian church prevented his approximation to the full stature of a man in Christ Jesus. He will see that it shut him out of the possession of a large part of his Christian heritage. He will see that it narrowed his horizon to the dimensions of his denomination and foreshortened his vision of the majesty of the cause of Christ in the world. He has now become an *ecumenical Christian*.

Looking back, he will see how dim and unrealistic was his sense of belonging to any church beyond that of his own denomination. True, he will recall that he used to repeat the words of the Apostles' Creed: "I believe in the holy catholic church." But he will now see that his churchly experience in a mere fragment of the church provided him with no realistic understanding of what these words meant. His consciousness of actually belonging to the holy church catholic was vague, sentimental and unempirical because that church itself had no experienceable existence. He could not lay hold of it, and it could not lay hold of him. Recalling his ever so devoted loyalty to his denomination, the ecumenical Christian will be conscious that his spiritual life suffered distinct impoverishment by this very loyalty to a sectarian church whose perverted freedom, whose unchristian classism, whose theological provincialism, and whose lack of spiritual dignity shut him out from much of the spiritual treasure of the Christian faith.

If this contrast seems too sharply drawn, it is drawn under the prompting of a great declaration by St. Paul. Let us look carefully into the apostle's words. He had learned that there were sectarian factions emerging in the church at Corinth. The Corinthians were in danger of being split into three sects, perhaps four. Some said, I am of Paul; others, I of Apollos; others, I of Peter; still others, I of Christ. Here was an incipient sectarianism, the potential equivalent of our present-day Protestant denominationalism. Paul was determined to nip it in the bud. He saw that these threatened divisions would be, in the eyes of the world, a scandal upon the Christian faith and that it might mean the extinction of the church he had so recently planted in Corinth. But he also foresaw the impoverishment of spiritual life which any sectarian division among them would entail. Upon this spiritual result of division he centered his emphasis. All these leaders, he told them—Paul, Apollos and Peter—all are yours, because they and you all belong to Christ.

Now, there were profound differences among these three leaders. Their differences were incomparably more crucial than those represented by our various denominations. But all these differences were swallowed up in their common allegiance to Christ. The Corinthians should not build a sectarian church upon Paul himself, nor upon Apollos, nor upon Peter. To do so was to be carnal, to be unspiritual, to be no better than the pagans around them. Sectarianism was never more sharply castigated than in these opening chapters of I Corinthians. Paul's mind was ecumenical, and he admonished the Corinthian Christians to remain ecumenical in order that they might possess the full richness of spiritual life which only the ecumenical fellowship in Christ could supply.

What Paul foresaw as the spiritual result of division is precisely what has come to pass in our Protestant sectarianism. Our spiritual life has been incalculably impoverished by it, in the church as a whole, in our parish churches and in the soul of the individual Christian. This result is not generally recognized by those who are its victims. We should not be surprised at this. The deficit in spirituality, due to our sectarian insularity, can hardly be realized by those whose concept of spirituality has been fashioned by their membership in an isolated fraction of the Church of Christ. The human mind does not consciously miss something it has never envisaged as a possibility. Yet we are beginning to comprehend St. Paul's sweeping dictum: "All are yours!" And we are becoming aware that the spiritual heritage of the whole church really belongs to us and that we have actually been cheated of something inestimably precious by the sectarian system in which we have to live the Christian life.

Who are those who are awakening to the spiritual deficit in our sectarian Protestantism? They are those who have come into vital contact with other denominations than their own and found there treasures of the spirit which they yearn to appropriate for themselves. The number of such people in both the laity and the ministry has greatly multiplied in the past half-century. A fast-increasing multitude of Christians have been awakened to the spiritual poverty of their own denomination as compared with the total richness of an ecumenical fellowship. This is a dynamic source of the ecumenical awakening.

May I speak quite personally? The span of my public life has covered the period in which the ecumenical awakening has occurred. My vocation as a Christian journalist has brought me into intimate relation with all our denominations. In all of them I have been received as a brother. I have participated in innumerable ecumenical conferences from Edinburgh 1910 to Amsterdam 1948. As a journalist, I dedicated my editorial responsibility to many causes, but to none more ardently than to the achievement of a united Protestantism. I hardly dare to confess what all this has done to my mind, or to assume that such a confession would be of interest to others. Yet I feel that I may be indulged in doing so. *This experience has made me deeply dissatisfied with my denomination.* I do not mean that I would prefer another denomination to my own—no, God forbid! I do not know where I would find a better one! I cannot treat lightly the fellowship in which my whole Christian life has been nurtured. I feel that my own denomination is as good as any other. And, if I may be allowed to express a childish idea in childish words, I think that, in some respects, my own denomination is a tiny little bit better than any other, and certainly my fellowship within it is precious beyond words. But none of our denominations is good enough.

My membership in my denomination shuts me out from the treasures of fellowship and tradition and truth carried by all other denominations. The treasures of Lutheranism should not be kept alone to the followers of Luther—they belong also to me. The treasures of Presbyterianism should not belong alone to the followers of Calvin—they belong also to me. Nor should the treasures of Anglicanism belong alone to the followers of Cranmer, nor those of Methodism belong alone to the followers of Wesley— they belong also to me. "All are yours!" I hear the apostle declare, as if he spoke directly to me. So also the treasures of the Disciples of Christ—and I bear witness that they are precious treasures— should not belong alone to the followers of Campbell—they belong also to everyone who names the name of Christ.

But we cannot possess these rightful belongings because they are all held by a monopolistic churchism which says, *We* are of Luther, *we* of Calvin, *we* of Cranmer, *we* of Wesley and *we* of

Campbell. Yet these great leaders and their followers all belong to the same Christ who was crucified for us all and rose again to be the Head of the whole church which is his living body. Our denominational churchism thus cheats us all of inestimably precious spiritual riches which, under Christ, belong to us all.

A great multitude of American Christians long to escape from the whole denominational scheme of things and take membership in the true Church of Christ, so that all the spiritual goods now held in all the churches might really belong to them. This they would do tomorrow if they could. But they cannot. They cannot even find the Church of Christ. It eludes their touch. They do have a haunting feeling that it is mystically present, and they know by faith that it really exists in the mind of Christ. But the Church of Christ—the ecumenical church—has no empirical habitation, no organization, no meeting times, no meeting places, no visibility at all which would enable them to have empirical membership in it. This is the tragedy that has overtaken the Protestant Reformation. And the sense of this tragedy has awakened in a great multitude of Protestant Christians a longing for the emergence of the ecumenical church into visibility—having its own structure and its own organs—so that each of us could cast in his humble lot with it, and give his allegiance, under Christ, to it alone.

In a united church, each of us would experience something like a transfiguration of his spiritual life. In such a church, the soul of every member would be enlarged and ennobled. His Christian faith, liberated from its walled-in sectarian isolation, would be exalted. His ardent devotion would then be given, under Christ, to a church whose moral and spiritual dignity would command the respect in the local community, in the nation and the world which the Lordship of Christ deserves and which our sectarian churches cannot evoke. Every believer would be a participant in this majestic and holy brotherhood. The glory of its world-wide mission and the depths of its ecumenical fellowship would be registered in his own soul. As an ecumenical Christian, his membership in the whole church would be invested with a sense of high reality, of profound religious meaning and of certain triumph.

All this, let us repeat, would mean that the attainment of an ecumenical church would produce a new kind of Christian.

We can expect no spiritual awakening in Protestantism until its leaders and its people set their hands and their hearts to the great task of giving back to Jesus Christ the church of which our sectarianism has robbed him and which his divine Lordship deserves —the church for whose unity he prayed and for whose life he died. Perhaps this united church will not be called Protestant. We may dare to hope that its historical genius will find a new name for it, an ecumenical name, answering to its long-hidden ecumenical character and the ecumenical intention by which the Reformation was motivated.

V

Protestant Unity and Roman Catholic Unity Compared

THERE are some Protestants who fear that a union of the forces of Protestantism would represent or lead to the same kind of unity as that which is embodied in the Roman Catholic Church. This misconception of the ecumenical goal inhibits their wholehearted response to the ecumenical movement. Put bluntly, it is said that Protestants should not create a *Protestant* Roman Catholicism. In some minds this attitude is adopted partly as a rationalization of an unwillingness to yield the cozy familiarities of the sectarian fellowship. But, as we have seen, these familiarities need not be given up but may be carried over into a united church. However, insofar as this fear is conscientious and sincere, it deserves considerate attention. We shall undertake to show that it is a needless apprehension and that a united Protestantism will be radically unlike the unity represented by the Roman church. The fear that Protestant unity will sacrifice or endanger its Protestant character is groundless. On the contrary, the attainment of its unity will be the realization of the ecumenical intention of the Reformation itself, the intention which, as we saw in Chapter I, has never been without witness through all the centuries of our denominational divisions.

Before entering upon a comparison of the two types of unity, let us examine the state of mind from which this fear arises. It is a state of mind which, in effect, makes a virtue of weakness. It shrinks from allowing Protestantism to be strong. The spirit of unconcern for Protestant strength is the natural result of the state of mind produced by sectarianism. Most of our denominations began as relatively small and humble groups. The great majority

100

7859

of these groups remain small to this day. Only a few have attained substantial strength either in numbers or in influence. Their launching out upon an independent existence was a highly precarious adventure. The secession of a group from a parent denomination, followed by secessions from the seceders in an endless process of chain reactions, required, especially at the start, that littleness and apparent weakness should be fortified by the dogmatic assertion of one aspect of the Christian faith, namely, that God uses "the weak things of the world to confound the mighty." In this faith they were sustained. Though most of them have not experienced any startling confirmation of their faith, they still cling to the principle that littleness and weakness are the special favorites of divine providence.

Those denominations which have surpassed their lesser neighbors have also cherished the same principle which they now have grounds for believing has been amply confirmed by their gratifying success. And yet these denominations, especially those numerically in the top brackets, are in a paradoxical state of mind. Having experienced God's blessing upon their weakness, they are now inspired by the ambition to be as strong as they can! Their faith that God blesses the weak things of the world has yielded to the demonstration that God blesses also the mighty. The ecumenical movement has considerably tempered the sense of sectarian self-sufficiency in most of our denominations. But we still have denominations whose spirit, untouched by the ecumenical imperative, indicates that they would rejoice if their own strength should increase and their own growth so far surpass others that eventually they would absorb them all and thus become the whole of Protestantism—as Aaron's rod swallowed up all the rods of the sorcerers before Pharoah. It is chiefly in these denominations that the warning signal is raised against allowing Protestantism to become strong. They are willing for it to become strong by the absorption into their own denomination of the whole of Protestantism, but unwilling for it to become strong by the union of its now divided forces! Hence their warning that the ecumenical movement may lead Protestantism to become just another Roman Catholic Church can hardly be taken seriously.

That divine providence does bless weakness is a firm article of Christian faith. But that God blesses strength is also an article of our faith. He blesses the mustard seed at the moment when it is first planted, but also blesses it when it becomes a full-grown tree. He blesses the little bit of leaven at the moment when it is thrust into the lump of dough, but he also blesses it when the whole lump is leavened. He blessed Martin Luther at the moment when, standing alone, he ushered in the Protestant Reformation, and he will also bless the Reformation when it fulfills the intention of the Reformers and becomes ecumenical.

Nevertheless, the mood which fears that a united Protestantism would tend to become another Roman Catholicism is characterized by an admirable and sound, though undiscriminating, intention. It is a well-founded conviction of Protestantism that the kind of power exercised by the Roman church is a perversion of the Christian faith. The Protestant conscience rightly shrinks from any movement whose outcome would clothe Protestantism with that kind of power. Happily, as we shall see, the ecumenical movement in Protestantism is oriented in a direction precisely opposite to that which leads to Rome.

We shall state our conclusion at the outset. It will appear increasingly as we proceed that Protestantism and Roman Catholicism are two radically different kinds of religion, this despite the fact that, in terms of history, they both stem from the same original event, namely, the appearance of Jesus Christ, together with the faith concerning him upon which his first followers founded, or better, became, the Christian Church. But this bare historical continuity to which both Protestantism and Catholicism can equally lay claim, must not be taken as a proof or a presupposition that the two religions are identical or even that the affinities between them are of such a nature that their differences can with sufficient patience be finally reconciled. Such a conclusion cannot be drawn from the bare fact of a common historical origin and continuity. Continuity is no guarantee that a historical entity may not have radically changed its character in the course of history.

The Roman Catholic Church has in the course of history so

radically departed from the essential character of the Christian Church that it can rightly be described in the terms used by the Reformers as an apostate church. This judgment, however, does not imply that Roman Catholic people, either as individuals or as a community, are not Christian. On the contrary, in both the Reformation and most of modern Protestantism such an idea is heartily repudiated. Unlikely as it is that the unchristian system under which the Roman church holds its Christian people in a state of bondage will ever be *voluntarily* relinquished, Protestantism must always maintain the distinction between the Roman Catholic community of Christians and the system which denies them their true Christian inheritance.

We should recognize at this point that there has emerged in the United States a spirit and a formidable organization either designed to neutralize, or having the effect of neutralizing, the differences between the Roman church and Protestantism. In the interest of social "brotherhood," the American principle of non-recognition of religious differences by the state has been subtly, and perhaps unawarely, taken over into the religious realm with the effect of obscuring, especially among Protestants, the profound dissimilarities and contradictions between Protestantism and Roman Catholicism. The principle of tolerance of one another's religion in the political and social spheres, which is the ethical expression of religious liberty, has been transferred to the religious sphere where it has become a false tolerance amounting to religious indifferentism. Its effect has been to suppress the discussion of Protestant principles *vis-à-vis* those of Catholicism.

The general public and many Protestants think of the Roman Catholic Church as just another denomination in the same category as the many Protestant denominations. Though the Roman church shares at least mildly in the activities of this interfaith organization and subtly furthers the propaganda of tolerance for its salutary effect upon Protestants, it continues in season and out of season to propangandize its own faith in contrast with Protestantism. Those Protestants, however, who follow a similar practice are likely to be branded as "bigots," not only by Catholics but by a considerable portion of the public, including some Protestants who have been inoculated with this false conception of tolerance.

The ecumenical movement itself has been tinctured in a slight but appreciable degree by this same failure to recognize with sufficient clarity the profound and irreconcilable differences between Protestantism and Roman Catholicism. It is one thing to "leave the door open" to the participation of the Roman church in this movement for Christian unity, and quite another thing to cherish any expectation that the invitation will be accepted. And it is still less realistic to allow so remote a possibility to affect either the conception or the planning of a union of the non-Roman churches. It is little short of a betrayal of the ecumenical aspiration to inhibit its progress and realization in American Protestantism by complicating the problem with any hint that Protestant action should be slowed down in any degree by the fatuous hope of co-operation on the part of the Roman church. Rome draws the line with absolute sharpness between itself and Protestantism. Its leaders know how wide is the gulf that separates them. Protestants should be no less aware of it.

Keeping in mind the consideration that prompts the writing of this chapter, namely, a certain fear that a united Protestantism would prove to be another Roman Catholicism, let us enter upon a comparison of the two types of unity—that embodied in the Roman Catholic Church and that toward which the eyes of Protestantism are hopefully turning. It is, of course, not our purpose to present a systematic comparison of these two faiths, but only to point out some of those features which characterize the unity of each and would illuminate the contrast between them. In the case of the Roman church, we have the actual entity before us. In the case of an ecumenical Protestantism, we have no such realized entity, but we do have the principles, the practices and the ethos or traditions of the Protestant churches. These will enter into and determine the character of a united Protestantism.

We shall compare first, the religious content, and second, the ecclesiastical forms of the two faiths. By "religious content" is meant the religious experience of the believer—his religious consciousness, the nature of his actual participation in his religion, in a word, his religiousness. By "ecclesiastical form" is meant the nature of the organization or institution, that is, the church, which provides for, inculcates and administers the characteristic religiousness of its members. The remainder of this chapter will be divided into two sections—one comparing the religious experience of the two religions, the other their institutional organization. Obviously the unity or cohesion of each will be found to derive from these two factors, and the contrast with respect to both of them will be expressed in a contrast between two types of unity. We shall find that the unity of Catholicism is radically different from the unity we may expect in a united Protestantism.

COMPARISON OF RELIGIOUS EXPERIENCE

1. *A unity gained by the depersonalization of the individual believer* versus *his personal fulfillment.* The religious life in Catholicism is fundamentally characterized by the reduction of the individual believer to the status of an observer of something done apart from him. This stands in contrast with Protestant religious life whose central characteristic is personal fulfillment by actual participation in the thing done. This marks the fundamental difference between the Roman Catholic and the Protestant celebration of the sacraments. In Catholicism, the divine presence is localized and focused, and sensuously apprehended by the believer, in seven sacraments—baptism, the mass or eucharist, ordination, penance, confirmation, matrimony and extreme unction. These all, it is claimed, were instituted by Christ and entrusted to the control of the priesthood which administers them by an inherent power or divine grace with which the priest has been uniquely endowed. The divine presence flows into the physical element or the action of the sacrament through the priest who alone is able to perform this miracle. Thus the believer participates as an observer in the real presence of Deity, an experience which occurs only then and there.

Chief among these sacraments, not because of any inherent pre-eminence, for all sacraments are equally significant and efficacious, each in its own place, but because it is most frequently and publicly performed, is the sacrament of the mass. The bread and wine are actually changed into the body and blood of Jesus, who thus becomes objectively and physically present and may be apprehended as present by the worshiper. However, the sacrament requires for its efficacy no active co-operation on the part of the worshiper. It is fulfilled, not by his participation in it, but by the sheer fact that it is performed. It is totally a priestly act, complete in itself, and its effect is communicated to the worshiper by the simple fact of his being present when the act is performed. Its efficacy for the individual is *ex opere operato,* by virtue of the thing done, not *ex opere operantis,* by virtue of the individual's participation. This does not imply that the sacrament is not to be received devoutly, but whether so received or otherwise, the thing done has its own efficacy. The emphasis upon the absolute objectivity of the sacrament, in contrast with the personal contribution of the worshiper, clearly indicates, as Professor Wilhelm Pauck says, that "the religious encounter between God and man is understood in such a manner that it is deprived of the feature of a personal relationship."

What we have said of the mass applies with only circumstantial modifications to all other sacraments. The central and substantive religious content of Catholicism is this miracle-working power which acts quite apart from moral or spiritual qualities in either the recipient or the administrator.

This depersonalization of the sacraments places Roman Catholicism in radical contrast with Protestantism. The contrast is often stated erroneously by Protestant apologists. For example, Catholicism claims that its sacramental system is integral with the sacramental character of the church itself. Protestants should not fall into the error of denying that the Church of Christ is a sacramental community, and that the sacraments are integral to the church as the sacramental body of Christ. Again, to the Catholic claim that its sacraments are corporate acts of the church, it is an erroneous answer to say that in Protestantism they are only individual acts. Such an understanding represents a departure not only from classic Protestantism but from classic Christianity. Once more, the clothing of the sacrament in absolute objectivity (the thing done), thus depersonalizing it, must not be answered by repeating the statement that Protestant sacraments are individual acts. This individualization of the sacraments as against both the corporate and the depersonalized concept, while representing a certain strand of Protestant thought, is contrary to the New Testament conception and to the deeper understanding of Protestantism. It degrades the sacraments to mere ordinances. Against such erroneous replies to Catholicism, Protestants should be on their guard.

Where, then, is the real point of contrast between the two faiths on this matter? The contrast is between the Catholic depersonalization of the sacraments resulting from their absolute objectivity, and the Protestant integration of personal participation in the corporate act itself. It is because of the contrasting convictions at this vital point that Protestantism has retained only two of the seven sacraments—baptism and the Lord's Supper, both of which it has reinterpreted in personal, though not individualistic, terms. It rejects the absolute objectivity of both, and gives each believer as a member of the corporate community a spiritual and creative part in the sacramental action. In Protestantism there is no sacrament apart from the actual participation of the Christian community, either as a congregation or through a representative acting in its behalf. Its rejection of the absolute objectivity of both baptism and the Lord's Supper carries with it the rejection of baptismal regeneration and transubstantiation. (Conceivably, while rejecting penance and extreme unction, Protestantism could consistently have retained ordination, confirmation and, possibly, matrimony. But for lack of biblical precedent, it did not do so. These are true sacramental acts in Protestantism, though not given the status of sacraments.)

That this fundamental difference between Catholicism and Protestantism would be endangered by a united Protestantism is inconceivable. Throughout all its denominations, despite some diversity of theory concerning the locus of the real presence of Christ in the sacrament, there is no divorce of the sacrament from faith, repentance, sincerity and self-commitment on the part of the participant. The divorce of the thing done, the event, from the spiritual contribution of the participating congregation and its members, is unknown in Protestantism. The sacrament as miracle is incontinently rejected as a superstitious pretension in the exercise of the absolute power assumed by the rulers of the Roman church. This we shall consider further on.

For further treatment of this feature of Roman Catholicism, the reader is referred to an illuminating chapter by Professor Wilhelm Pauck in his book *The Heritage of the Reformation*. His exposition of "depersonalization" as inherent in Catholic sacramental experience prompted the present development of the same idea in relation to Roman Catholic unity in comparison with the unity of a united Protestantism.

2. *A unity gained by the passive obedience of the Catholic laity in contrast to a unity resting upon the active responsibility of the Protestant laity in every aspect of the religious life.* This contrast is closely related to the depersonalization inherent in the absolute objectivity of the Catholic sacraments. In Catholicism the church is sharply divided into two parts—the clergy and the people. The clergy, that is, the hierarchy, really constitute the church, and the religious life of the people consists of their passive acceptance of the religion offered by the clergy. We have seen how this operates in the celebration of the sacraments where the believer's participation is virtually reduced to that of an onlooker, albeit a devout onlooker.

This status of an observer carries through the entire Catholic system. The layman is totally without ecclesiastical responsibility. He has no part in the determination of the church's doctrine, or worship, or morals, or policy, or in the management of its property or the expenditure of the vast sums of money which he himself gives. Indeed, he does not know how much money the church receives, nor how it is expended. The hierarchy makes no accounting to the faithful nor to the public. The parish priest may report to his people the earnings of a bingo game and similar pious money-making activities of the parish, but above that level the layman is in total darkness. Even the parish priest may know but little, as the overall affairs of the church are tightly held within the counsels of the upper echelons of the hierarchy.

This "unofficial observer" status of the layman in the ecclesiastical affairs of the church, combined with his status of an observer in the sacramental system, produces a quality of religious experience as unlike that of Protestantism as is the religious experience produced by a totally non-Christian religion. Indeed, at the point of the impassive and nonresponsible receptivity of the laity, there would seem to be more kinship between Catholicism and certain non-Christian religions than with what Protestants believe to be true Christianity.

The Protestant religious experience arises from the active and responsible participation of the whole church in its ecclesiastical affairs and its religious life. The whole church consists of the people of the church, the whole Christian community. In Protestantism, the distinction between clergy and laity is strictly a functional one, not a distinction which divides the church into two classes—one class, the absolute custodian of divine revelation and the sole channel through which divine truth and the grace of God flow into the lives of the faithful; the other class, the obedient and passive recipients of this divine grace. In Protestantism, the Christian revelation is God's gift to the total community of the church, not to a part of it. And the operation of divine grace is a communal possession of the Christian fellowship in which every believer actively and responsibly participates. A Protestant can conceive of nothing ecclesiastical that is more repugnant to the mind of Christ than the claim that the relation between God and man requires the mediation of a self-constituted, self-contained, self-perpetuating and sacrosanct professional class which possesses a monopolistic control of the grace of God.

Protestantism does not, however, reject the principle of mediation, but it finds it in "the priesthood of all believers." Every Christian is a priest to others and they to him. The Protestant minister is primarily a layman, and becomes a minister by his consciousness of a "call" from God and ordination by the church which takes into account his human gifts as well as his spiritual devotion. He is set apart to devote his life to this priestly and prophetic function, but he has no unique power to convey divine grace beyond the influence of those special gifts of teaching, of preaching, of counseling and of personal character with which he may be endowed.

In ecclesiastical affairs, the whole membership of a Protestant church has an active and responsible part, from the local congregation to its most comprehensive connexional relationship. This active responsibility of every Christian in both the spiritual life and the practical affairs of the church produces a religious experience essentially and radically unlike that produced by the obedient receptivity of the laity in the Roman Catholic system.

The total commitment of the soul of man to the keeping of a hierarchy, which Protestants hold to be a humanly constituted professional class, appears to them as nothing less than an abdication of human dignity. For a church to demand such a commitment from its members is a violation of the nature of man. And for any man to make such a commitment is an act of self-abasement. The religious experience that results from this abdication of the freedom of the human mind and spirit in the soul's relation to God and to the church, under Christ, is so completely incommensurable with the religious experience of Protestant believers that even conversation between them in this area is impossible.

That the churches of Protestantism, carrying their undeviating traditions of Christian liberty and human dignity into a united church, could become another Roman Catholic Church, is unthinkable.

3. *A unity of uniformity* versus *a unity of diversity*. Perception of this contrast between Roman Catholic unity and the unity toward which the ecumenical movement is carrying Protestantism should definitely aid in allaying the apprehension that a united Protestantism might take on the character of Roman Catholicism. The Roman church claims for itself absolute uniformity in its structure and practices, and in its beliefs and dogmas. Not only so, but it claims that its uniformity has been consistently maintained from the time of the apostles and of Christ himself throughout the entire history of the church. What the church now teaches is claimed to be the same as that which it has always taught. One of its mottoes is *semper idem*—always the same.

To the historian this claim is preposterous. He points out that the church has developed from its almost amorphous state in the first generation when numerous divergent views were represented not only in its membership but in the apostolic circle itself, down to our own day. The historian is able to place his finger on the actual circumstances when, in the fourth century, the claim of the Bishop of Rome to be the successor of Peter was first put forward. Prior to that date the church had undergone a distinct evolution in its structure and its doctrines. Subsequently, through the Middle Ages, the Renaissance, the Reformation period and down to our time, the church added many innovations of doctrine, organization and practice. Among these are few that had not been previously repudiated by authoritative theologians and councils, and even by certain popes themselves. The dogma of the immaculate conception was not promulgated until 1854, that of papal infallibility until 1870, and that of the bodily assumption of Mary into heaven until 1950.

These are merely a few illustrations of actual development of the Roman system in history. To these and innumerable other developments of hierarchical claims and authoritative doctrines, the church answers that there was no change, that what the church now says is true was always true, because it was "implicit" both in tradition and in Scripture. The faithful must not bother with history. Since the papacy affixed its dogmatic and now infallible seal upon history the faithful must accept as history what the church declares history to have been. Thus the Roman church, by dogmatic fiat, supports its claim to absolute uniformity throughout the ages. One hesitates to characterize the kind of spiritual life which results from the acceptance of this arbitrary and high-handed method of dealing with historical fact.

Catholic writers point with scorn at the changes which have admittedly occurred in Protestant history, and at the diversities which characterize its contemporary life. But Protestantism reacts to this derisive charge, not with apology, but with reassurance and gladness. Having turned away from the static and dogmatic uniformity claimed by Rome, it welcomes and rejoices in its diversity as marks of its spiritual vitality. It cultivates an honest mind in dealing with history. Its religious experience cannot be separated from this intellectual integrity. Indeed, it is the interaction of its faith and its knowledge that creatively nourishes its religious experience. In the long run, Protestantism rejoices in the discovery of new truth, though faith is always by its nature reluctant to accept new truth until its validity is clearly demonstrated.

Protestantism anchors its faith in one supreme historical event, namely, the revelation of God in Jesus Christ. And it holds that that momentous event is too great for our small minds. It therefore refuses to set a final seal upon any human interpretation, but welcomes diversities and even differences which do not dislodge or dissolve that supreme event. It finds the inspiration of its spiritual life in the unending experience of creatively reconciling these differences and in the expectation that new insights will emerge from age to age. Protestantism reads the Scriptures with a mind unshackled by any authoritarianism, and with the alert expectancy that more and more truth will yet break forth from the Word of God. And it cleaves to the pledge of Christ that the Spirit whose continuing presence he promised to the church would reveal many things which he had not imparted to his disciples because they could not then understand them.

It is not often observed nor commented upon that Catholicism has no place for the Holy Spirit in the New Testament sense of its manifestation. The church drained off the operation of the Spirit into a theological dogma where it remains isolated in majestic inactivity. Even the priesthood does not depend upon the Spirit, for the powers of the priest are an original endowment legally authorized by Christ to the successors of Peter. In Protestantism, as in the New Testament church, the Holy Spirit is the life-giving source of the spiritual experience of every believer. The Spirit is the living presence of Christ in the corporate life of the church, who takes the variety of gifts represented in its individual members and integrates them in the one body. This variety of gifts makes room not only for diversity of function but also of interpretation. It makes for the enrichment of the spiritual life of every member of the body. Between the quality of religiousness in a free Protestantism and that of a sacrament-bound Catholicism the difference is immense.

In looking forward to its own unity, Protestantism is learning from the ecumenical movement to hold its diversities as an asset to its spiritual life, rather than as a liability. The denominational system has not only stressed uniformity but embodies it and is based upon it. But the ecumenical movement is shaking the churches of Protestantism out of their obsession with this unbiblical impoverishment of the spiritual life. The insistence upon uniformity is a Roman Catholic deviation, not to say an apostasy, from the Christian faith, and the ecumenical aspiration is leading Protestantism in the opposite direction where change and diversity are welcomed and embraced. The greatest change which Protestantism has ever experienced since the Reformation would be the achievement of its perennial aspiration for its own long-deferred unity.

4. *A unity based upon a superficial morality* versus *a morality of personal depth and dignity.* One cannot help sensing a certain delicacy in the attempt to analyze and state the contrasting differences between any two religions in the area of their religious life. This feeling has been a constant accompaniment of our procedure thus far. But the sensitivity becomes even more keen when one accepts the task of showing the contrast between the quality of morality in Protestantism and Catholicism, respectively. We are, however, compelled to say that in no respect has the Roman church departed further from the Christian faith than in its standards of the moral life. Protestant critics of Catholicism are bold enough in exhibiting its theological and ecclesiastical deviation from Christianity, but they shrink from exhibiting its ethical deviation. Indeed, these critics often cushion their radical strictures of the Roman system by paying a tribute to the quality of devotion which that system produces.

Because Catholicism has produced its share of saintly characters, both canonized and uncanonized; because its priesthood, monks and nuns have foresworn involvement in family life and wordly affairs and devote their lives to the service of the church; because these dedicated persons obediently accept assignment to missionary labors often in faraway places, or philanthropic service in hospitals and other humanitarian institutions; and because its people in general manifest a high degree of reverence for the church and devotion to the duties which the church has taught them to regard as essential to their salvation—because of these indisputable evidences of human virtue and loyalty it is easily inferred that the moral standards of Catholicism are not only above criticism but are truly Christian.

It is a delicate task to challenge this inference. But it must be challenged, because it leads many to assume that such fruits are clear evidence that the tree is good, and therefore the ideological and institutional differences between Protestantism and Catholicism are unimportant and negligible. Hence, an attitude of indifferentism as between the two faiths is felt to be justifiable. Into this mood, a large body of American public opinion, including much Protestant opinion, has fallen as the result of a purely sentimental appreciation of Roman Catholic devotion.[1] The matter requires thoughtful attention.

In the first place, it should be noted that the devotion manifested in Catholicism is not unique. In other religions also we find saints and ascetic devotees and popular piety—in some even more pronounced than in the Roman church. No Protestant—nor any Catholic—would judge Buddhism or Hinduism or Islam as worthy of acceptance, or regard them with the tolerance of indifference, on the ground that, forsooth, their saints and priests and ascetics and people exhibit great devotion. Protestantism, on its part, though it does not regard celibacy and asceticism as Christian or even ethical principles, has its saints also, who compare not unfavorably with the saints produced by any other faith. It could be argued, though we are not concerned to do so, that Protestant saints and, indeed, the moral character of Protestants compare more favorably with those of other faiths because their saintly or moral character has been achieved, under Christ, not by withdrawal from the world, but in the midst of the difficulties and temptations of the common life.

It would, then, seem clear that in comparing the ethic of one religion with that of another, a basis must be found elsewhere than in the devotion of its members to the religious institution. In the two cases of Protestantism and Catholicism, it is not difficult to establish the true basis for such comparison. In Catholicism the

---

[1] For a brief discussion of this observation, see p. 35 ff.

moral standard is inflexibly set by the church, that is, by the hierarchy. The individual believer submits his intelligence and conscience to this external authority to tell him what is right and what is wrong. In Protestantism, the moral standard is the will of God apprehended by the Christian believer in his direct responsibility to God for the exercise of his God-given freedom, intelligence and conscience. Between these two standards the gulf is immense, and the moral life that is produced on one side of the gulf is qualitatively different from that produced on the other side. We have stated it as the difference between superficiality and depth. These mild terms have been chosen because it is not profitable to press the contrast into the area of more empirical difference.

Let us consider, then, the ethic of Catholicism. it could be described in a term current among theologians as an ethic of *heteronomy,* which means the rule of oneself by another who stands between himself and God. To such a rule every Roman Catholic submits. From childhood every member of the church is trained to accept the domination of the hierarchy over his moral life. Through the priesthood he is told what is right and what is wrong, and he has vowed to accept its decree as absolute authority over his behavior. Every priest is thoroughly instructed, not only in the general principles of authoritative morality, but in the most elaborate details of their application to specific cases. The refinements of casuistry with which the priest is equipped surpass in their coverage of the whole moral life the system of the Pharisees which Jesus denounced with his most vehement invective. It is true that certain remnants of this system of pharisaical Judaism were carried over into the early Christian church. But, chiefly by the teaching of St. Paul, the moral freedom and responsibility of the Christian man, under Christ, was established as the true ethical principle of the Christian faith.

The ethic of the Roman Catholic Church is a denial of this principle by the adoption of a moral standard not unlike that of pharisaic Judaism. The development of this crucial deviation from the Christian standard is historically understandable. It arose during the rapid expansion of the church among pagans of crude moral conceptions, and especially among the barbarian tribes of

Western Europe. But the permanent institutionalization of the confessional, the system of penance and the granting of indulgences on the assumption of authority over the soul of man, constitutes a complete letdown from the moral ideal enshrined in the New Testament. By divesting the Christian man of his dignity and moral responsibility, under Christ, and by the priestly obstruction of the open possibility of direct access to God for both moral guidance and forgiveness, the Roman church fell back into an alien and pre-Christian morality. However this deviation may be condoned by the exercise of historical charity, it cannot be justified. And it most certainly canot be justified in a society whose ethos has been permeated by the principles of Christianity. This static authoritarianism in dealing with man's moral life is superficial, and it is unwholesome in its effects.

The essence of the Catholic penitential system—confessional, penance and indulgences—inheres in its authoritarian sacerdotalism and its presumption. The priest is divinely endowed with the power to forgive sins, to absolve the penitent, and to impose penalties. He stands in the place of Christ who, it is claimed, has committed this power and authority to him. He is more than a counselor whose wisdom and experience may be drawn upon for guidance in the moral perplexities and misbehaviors and gross sins or crimes which may be brought to him. The priest speaks with an ultimate authority which lifts the responsibility from the conscience of the penitent and takes into his own hands the right to dispose of the sin. He disposes of it by declaring absolution— "I absolve thee"—and by imposing penance. The penalty is graded according to the priest's judgment of the seriousness of the sin, a judgment which has been trained in the elaborate refinements of casuistry. Sins are classified as either venial or mortal. In each of these categories there are innumerable degrees of seriousness. The penalty imposed is measured by these variables.

The crucial point here is that the priest *does something*. He does not merely advise; he acts. His action is effective and binding. In declaring absolution and imposing the penalty, he is performing a sacrament. This, as we have seen, is a superhuman act which no man but himself, as priest, can perform. The efficacy of this sacrament of penance is *ex opere operato,* by virtue of the thing done, and is on a parity with the miracle of the mass. In the sacrament of penance the penitent is in the position of a recipient observer, as in the mass the worshiper is only an observer, albeit in one case a devout observer and in the other a penitent observer. In each case something is done by priestly power *for him,* something which could not have been done for him in any other way. The dependence of the faithful upon the priest for the forgiveness of sin is absolute.

The penance imposed may have some relevance to the wrong done, such as restitution of stolen property or reconciliation with one whom the penitent has injured, but for the most part the penalty has no inherent relation to the sin. It usually takes the form of certain religious acts—so many paternosters, so many prayers, so many fasts, and so on. It might even include the payment of money to the church, though the money penalty is usually reserved for indulgences. The essence of penance is a deed to be performed—what Luther and the other Reformers called "works" —by which a *quid pro quo* is matched against the sin committed, thus assuring God's favor. The ethical principle in Catholicism is thus a debasement of Christian morality.

It was not until the thirteenth century that penance became a sacrament, and it was not dogmatically recognized as a sacrament until the Council of Trent in the sixteenth century. From the second and third centuries, penance had been practiced for disciplinary purposes. The element of authority was present, but the sacerdotal element came in long afterward. With the recognition of the sacerdotal character of the penitential system the element of compulsion enters. The faithful are required to go to confession at least once a year, but more frequent confessions are marks of piety and merit.

Protestantism has historically, and to this day consistently, rejected the whole system of ethics embodied in the institution of penance. It sees not only the ethical superficiality of the system but the easy hypocrisy and the moral complacency that it breeds. It sees that the formal requirement of contrition as a condition of absolution is a temptation verbally to make a protestation of contrition in view of the great gift the priest is expected to bestow. Or a conscientious believer can be self-deceived and believe that he is contrite when he is only fearful of consequences or feels only a momentary regret. The substitution of specific sins for the generic reality of sin in human nature fosters an inferior type of morality.

Catholic theology itself has drawn up a list of the seven deadly sins—pride, covetousness, lust, anger, gluttony, envy and sloth. But these lie deep in the heart of man, beyond the reach of any priest and beyond the reach of any penalty he may impose. Indeed, they are bound to be comfortably eclipsed and ignored by concentration upon overt sins. The fact that these overt sins can be disposed of by confession, absolution and penance at the hand of a vicar of Christ, tends to cheapen the whole moral life by setting up a standard that is too low to activate the deeper motivations which lie in the heart of man where the ethic of Jesus and of the New Testament reveal them as the source of all moral good and evil. Protestantism sees that the system under which an arbitrary and authoritative penalty is imposed by one who stands between the soul and God involves the usurpation of a prerogative that belongs only to God. The acceptance of such a penalty as a *quid pro quo* for the sin committed provides a superficial and premature relief of conscience and precludes the full working of God's grace in the depths of the penitent's soul.

Protestantism has cast out, root and branch, this whole system of heteronomy in which a sacred man stands between the believer and God and presumes to act for God with divine authority over the believer's conscience. To the Protestant, this system perpetrates a monstrous indignity upon the human soul. And for any man to subject himself to it is, though unwittingly, an act of self-abasement. In contrast to this elaborate apparatus of managing the moral life of the believer, Protestantism points him directly to God whose will is apprehended by faith and whose forgiveness waits only to be appropriated by deep and sincere repentance. The way to God is always open and unimpeded by any priestly mediator. There is only one Mediator, Jesus Christ, in whose incarnation God the Father acted to reveal his own immediacy and the unmediated accessibility of his forgiving love. The divine absolution, the divine forgiveness, is bestowed so freely upon the truly penitent that its unmerited fullness and freeness brings with it the poignancy of an inward penalty which opens the springs of regeneration.

In order to present this contrast as sharply as the differences are profound, we have stated the Protestant ethic in terms which the reader may feel are quite too individualistic. This impression must be corrected.

(a) Protestantism does not deny the place of the church in the believer's apprehension of the will of God. On the contrary, it is in the fellowship of the Christian community that the believer's intelligence and conscience are fashioned to perceive the will of God. The ethic of Protestantism is both individualistic and social. It is within the community of the faithful that "the Spirit bears witness with our spirit that we are the children of God," and therefore ought to behave as his children. But each believer's intelligence is kept free of authoritarian control by his participation in the fellowship of the community.

(b) Nor does the grace of God, directly available to every believer, operate in individualistic isolation. We have said that Christ is the only Mediator between the soul and God, and that Protestantism rejects as blasphemous the priestly claim to act in Christ's stead. But it accepts the New Testament conception of the church as the *medium* in which and through which the grace of God is conveyed to the faithful by the living presence of the Mediator. Rome sees Christ departing from the earth and taking his place at "the right hand of God," leaving his divine work in charge of an authoritative and infallible vicar whom he has endowed with full power to rule in his absence. Protestantism also sees Christ enthroned at the right of God, but this honorific ascription is correlated with the truth of his living presence in the church of which he is the head.

We have previously referred to the great Reformation doctrine of "the priesthood of all believers." Every Christian, said the Reformers, is a priest, not in the sense often misunderstood as "every Christian a priest unto himself," but every Christian a priest to others and others priests to him. This is the true conception of priesthood—the mutuality of interaction among the members of Christ's body, each conveying to all and all to each the grace of God in guidance, in consolation, in instruction, in confession, in forgiveness, and even in discipline. "Ye are a holy priesthood," says the writer of Hebrews. "We are all kings and priests unto God," he says again. And the author of the Epistle of James writes: "Confess therefore your sins one to another, and pray one for another that ye may be healed." No other conception of Christian priesthood can be found in the New Testament.

We have been viewing the Roman system from the side of the individual's submission to its authority. We have seen, under four headings, that its authority is maintained over its people (1) by the depersonalization of each individual, (2) by his passive receptivity of divine grace and forgiveness through priestly mediation in a sacramental action which is uniquely and exclusively in the power of the priest to perform, (3) by the dogmatic determination of truth which the faithful must receive without question, and (4) by a superficial ethic which transfers the burden of misbehavior and sin from the soul of the individual to the hands of a priestly mediator who disposes of it under divine authority by the imposition of an external penalty of things to be done not necessarily related to the sin committed. Upon the submission of the faithful to the church's authority to demand and power to perform these acts, the unity and the power of the Roman church is based. Disobedience is punished by numerous penalties, the supreme penalty being excommunication and punishment after death in purgatory or in hell.

COMPARISON OF THE INSTITUTIONS

We now turn to a comparison of the two institutions in which Protestantism and Catholicism are, respectively, embodied. Here, again, in the case of the Roman church we have the actual entity before us, while in the case of an ecumenical Protestantism we have the principles and practices of the Protestant churches which will enter into and determine the character and structure of a united Protestantism. It is probable that the feeling of apprehension which the writing of this chapter is intended to allay, arises from the contemplation of the vast power which the Roman church wields in the political order. It is vaguely felt that, with the access of strength derived from the realization of its unity, Protestantism might be unable to resist the temptation to follow the Roman Catholic example. This apprehension arises, in our judgment, from a sheerly fantastic possibility. It fails to distinguish the kind of power exercised by Rome from the wholly different kind of strength which a united Protestantism would or could possess.

How strong, then, should the Church of Christ be? The only answer on moral or Christian grounds is that it should be as strong, with the right kind of strength, as its God-given resources will enable it to be. We shall see, as we proceed, that the strength of a united Protestantism will lie in a wholly different dimension from that in which Catholicism operates. Our task, therefore, is to examine the kind of power embodied in the Roman church, in contrast to the access of strength which will come to Protestantism with the achievement of its unity.

We cannot understand how the Christian Church could have been transformed into something so unlike itself unless we see the Roman Catholic Church as the residuary legatee of the disintegrating Roman Empire. The church emerged as the only unifying force in the feudal ages of political and social disintegration, and accrued such political and material power that it became itself a state as well as a church. For more than a thousand years it ruled some of the most important territories of Europe, containing large populations and, besides, asserted its spiritual dominance over all other rulers and peoples. Its "spiritual dominance" was exercised by its own military forces, by a network of alliances with other rulers and by the attempt to maintain a balance of power in which its own political and material interests would be assured and furthered. Kings and emperors received their crowns from the papal hand. Bloody wars between the church and other states marked the whole period. In these wars the Roman church always had a stake and took a military part. After the Protestant Reformation which was accompanied by the emergence of strong national states, the political dominance of the papacy was cast off and its spiritual power repudiated in many European countries. By 1870, all the papal territories were taken over by the Italian revolution and the papacy itself was reduced to the confines of the Vatican. Though shorn of its historic political power, the papacy has never surrendered its claim to be a state as well as a church.

What was the secret of the enormous political power that the church exercised in medieval Europe? It can be explained only in connection with the enormous *religious* power which the church claimed and had taught both rulers and peoples to respect. The church had supernatural benefits to confer and supernatural penalties to impose before which the common man and the mightiest rulers stood in awe. The penalty of exclusion from the sacraments and the threat of excommunication caused men, high and low, to tremble. The political power of the papacy was grounded in its religious power over its own people. The unity of the church as an institution was maintained by the tremendous claims of the papacy to possess the power of eternal life and death, symbolized by the keys of the kingdom of heaven which Christ had given to Peter and his successors.

It is this same religious control of its "docile multitude" which is the secret of its institutional unity and the power it is able to exercise in the political and social orders of those countries where its numerical strength is sufficient to give it a substantial base of operation. Some non-Roman interpreters of Catholicism are inclined to put this the other way around and say that the essential character of the Roman church is that of a formidable power system which uses religion as a "front" behind which the hierarchy operates for the aggrandizement of its own power. This cynical judgment is, if not unwarranted, at least unnecessary. The truth would seem to be that the religious and the power motivations are so intertwined that neither can be regarded as having precedence over the other. It is doubtful that the pope himself, on searching his own heart, could tell where his religious motive leaves off and his power motive takes over. The two have historically grown by mutual interaction and are inseparable.

However, this is an unfruitful issue for critics of the Roman system to raise, because it assumes that the religion of Catholicism is less noxious than its power system. But the religious power exercised by the hierarchy over its people is, in the eyes of Protestantism, such a radical perversion of the Christian faith and of human dignity that it inevitably requires a secular power system to maintain and propagate it. Thus it is impossible to treat of the Roman church as an institution in complete detachment from its religious content which we have previously examined. The character of this system was formed, as we have seen, in a period of popular ignorance, superstition and docility, and it carries over this same character into an age of critical enlightenment, not only unchanged in its essential nature, but actually tightened more rigorously in defensive reaction to the Reformation and the human freedoms with which Protestantism is historically identified.

We cannot be reminded too often of the purpose which started us upon the comparison of Protestantism and Roman Catholicism. Our analysis of the two faiths in contrast with each other is not directed as a polemic against the Roman church. Such a polemic would have no place in a book devoted to the unity of Protestantism. Our comparison has been prompted by the purpose of showing how unfounded is the notion that a united Protestantism would be in danger of becoming another Roman Catholicism.

Our examination of the religious and ethical content of the Roman Catholic faith has shown that the church maintains its unity by subjecting the faithful to a system of authoritarian control in the spheres of religious experience, religious belief, moral behavior and education. That this subjection is voluntarily accepted, either initially by a convert or by a strict process of inculcation from childhood, does not modify its authoritarian character. Indeed, the education of Catholic children is designed so to mold their mentality that their "voluntary" acceptance of churchly authority is virtually beyond their power to question or challenge. As for the convert, he or she is usually a person who has given little or no attention to matters religious, or one who has been driven into disillusionment by oversophistication. It is easy for persons of both of these types to accept with a deep sigh of relief the overwhelming claim of Mother Church that in her bosom all their problems—spiritual, moral and intellectual—are already solved and full provision made for the perpetual relief of a burdened conscience.

Turning our attention more directly to the institution through which this tremendous power over human souls is exercised, the first thing that strikes the Protestant eye is the fact that the Roman church is sharply divided into two parts—the hierarchy and the people, the rulers and the ruled. To show that this is not merely a Protestant way of looking at the Roman church we may quote the language of an encyclical by Pope Pius X. He said in 1906:

> The church is the mystical Body of Christ, a body *ruled* by pastors and teachers, a society of men headed by *rulers* having full and perfect powers of governing, instructing and judging. It follows that this church is essentially *an unequal society,* that is to say, a society composed of *two categories of persons:* pastors and the flock: those who rank in the different degrees of the hierarchy and the multitude of the faithful; and *these categories are so distinct in themselves* that in the pastoral body *alone* reside the necessary right and authority to guide and direct all the members towards the goal of society. As for the multitude, *it has no other right than that of allowing itself to be led, and, as a docile flock, to follow its shepherds.* (Italics mine.)

In our present context we have no occasion to dwell upon the deep chasm which separates this conception of the church from that of the New Testament and the beginnings of Christianity. It is sufficient here to let it stand as a measure of the great gulf which divides Catholicism from Protestantism. Throughout the whole of Protestantism, this conception of the church is incontinently rejected. The church as the body of Christ is the church of Christ's *people*—what Pope Pius X called, with a hardly disguised tone of condecension from his lofty eminence, "the multitude." This "multitude" of those whom Christ has received—they, says Protestantism, constitute his church. With one voice, throughout all its separate denomintions, it proclaims a common and united revulsion against the Roman Catholic apostasy from the spirit and the truth of the Christian faith. Before one falls victim to the fear that a united Protestantism would be in danger of becoming another Roman Catholic Church, it will be necessary to imagine that Protestantism could empty itself of its own historical and universally held conception of the church and set up this flagrantly apostate conception in its stead.

It remains, now, to gather the whole system of Catholicism into an inclusive concept and compare it with a similarly inclusive concept of a united Protestantism. In a word, Catholicism must be seen whole and compared with a united Protestantism also seen whole. Recent writers have pointed out the importance of this procedure in the case of Catholicism. In 1945, Harold E. Fey, published in *The Christian Century* a series of articles which were later issued as a brochure entitled *Can Catholicism Win America?* Dr. Fey undertook a survey of the operations of the Roman Catholic Church in the United States from the standpoint of the church as a system of power, both religious and political. In 1949, Professor George La Piana, of Harvard University, published in *The Shane Quarterly* a scholarly series of articles under the title "A Totalitarian Church in a Democratic State," in which the same concept of an organized system of power was used as the key to an adequate understanding of the nature of the Roman church. More recently (1951) Paul Blanshard, in his book, *Communism, Democracy and Catholic Power,* took this overall concept of Catholicism as a system of power and demonstrated its irreconcilable contrast with democracy. He drew an illuminating parallel between this system and the totalitarian system of Soviet communism. These writers performed their several tasks so well that it remains only for us to compare the system of power which is the Roman church with the character of the united church toward which the ecumenical movement is carrying Protestantism.

It must be emphasized that the political power of the Roman church, if not derived primarily from the religious power which it exercises over the "docile multitude" of its people, is at least inseparably associated with it. By what means is this power exercised? By means of the finest instrument for the coercive maintenance of unity, uniformity and loyalty that was ever invented: an army of sacred men sworn to poverty, chastity and obedience, and trained from youth to an outlook upon the church, the world and life which insulates them from all temptation to doubt or challenge the authority under which their vocation is pursued. This army of priests, called the hierarchy, is a body of holy men headed by an infallible monarch who is believed to derive his authority from Christ himself, whose vicar he is, and whose power flows down through the ranks of cardinals, archbishops and bishops to the lowliest priest. In addition to the priesthood are innumerable orders of ascetic monks and nuns most of them directly responsible to the papacy.

In this great ecclesiastical army of dedicated persons, trained and sworn to absolute obedience, the papacy has the perfect instrument for maintaining the kind of unity which the Roman church embodies. We have here a prototype upon which the political systems of modern totalitarianism have been fashioned. Into the details of this analogy it is not relevant for us, in the present context, to go. But it should be obvious that any Protestant who hesitates to support the ecumenical movement because he fears that it may eventuate in another Roman Catholicism is thinking fantastically.

Turning our thoughts, now, to the kind of church which a united Protestantism will represent, the first thing to note is that its unity will not be maintained by any authoritarian principle or any authoritarian professional class. In Protestantism, the Christian people *are* the church. This is the most fundamental difference between Protestantism and Catholicism. Protestants are not a "docile" multitude "allowing itself to be led" by any human authority, even one that claims divine sanction. They reject that claim as a sheer façade behind which a ruling class maintains its power. In no denomination throughout the whole of Protestantism is there a division between the rulers and the ruled. The people are their own rulers, under Christ, who has appointed no man or succession of men to act as his vicar.

The living presence of Christ in the church is the most precious reality which Protestants cherish. It stands over against the periodic or occasional materialization of Christ's presence in the sacrament of the mass. How wide is the gulf that separates the two faiths at this crucial point can be made clear by quoting from a pastoral letter written by a German cardinal of the church in 1905, who said:

Where in heaven is such power as that of the Catholic priest? . . . One time only Mary brought the heavenly child into the world, but, lo, the priest does this not once, but a hundred and a thousand times, as often as he celebrates [the mass]. To the priests he transferred the right to dispose of his holy humanity; to them he gave, so to speak, power over his body. The Catholic priest is able . . . to make him present at the altar, to lock him up in the tabernacle and to take him out again in order to give him to the faithful for their nourishment. . . . In all this, Christ the only begotten Son of God the Father, is yielding to his will.[2]

Protestantism turns away in disgust from such an exhibition of primitive magic. It thinks of Christ as livingly present in the whole community of the faithful. The Holy Spirit is the empirical manifestation of his presence. For the Holy Spirit, Rome has no place. Its place and function have been usurped by authority. What Christ promised to do by the Spirit who would come to his disciples after his departure, Rome does by the hierarchy. It has taken the Spirit away from the "docile multitude" of the faithful and controls the presence of Christ by sacramental incantations. Against this magic, the Reformation revolted and all Protestant denominations have consistently been in revolt to this day.

Protestantism gave Christ back to his people. It released him from the sacrilegious control of a small part of the church and set his Spirit free to work where it would and as it would in the lives of the faithful. There is nothing magical or weird about the operation of the Spirit. Its working is as familiar as the common practice of democracy. Indeed, the guidance of the Spirit is the Christian counterpart of the democratic principle. It would be more accurate to put it the other way around and say that the principle of democracy in the secular order is the political counterpart of the same principle in the Christian Church. Protestantism is the embodiment of this democracy.

But there is a difference between the democracy of the church

[2] Quoted by Wilhelm Pauck, *The Heritage of the Reformation* (Boston: The Beacon Press, 1950), p. 161.

and the political practice of democracy. This difference derives from the fact that the church is consciously a sacramental community. It is sacramental because of its conscious dependence upon the Holy Spirit, and its democracy partakes of the sacramental character which is of the essence of the church itself. Its sacraments also are acts of this sacramental body, rather than acts of a professional class to whom supernatural power has been committed.

There is one other important difference. In political democracy the people are sovereign. But in the Christian Church, the people are not sovereign. Christ alone, its living head, is sovereign. All its members and office-bearers acknowledge his Lordship and all its corporate activities are carried on under it. In contrast with political democracy, the sovereignty of Christ demands the rejection of the ultimate sovereignty of the community and saves it from the *vox populi, vox Dei* fallacy.

The will of Christ is made known by the church's dependence upon the Spirit which is immanent in the devotion and intelligence of the community. The secular form of democracy which rests upon the "consent of the governed" as expressed by a majority, is embodied in the church, but exalted into another dimension by the Spirit.

Using the term "democracy," then, in this sense of a Spirit-guided community of the Christian people, Protestantism historically and universally rests upon a democratic basis. It has no place for any human authority whatever. The concept of "authority" has historically bedeviled the Christian Church more than any other concept, and its use has wrought confusion in Protestantism itself. Because of its ambiguity it should be outlawed from the Protestant vocabulary. In its place, the good word "responsibility" should be substituted. For in Protestantism no office-bearer possesses any authority. Instead, he has been invested by the church with *responsibility* to perform specific acts and services in behalf of the church. Every office-bearer, be he called bishop, presbyter, priest, minister, pastor, deacon or whatever, derives the function of his office and his responsibility to discharge it from the community of the Holy Spirit whose representative he is. In the church of Protestantism the principle of democracy attains its most exalted conception and manifestation because it is the method by which the Spirit of Christ operates in the community of those who remember and love and honor him.

In a united church of Protestantism no other principle for the maintenance of its unity is conceivable. It will be a church of the Christian people. In them, under Christ, will be vested the sole responsibility to determine its character and work. It will thus be a growing church, not a static one. It will be, under Christ, a responsible church, not dependent upon any priestly class. It will be a church characterized by diversity, not by uniformity, for the Spirit is not manifested in uniformity, but in diversity. It will be a perennially reformable church, for it will not always follow the Spirit's guidance and will never claim infallibility. It will be a fellowship within which each member attains, under Christ, the full freedom and the highest fulfillment of his personal life, not a "docile multitude" of depersonalized followers who have yielded their souls to the management of any self-constituted human authority. In the content of its religious and moral life and in the ecclesiastical form which it will assume, a united Protestantism will bear no substantive likeness to the Roman church whose apostasy from the Christian faith it was historically called of God to reform.

VI

The Illusion of Restorationism

THE ecumenical ideal evokes two different kinds of feeling-response in the churches of Protestantism. The difference is not due so much to diverse theological doctrines, though this element cannot be excluded. It is rather a psychological difference, a difference in what might be called the ethos of two types of denomination. On the one hand are the denominations of classic Protestantism, on the other hand are the denominations which had their origin in dissent and defection from one or the other of these original denominations.

Both groups share in the ecumenical awakening, but their collective mind has been historically molded by different feelings for the Christian Church. The former carried with them a strong sense of the continuity of the church in history. The Reformation in its three original tributaries clearly recognized that the Church of Christ was actually in existence, and had always existed since its beginning. It had been led astray under historical conditions and assumed a form which the Reformers called an apostasy. They conceived their task as that of reforming the church by emancipating it from its "Babylonian captivity." But they had no idea that they were starting new churches.

The denominations which originated in dissent from one or another of these original denominations naturally conceived themselves in quite different terms. They were in reality dissenters from the Reformation itself, which, they said, had not been radical enough. Instead of reforming the existing church, they conceived themselves as restoring the New Testament church in its original purity. Thus their feeling of continuity was dimmed, if not neutralized. The feeling was established in each dissenting group that it was beginning all over again and making direct connection with the apostolic church. The distinction which the Reformers had made between the historic church and the corruptions of it by unscriptural forms and practices was disregarded and more or less consciously rejected.

The sharp edges of these divergent conceptions of the Reformation have been greatly worn away in modern times. The present generation of the classic group of denominations and of the dissenting group have become assimilated to each other in such a degree that this particular difference between them is hardly noticeable. Nevertheless, when the ecumenical movement touches them, it finds that their difference in origin has left a deposit of feeling which appreciably helps one group to take the ecumenical imperative wholeheartedly, and makes it less easy for the other group to do so.

Our chief concern in this chapter is with those churches of Protestantism whose collective psychology has been appreciably molded by the experience of dissent and the attempt to restore the primitive apostolic church. We can understand them better and their place in Protestantism as a whole if we turn back to their antecedents both before and in the period of the Reformation. From time to time throughout Christian history there had emerged intransigent groups who sensed the profound deviation of the Roman church from the true Church of Christ and undertook to restore the church of the New Testament. As persecuted heretics, they were compelled to maintain a more or less underground existence. Such survivors of these various and unconnected groups of heretics at first hailed the Reformation as the fulfillment of their hopes and prayers. But they were soon disappointed. Chief among them were the Anabaptists whose name is generally, though indiscriminately, used to apply to them all. Though they differed widely among themselves, they were alike in their claim to have discovered the true church in the New Testament and in their determination to restore it.

The Reformers also, of course, had rediscovered the New Testament. But they differed from the Anabaptists in the use to which their discovery was put. Luther, Zwingli, Calvin and Cranmer had no idea of restoring the New Testament church in disregard of the existing church. They all took over large geographical sections of the Roman church and proceeded to reorganize their people in conformity with what they regarded (with whatever differences among themselves) as New Testament principles. In all the original Reformation countries—Germany, Switzerland, England, Holland, Scotland and the Scandinavian countries—the actual event could be described as the casting off of the trappings of the Roman system and the reclothing of the existing church in garments believed to be consistent with New Testament Christianity. But the reclothed church was the same church of Christ's people that had long worn the habiliments of its Roman captivity. The idea of creating a new church, or of re-creating the primitive church, was alien to their intention.

In contrast, the Anabaptists and the other sectaries were "come-outers," radical dissenters, not only from Rome but from the Reformation churches. In some respects they had good reason for their radical criticism of the reformed churches. Had the Reformers given heed to certain of their criticisms, the Reformation would have profited greatly. This was notably the case in the matter of their insistence upon the separation of the church from its entanglement with the state. On this point, the radicals were ahead of their time. But they discovered many strange things in their New Testaments which the Reformation could not digest. Among these were radical social theories which led some to adopt obnoxious social practices and, in some instances, politically subversive activities to the point of rebellion. This smeared the whole group of dissidents with a bad name to the great injustice of some of them, notably the Mennonites and the followers of Conrad Grebel.

With the idiosyncrasies of these numerous sects, referred to by the name of one of them, the Anabaptists, we are not here concerned. What concerns us is their fundamental presupposition, common to them all, namely, the concept of restoring the primitive church. Underlying the endless proliferation of their differences in interpreting the New Testament, this was their conceptual common denominator. Each sect believed that it had found the true church in the Bible and set out to re-create it by waging what we would describe as evangelistic campaigns to call out, not only from Rome, but also from the Reformation churches, as many as would join them. Their break with the historic church was complete. This was signalized by their proselytism, and by their practice of rebaptizing their converts. (The name "Anabaptists" means "rebaptizers.") Their sectarian denominations were new churches, newly constituted by those who accepted their doctrines. They were new, both in being conceived as replicas of the primitive church and also as totally severed from both Rome and the Reformation. They thought of themselves as making a new start in the history of the Christian Church.

By the end of the sixteenth century, all save a few remnants of the Anabaptists had been effectively suppressed. Those remaining, notably the Mennonites, were chiefly in Holland whose more tolerant government gave them refuge. But their spirit and fundamental idea were soon to re-emerge amid the tensions developing in the Church of England where the Reformation had been less thoroughgoing than in Scotland and on the Continent. Out of this tension there began the long process of fissiparous proliferation of separate denominations which has continued down to our own time. Each new denomination was animated by the intention of restoring the church of the New Testament.

We thus have in modern Protestantism two groups of denominations whose instinctive reaction to the ecumenical appeal is appreciably conditioned by an ethos formed under one or the other conception of the Church of Christ—the conception of continuity and reform or that of discontinuity and restoration. On the one hand are the denominations representing the tradition of classic Protestantism—Lutherans, Presbyterians and Anglicans, together with certain offshoots which still cling to their particular family tradition. On the other hand are those denominations which have sprung from one or the other of these classic bodies by radical dissent from its doctrine, polity, liturgical character or in puritan protest against the low estate of its religious life. These denominations are too numerous in the United States to consider within reasonable limits of our space. So we shall select the four largest of them as representative of the entire group—the Congregationalists, Baptists, Methodists and Disciples of Christ.

These denominations are the spiritual descendants of the Anabaptists. They are all "come-outers" from one or another of the Reformation churches. We shall not be surprised to find in them a perceptible difference in feeling toward the Christian Church from that of the other group of denominations. And also a different feeling-response to the ecumenical movement. We are not thinking, here, of theological differences which, as we have seen in other chapters, have been greatly diminished or toned down under the influence of the ecumenical spirit and the enlightenment of modern biblical and theological scholarship.

These conceptual differences are now less easy to recognize in either group than the instinctive feeling which comes to the surface when the denomination is confronted by the ecumenical imperative. This feeling-response arises chiefly from the ethos of a denomination which was formed under the psychology of continuity, on the one hand, and by the psychology of dissent and rupture, on the other. The ecumenical movement has not yet taken this more cryptic or elusive characteristic of the several denominations into account and sought for the means of reconciling them by (1) laying bare the historical cause of the dissimilar feeling and (2) subjecting this cause to critical examination as to its validity.

It is, admittedly, a delicate task to interpret the contrast between the two groups with respect to their feeling for the Christian Church. We may essay such an undertaking only with the frank admission at the outset that our classification oversimplifies the facts by omitting certain features of certain denominations that do not fit neatly into it. To these qualifications, however, we shall give brief attention when we come to them. For convenience, let us give a name to each group. Let us call the first mentioned the Reformist group, and the second, the Restorationist group of denominations.

Our subject can hardly be discussed without some reference to the different nomenclature with which Ernst Troeltsch christened virtually the same groups to which we have just given names. In his monumental work, *The Social Teaching of the Churches,* he distinguished one group as the "church type" and the other as the "sect type" of denomination. His treatment under these heads greatly illuminated the sociological aspects of the many churches of Protestantism, and his nomenclature has been widely adopted. But his two categories were conceived with a different problem in mind from that which here concerns us. As a sociological historian, he was engaged in explaining the varieties of social idealism and practice which he found in the churches of Protestantism. He took the churches, both those now extant and some long since extinct, as he found them, and saw no impropriety in calling one group the "church type" and the other the "sect type."

But Troeltsch's categories are unsuitable for the problem with which we are dealing. He was concerned with the relation of each of these churches to society; we are concerned with their relation to the ccumenical church. In this latter relation, it only makes for confusion to say that one denomination belongs to the "church type" and another to the "sect type." This is because both "church" and "sect" must be defined in one way in relation to society and in another way in relation to the ccumenical church. In Chapter III we have defined each Protestant denomination as both a sect and a church. It is a sect just because it is a church. Every denomination, even the most venerable and, in Troeltsch's terms, the most "churchly," is a sect in its relation to the ecumenical church. We have defined a denomination, or sect, as "a part of the Church of Christ existing in a separate structure and exercising by itself and for itself those functions which belong to the unity of the whole Church of Christ." The sectarian character of such a body is not concealed by calling it a church. Indeed, by claiming the embellishment of that title, the denomination only compounds its sectarianism in seeking to dignify it.

The categories we have chosen have the additional advantage of being historical and objective, in contrast with those of Troeltsch which are more subjective and arbitrary. Moreover, our categories explain why Troeltsch could find grounds to classify some denominations as "sects" and others as "churches." The dissimilarity which he discerned arises from the fact that the consciousness of continuity is stronger in one group and, in the other, the consciousness of dissent and separation.

The ethos of the reformist group carries on the spirit of the Reformation; that of the restorationist group represents dissent from the Reformation. In the mood of one, Protestantism is regarded as a continuation of the historically unbroken church; the other tends to think of Protestantism as a break with the historical church and a junction with the true church of the New Testament which was lost in the medieval darkness of Romanist domination. In one, the feeling for catholicity is more realistic; in the other, more abstractly ideal or sentimental. In one, the ecumenical church is felt, though vaguely, as prior to and transcendent of the denomination; in the other, the denomination tends to absorb the concern of its members. In one, the church is felt as *given* in history and is perennially reformable; in the other, it is felt as *given* in the New Testament and is re-created according to a fixed norm or pattern by evangelism, including proselytism, and often by rebaptism. Finally, these differences in mood and feeling give to one group a certain flexibility of action in response to the ecumenical movement, and to the other, a certain fixity of sectarian purpose which retards their response to it.

It must be noted that in neither group is the denominational self-consciousness canceled out. All the denominations of Protestantism are equally conscious of and devoted to their independent and autonomous churchism. Our classification is not intended to be complimentary to either group in this fundamental respect! It is intended only to suggest an explanation of the differing reactions of the two groups as each is confronted by the ideal of Christian unity. The ethos of the reformist group provides a background from which may be expected a more prompt and understanding response than is provided by the ethos of the restorationists. That is to say, the negative psychology of dissent, coupled with a denomination's conviction that it has discovered and actually restored the true church of the New Testament, creates a special problem in the feeling of such a denomination which is not experienced in the same degree by a reformist denomination when they turn their faces, as both are now doing, toward the ecumenical goal.

We must now take up the denominations one by one to clarify our inclusion of them in one or the other of the categories. We must also indicate whatever exceptions are necessary where a denomination does not fit too neatly in its classification. It should be kept in mind that the scope of our entire study has been delimited to American Protestantism, with only an occasional excursus into Reformation history where necessary to explain the situation in this country. Our concern in this chapter, as we have said, is, chiefly, with the restorationist group of denominations, but somethng must be said, first, of those of the reformist group.

THE REFORMIST CHURCHES

The Episcopalians. We begin with the Episcopalians because their feeling of continuity is most marked. The Church of England, with which the Protestant Episcopal Church in the United States is in communion, underwent the least radical reform of any of the three tributaries of the Reformation. With one stroke it cut its connection with the papacy and proceeded to organize itself as the national church with the king as its head. In this political aspect of the Church of England the Episcopal Church in the United States does not share. The reformed Church of England retained more of the elements of the medieval church than were retained by the Reformation churches of the Continent. Yet in its theology and its evangelicalism it was profoundly influenced by both Luther and Calvin. It discarded the magical conception of the sacraments and all but two of the sacraments themselves— baptism and the Lord's Supper. Its strong sense of continuity with the historic church was reinforced by the historic episcopate which it retained. The interpretation of this unique organ of connection with the past (which no other Protestant church in America claims to possess) has led to a deep cleavage of opinion in Anglicanism. An Anglo-catholic minority both in England and the United States holds a view hardly distinguishable from the sacerdotal conception which attributes the origin of the episcopate to the apostles and Christ himself. The evangelical majority, however, holds a more flexible view, being content to emphasize the historical dignity and permanent value of the episcopate while admitting that its origin cannot be historically attributed to Christ.

The possession of the historic episcopate has been both an inspirer of action in the cause of Christian unity and an impediment to its achievement. An inspirer, because the Episcopal Church earnestly desires to contribute this possession to the whole of Protestantism; an impediment, because, so far, the other churches of Protestantism have been unwilling to accept it; and an impediment also because the Episcopal Church cannot gain its consent to unite with others on any basis that would involve the surrender or the jeopardizing of this chain of succession in which its ministry stands. Nevertheless, this church has been ardently responsive to the ecumenical appeal, as might be expected in the light of its profound conception of the Christian Church as the ecumenical body of Christ.

The Lutherans. This denomination, or family of denominations, presents a paradox which other Protestant churches have difficulty in understanding. We might expect to find modern Lutheranism imbued with the ecumenical spirit of Luther himself whose conception of the church, as church, was profoundly ecumenical. Instead, it seems to others to be one of the least ecumenical-minded of our denominations. This paradox can perhaps be historically explained by the fact that the ethos of modern Lutheranism has been molded by the creedal orthodoxy into which the German Reformation began to be frozen even before the death of the great Reformer. Luther was a protean figure, many-sided and by no means always consistent. Especially do certain inconsistencies appear as between the views which he expressed in the earlier years of the Reformation and those of the later years of his life. Under various influences, and especially under pressure to keep the Reformation unsullied by association with the extreme Anabaptist radicals, Luther acquiesced in the trend of his coadjutors toward the crystallization of the Reformation faith into virtually an orthodoxy of belief.

It is by this period of the Reformation that historical and

modern Lutheranism has been conditioned. Its feeling for the ecumenical ideal which characterizes Anglicanism and, as we shall see, Presbyterianism, has been dimmed by the biblical theologism[1] which developed after the adoption of the Augsburg Confession to which all Lutheran bodies still devoutly adhere. This has produced a self-contained and self-sufficient ethos more akin to that of the restorationist denominations than to those of the reformist group.

But Lutheranism cannot be denied its historical place as a representative of classic Protestantism. Besides, grateful evidences are appearing in our time which indicate that its encounter with the ecumenical movement (in common with the rest of Protestantism) is proving that in Lutheranism the deeper Reformation feeling for the ecumenical church has not been irrecoverably repressed. Like live embers smothered under the ashes of burned-out sectarian issues, we may expect them to kindle again at the touch of the ecumenical imperative. No doubt, also, the modern scholarly research into the history of the Reformation which throws new light upon Luther himself and his conception of the church, will have its effect in reviving the ecumenical feeling in the churches that bear his name.

The Presbyterians. The Reformation in Switzerland, led by Zwingli and Calvin, was more thoroughgoing than in Germany or England, but it shared with the two other tributaries the concept of reform or purification of the existing church. Indeed, this branch, which we know as Presbyterianism, bore and still bears the name "Reformed Church" on the Continent and in those American churches which were originally constituted by immigration from the Continent. Thus "German Reformed," "Dutch Reformed," and so on. The major bodies of Presbyterians in the United States originated chiefly by immigration from Ireland and Scotland. We find in modern Presbyterianism a strong sense of the ecumenical church and of the continuity of the church in history, fully equal to that which informs Anglicanism. Presbyterians, however, conceive continuity, not in terms of the histori-

[1] Contrasted with both restorationist "biblicism" and modern "biblical theology."

cal succession of any organ or order, such as the episcopate, but in terms of the ecumenical church itself, that is, the Christian community. This community never lost its identity even in its captivity under the papacy.

With this background, we could expect that the movement for Christian unity would meet with an instinctively favorable response from the Presbyterian denomination. This has proved to be the case. Presbyterianism has not only contributed leadership to this movement equal to that of the Episcopalians, but has gone further in expressions of willingness to subordinate its denominational existence in order to achieve a united church. In 1918, its general assembly, by a vote of some 900 to 1, authorized a public overture to all evangelical churches calling for a conference looking toward their union. This was accompanied by a declaration of the readiness of the Presbyterian Church, U. S. A., to enter such a union. The failure, after two years of formal conferences resulting from this overture, was due to no reluctance on the part of this denomination. In 1945, a plan for the union of Presbyterian and Episcopal churches, involving a solution of the problem of the historic episcopate, was adopted by a large joint committee, but was defeated in the General Convention of the Episcopal Church, chiefly by the intransigence of the Anglo-catholic minority. The Presbyterian Church, U. S. (Southern) has been less responsive, but it is now a member of the National Council of Churches and actively participating in negotiations for a union with its northern sister church and the United Presbyterian denomination. Both churches (Northern and Southern) are officially participating in the so-called Greenwich movement for the union of those denominations which "recognize one another's ministries and sacraments."

It should be borne in mind that we are dealing with these denominations in no other aspect save that of their feeling-response to the ecumenical appeal. We have classified them as reformist denominations because their Protestantism, insofar as it has conserved the sense of the essential unity of the church which characterized the main stream of the Reformation, should, and actually does, predispose them understandingly, and even favorably, toward the ecumenical ideal. Whatever other obstacles they may present to a united church, their feeling-inhibitions are less pronounced than in the case of those denominations whose ethos bears the marks of their origin in dissent and separation.

THE RESTORATIONIST CHURCHES

We must now turn our attention to four representative denominations of the group which we have classified as restorationists. The origin of this the largest group of denominations, we have said, was in the tensions that emerged in the Church of England at the end of the sixteenth and the beginning of the seventeenth centuries. The infiltration of Calvinist, or Presbyterian, ideas into the established church gave rise to Puritanism and Independency. The former demanded reform, but remained resolutely in the church. The latter called for reform "without tarrying for any," and proceeded to set up independent churches in the spirit of the Anabaptists and in the firm belief that they were restoring the church of the New Testament. Into the details of this fascinating history, we cannot go. It must suffice to say that the dissenters from the Church of England, though persecuted as were the Anabaptists before them, met with no such ultimate fate as that which overtook their spiritual forebears. This was because the unexplored wilderness of the American continent offered itself as a providential haven.

The story of the *Mayflower* and the Massachusetts Bay Colony is the story of the beginning of a new type of church in Protestantism which, in intention, was foreshadowed but unattained by the Anabaptist sects. It also marks the beginning of that sometimes reasonable, sometimes wanton, division and subdivision of the church which has eventuated in the sectarian scene presented by modern American Protestantism as described in Chapter I. Into this scene, the ecumenical movement has come with a message from Christ, the head of the church. What response does it receive? We have already indicated the response of the reformist group of churches. What response does it receive from the churches whose ethos is informed with restorationism?

The Congregationalists. Whether to begin with the Baptists or the Congregationalists must be decided arbitrarily because they have, historically, a common origin. The Baptists represent the Separatist movement, while the Congregationalists represent both Puritanism and Separatism or Independency. These two movements were bitterly hostile to each other in England, their homeland, but their emigrants to New England were reconciled and merged in their new home in the American wilderness. The Pilgrims who came over in the *Mayflower* were an entire congregation of English Separatists who had lived in exile in Holland for twelve years and finally braved the hazards of the sea and landed at Plymouth Rock in 1620. Eight years later, a similar but larger group of Puritans settled at Salem, within fifty miles of the Pilgrim colony, and were reinforced during the next twelve years by the remarkable emigration of some twenty thousand Puritans from the homeland.

In organizing themselves as churches in their new habitat, neither Pilgrims nor Puritans followed precisely the intention with which they started. The isolated Plymouth church, having no neighbor churches, was not concerned with the problem of a connexional polity. They adopted for their single congregation an essentially Presbyterian polity with a ruling eldership. The Puritan colony, on its part, had left England with the tenderest feelings for the national church, and with feelings of revulsion at the very thought of breaking with it. But in their complete freedom from their Old World environment, the Calvinist ideology which informed the whole Puritan movement became dominant. The Anglican church with its episcopate, its prelacy and its strong sense of continuity, was abandoned, and a new church was formed on avowedly Scriptural lines. To this now truly separatist church the Pilgrim separatists were eventually drawn. The two bodies were reconciled and merged. This union became the mother church of American Congregationalism.

The Congregationalists have undergone a process of evolutionary change more marked than that experienced by any other denomination in America. In addition to the transformation of the Puritan founders into a separatist church, two later changes must be mentioned. One of these occurred at the beginning of the nineteenth century in connection with the Unitarian rupture. The original churches of New England had preserved the Anglican parish system which included all citizens of the community. But these "parishioners" were not all members of the church. The church, as such, was constituted by a covenant of the elect or spiritual elite, and this "parish church" was supported by a general tax. Who owned the church property and its funds—the church or the parish? This question was not settled until the rise of Unitarianism in the early years of the nineteenth century.

The *parishes* in and around Boston, with only two or three exceptions, had all gone Unitarian, though only a minority of the *churches* had done so. The state court decided that the property and all the accumulated funds belonged to the parish rather than to the church. Thus the Unitarians were enabled to take possession of the property of 120 churches and of Harvard College. This imposed upon the orthodox majority the necessity in good conscience of starting as new churches. In reaction against Unitarianism, the main stream of Congregationalism turned back into an extreme form of Calvinistic orthodoxy. But their churches, no longer dependent on the parish system for tax support, stood on their own feet as voluntary organizations. Their influence spread into Connecticut and other New England states whose churches gradually followed suit.

The recovery of the denomination after this incalculably costly defection was amazingly successful. Congregationalism developed a new zeal for expansion. Its people in large numbers followed the course of migration beyond the Allegheny Mountains to the western frontier. And wherever they settled they carried the consciousness of their uniqueness as a separatist church, a state of mind that was reinforced by a hardly less conscious awareness of their beloved New England as their homeland. For a time, the denomination co-operated with the Presbyterians under a "Plan of Union" for establishing new churches. But it was not able to hold its own under this arrangement. The new churches tended to become predominantly Presbyterian, and the "union" was abandoned.

The second great change in Congregationalism occurred in the middle of the nineteenth century. Theologically, it soon appeared that the first reaction from Unitarianism into an extreme form of Calvinism had gone too far. A Hartford minister, Horace Bushnell, published a little book on *Christian Nurture* inveighing against the abuses of the human soul by the current revivalism which reflected a crass interpretation of Calvinism. The thesis of his book and of Bushnell's other writings swept through the whole of Congregationalism, and, in an extraordinarily short period transformed it into one of the most flexible, adaptable and yet soundly evangelical, of our Protestant denominations.

It was admitted at the outset of this discussion that we would run upon some difficulties in neatly fitting all the restorationist denominations into the category to which they are assigned. The Congregationalists present the major difficulty. This is because modern Congregationalism has, perhaps more than any other of the restorationist denominations, exorcised the sectarian spirit. Its feeling-response to the ecumenical ideal is as favorably positive as any reformist denomination. This may be partly accounted for by its affinity with Presbyterianism, both in its origin and its American evolution. But it still carries the marks of its origin as a separate church. It had begun in the intense consciousness that it was a new church. Severed from one of the churches of the Reformation, it set itself to restore the true Church of Christ. Indeed, many of its local churches took the name "Church of Christ." In the absolute freedom of its wilderness isolation from the constraints of Old World associations, the sense of continuity gave place to the sense of uniqueness. The hope, long cherished by these Puritans, of reforming the existing church, faded out. Their deep revulsion at the idea of schism had been abandoned under the conviction that here, in their complete isolation, they were starting a new church which transcended history.

In the pages of the New Testament they found the pattern of the true church and were laid under the compulsion of conscience to restore it. Their Puritan consciousness of continuity was transcended by the sense of their uniqueness. It is out of this feeling of uniqueness—a feeling of being different from other Christians in ways that have divine sanction in the Bible—that most of our

Protestant sectarianism has grown. The Congregational sense of being unique did not carry them to the extreme form of sectarianism represented by the Baptists, and they differed from the Anabaptists in that they did not practice rebaptism. But they agreed with both in this fundamental conviction that the church of the New Testament must be restored and that their church had restored it. This use of the Scriptures is (as we shall maintain in Chapter VIII) the chief root out of which the denominational system has grown.

The feeling of uniqueness shows itself not only in those matters of creed and church organization which a denomination thinks of as so different from those of others, but in the irresistible tendency to magnify them out of proportion to their significance. Once a denomination is established on the basis of some special interpretation of the Scriptures, its institutional morale and momentum require it to make the most of its uniqueness. In the evolution of Congregationalism in the United States from the biblicism in which it was founded, through the period of its crass Calvinism in reaction to the Unitarian defection, down to its modern expression in terms of liberal evangelicalism, it has shed much of its sectarian illusion of biblical uniqueness. But this sectarian feeling still lies latent in the ethos of the denomination like a hidden nerve which reacts with pain and protest when touched by the ecumenical imperative. This has recently been dramatically illustrated in the violent reaction of a minority faction to the all but consummated union of Congregationalism with the Evangelical and Reformed Church.

Deeper and more subtle, however, is the deposit of pride which the sense of uniqueness gradually accumulates in the ethos of a denomination. If pride could be justified in the Church of Christ, no denomination could exceed the Congregationalists in claiming the right to it. Their New England was for centuries universally recognized as that part of American society where its finest culture was in flower. Congregationalism has carried this cultural heritage everywhere it has gone, even to the shores that mark the opposite boundary of the nation. It has been both an inspiration and a handicap upon the denomination which has not been able to follow the spirit of its best leadership and emancipate itself from the pride which is the by-product of its sectarian sense of uniqueness. The denomination yields too easily to the temptation of smugness. Its clannish psychology, decorously held in reserve in the normal course of things, tends to take charge of the collective will when a crucial decision has to be made that would involve the denomination organically in an ecumenical advance. Predominantly liberal and even ecumenical in its modern spirit, the remnants of the old sectarian pride in its cultural and separatist past still remain as an inhibition upon a decisive ecumenical response.

The Baptists. The family of Baptist churches—23 separate denominations—represents the largest body of Protestant Christians in the United States, with a total of more than 14 million members. The churches of the Southern Baptist Convention have 6 million members, two Negro denominations account for nearly 7 million, and the American Baptist Convention (Northern) represents 1,600,000 members. Of these, the Northern Baptists alone are federated with other Protestant denominations in the National Council of Churches. The spirit of self-sufficiency and of unconcern for co-operation, not to mention unity, with other Christians, is a marked characteristic of the ethos of most Baptist bodies.

Our discussion of the origin of the Congregationalists necessarily overlapped the origin of the Baptists, because, at birth, they were twin denominations. Appearing when the Reformation was nearly a century old, they have a common origin in the Puritan movement of dissent and separation from one of the classic churches of the Reformation, the reformed Church of England. We have seen how the Congregationalists represented both the "come-outers" and the loyalist Puritans who united on American soil to create a new church. The Baptists, on their part, were come-outers from the beginning, and developed an even stronger ethos of uniqueness than their twin denomination. Both are the spiritual descendants of the Anabaptists. But the kinship of the Baptists with these radical restorationists of the Reformation period is more marked than that of the Congregationalists.

The dissent of the Baptists was radical, deliberate and complete.

They took their congregational independence more seriously than did those who long afterward came to be called "Congregationalists." On this and other New Testament points, the Baptists were even more radical than the Anabaptists for whom the independence of the local congregation was less a conscious principle than a historical necessity. They also differed from the Anabaptists by finally (in 1641) adopting immersion as the Scriptural and only mode of baptism, whereas the Anabaptists had recognized and practiced both immersion and affusion.

The chief features which the Baptists shared with the Anabaptists were (1) their rejection of infant baptism, (2) their contention for the separation of church and state and, more fundamental, (3) their purpose to restore the primitive church. The rite of infant baptism was conceived not only as unauthorized by the New Testament, but also as the bulwark of a state church. By extending the sacrament of baptism to include every child, whether of Christian or non-Christian parents, and thereby limiting certain privileges such as marriage in a church and burial in a church yard to those who had been baptized, the idea of a national church was difficult to dislodge. In this connection, the Baptist emphasis on believer's (adult) baptism implied a church whose nature would be confessional, as opposed to the national idea. Thus arose the Baptist concept of a "regenerate church membership." This was not only a protest against infant baptism on Scriptural grounds, but was held to be a fundamental requirement of church-state separation.

Whether the history of Protestant denominations, most of whom practice infant baptism, bears out either of these contentions is debatable. It would be difficult for Baptists to demonstrate that their churches are more "regenerate" than the Presbyterian, Lutheran, Methodist, Congregational, Episcopalian and other pedobaptist denominations in the United States. Which suggests that the Baptist emphasis on a regenerate church was, and perhaps still is, relevant in a society dominated by a state church, but may not be relevant in a society like our own where church and state are separate.

The subject of baptism, including infant baptism, has rather surprisingly emerged in our time as a matter upon which our most famous theologians are taking strong positions. Karl Barth and Emil Brunner, so sharply opposed to each other on many theological issues, are agreed that infant baptism is incompatible with the biblical conception of the church. Their arguments have brought to the defense of the practice the powerful voices of such New Testament authorities as Oscar Cullmann and Joachim Jeremias who contend that infant baptism is not only compatible with the New Testament, but does not necessarily jeopardize the confessional character of the church.

The combination of all these features of radical dissent from the mother Church of England, sharpened as they have been by conflict with other denominations, has developed in Baptist mentality a sense of uniqueness little short of a self-sufficient sectarianism. The feeling of continuity with the church of history is hardly appreciable. Yet, paradoxically, the instinctive desire for some thread of continuity running back to the primitive church has produced a mythical chain extending through the Anabaptists not only to Christ, but to John the Baptist! Few, if any, recognized Baptist scholars take this myth seriously, and it should be clearly said that Northern Baptists, in general, reject it as fantastic. It is, however, part of the stock in trade of the aggressive evangelism of the Southern Baptists. Its effect, combined with the other distinctive features mentioned, is to etch more deeply upon the mentality of their membership the sense of the divinely constituted uniqueness of their denomination. This is often carried so far as to deny that Baptists are Protestants, and to inhibit the usual forms of cooperative fellowship which obtain among ministers and churches of a local community.

Naturally, the ecumenical movement makes its way slowly into the heart and conscience of a denomination so sure that it has uniquely restored the New Testament church. Yet the description we have given must be qualified by more hopeful observations. Even in the Southern church there exists a restlessness and solemn concern over the sectarian isolation into which their denomination has been driven by its dogmatic devotion to its own self-sufficiency. The ecumenical movement meets with a heartening response when it touches this more enlightened and fraternal spirit. In every

Southern city where the Baptists have multiple local churches, there is usually at least one which, led by its minister, openly and cordially takes its co-operative part with the churches of other denominations, as does its minister in association with other ministers. These churches and ministers are growing in number and gaining ground, despite the collective intensity with which the denomination as a whole magnifies its uniqueness by exploiting time-worn slogans and debatable interpretations of Scripture. If the ecumenical movement would shift its orientation so as to focus its attention not only upon the reformist denominations but also upon the restorationist denominations, the Baptists would at least feel that the controversial matters, on which they represent one side, were being given due consideration. We may well believe that such an approach would yield ecumenical results.

The Northern Baptists have already left behind them much of the sectarian dogmatism and isolationism which has characterized Baptists from the beginning. Their membership in the Federal Council, now the National Council of Churches, long held against bitter intransigency in their own ranks, is now happily established beyond any likelihood of dislodgment. And just because Baptist origin and tradition, representing the most extreme form of separatism, provided less of a foothold for the ecumenical idea than other restorationist denominations, this achievement of the Northern Baptists is the more remarkable and heartening.

The Methodists.   It may seem at first blush that the Methodists hardly fit into the category of the restorationists. This is because they have placed less emphasis upon the restoration of some distinctive New Testament doctrine or polity than have the other denominations so classified. The church polity of Methodism does not claim to be fashioned on literalistic New Testament lines. It was adopted pragmatically, as the type of organization best fitted for the work it was to do. Methodism has been and still is the least theological or creedal-minded of any of our leading denominations. This partly derives from the Arminianism of John Wesley which tended to wash out many of the controversial issues inherent in the prevailing Calvinism. "If thy heart is as my heart," said Wesley, "give me thy hand." It would be true to say that Methodism has been less sectarian in its internal fellowship, so far as doctrine is concerned, than any of our leading denominations. Its consciousness of difference from others does not derive from the meticulous biblicism which has informed other restorationist bodies. But it was derived nevertheless from the New Testament!

The distinctive characteristic of Methodist self-consciousness inheres in its belief that it had historically restored the spirit and substance of the New Testament *gospel*. Methodism reads the Acts of the Apostles with eyes focused upon other matters than those which other restorationists see. Others see certain features of a church polity—the independence or the integration of the local churches, immersion baptism, officers of the local churches and so on—and devote great pains to discover every organizational detail of the primitive church, so that they may meticulously restore it. But Methodism cares for none of these things, and fails even to see them. When it organized itself as a church, it went about the task with no feeling of subjection to the mandate of a New Testament pattern. Its eyes were focused upon the glowing faith, the ecstatic ardor and radiance of the New Testament *Christians* to whom the gospel came as deliverance and hope. This essential experience Methodism was out to restore. But to do so, it had to follow the same course of dissent and separation from one of the churches of the Reformation, the reformed Church of England. And, as in the case of the other restorationist bodies, the act of founding a new church, combined with the necessity of justifying it, and reinforced by the amazing success that has attended its venture, has produced an ethos informed by a consciousness of self-sufficiency which inhibits its wholehearted response to the claims of the emerging Church of Christ. Admittedly, this inhibition is not so difficult to penetrate and overcome as is the ethos of those denominations whose separatism is buttressed by organizational or theological convictions derived from the New Testament. But the schismatic act in which Methodism was born has left its mark upon it, as it has done in the case of every separatist denomination.

Unlike most other new churches formed by schism within Protestantism, the Methodists were already a formidable body be-

fore they became a separate church. At that time, 1784, their unecclesiastical societies within the Church of England included a
membership of 70,000, and in the American colonies their members have been estimated at 20,000. The plea came to John Wesley
from America to send ministers who could baptize their converts
and celebrate the Lord's Supper. There was great spiritual distress
over the anomalous position in which these early Methodist converts stood. They were united as Christians in a special fellowship
outside of any recognized church, and no provision for the sacraments could be made. Hence their only recourse was to send their
members to the Episcopalians or the Presbyterians for the sacraments.

Wesley, himself a loyal Anglican and a presbyter in that church,
was slow to respond with any solution of the dilemma which his
societies in America faced. For forty years, in carrying on his
work of evangelism, he had been breaking the rules of the church
which forbade preaching in parishes and dioceses without consent
of the ecclessiastical authority. Wesley was the most undutiful son
the Anglican church had ever had. His work had gained only the
grudging indulgence of the authorities. Naturally, the idea of making him a bishop so that he would have canonical authority to
ordain ministers for his societies was not cordially received. For
some years he had been studying the New Testament and the history of the episcopacy in the early church and had finally reached
the conclusion that "bishop" and "presbyter" were an identical
order and distinguished only in terms of function—the bishop's
function being that of a superintendent over an area including
numerous local churches, while the presbyter's function was
limited to his local church. He also found a precedent in the early
church of Alexandria for the election of a bishop by the presbyters.

With this conception well established in his mind, Wesley was
ready at the end of the American Revolution to take advantage of
the new situation created by the complete separation of the colonies from the mother country and of the Anglican church in the
colonies from the control of the mother church. He ordained
Thomas Coke, like himself an Anglican presbyter, as superintendent, and sent him with two other presbyters to America. Coke, on

his arrival, ordained as a superintendent Francis Asbury, who had long been in the colonies. Three years later, these men assumed the title of bishop. Thus Methodism passed from its anomalous position as a "society" into the status of the Methodist Episcopal Church.

This break with the Church of England was accompanied by bitter criticism of what was naturally regarded as a high-handed and disloyal proceeding on Wesley's part. But Wesley had always been vulnerable to such criticism, for, holding his societies in autocratic control, he had defied the constituted authorities which he charged with responsibility for the low estate to which the church had fallen and against which his movement was a profoundly religious and moral reaction. The best defense of Wesley is in the consideration that his action was historically inevitable. The growth of his societies had been so phenomenal, their anomalous position so distressing, the contempt in which they were held by the established church so unappeasable, that no alternative course seemed open but to constitute them into a separatist church.

The Methodist Church, since the recent union of the Northern and Southern branches, together with the Methodist Protestant denomination, is now the largest single Protestant body in the United States. Its phenomenal success, relative to the rest of Protestantism, is naturally interpreted by its people as a providential sanction of its historically independent course. No one can say that this interpretation is unjustified. But this success has tended to nourish in the ethos of Methodism, as does the parallel success of the Southern Baptists, a sense of self-sufficiency which has tended to retard a wholehearted response to the appeal of Christian unity. But this self-sufficiency is now being effectively penetrated by the ecumenical spirit. No more encouraging pronouncement has been made by any denomination than that of the unanimous Council of Bishops at the 1948 General Conference which put the Methodist Church clearly and openly on record as desiring the organic union of American Protestantism, including Methodism itself.

The Disciples of Christ.   This youngest of the four restorationist denominations which we have chosen as representative of the entire group, is the largest of the many denominations originating on American soil, with a present membership of more than 1,600,000. It presents a peculiar problem to the interpreter, but its classification in the restorationist category requires no qualification or reservation. The Disciples have always claimed that they were out to restore the New Testament church. Not only so, but, like virtually all denominations in this category, their dominant feeling until quite recent times has been that they had actually restored it. The particular features upon which they have relied to justify this conviction are (1) the independence and autonomy of the local church, (2) believer's baptism, (3) immersion baptism, (4) weekly observance of the Lord's Supper, (5) elders (or presbyters) and deacons in the local church, (6) "no creed but Christ," (7) a rational or "common sense" theory of conversion, and (8) a plea for Christian unity upon the basis of this pattern of the church which they found in the New Testament.

Such an atomistic enumeration of the salient features of the Disciples' restorationism does less than justice both to their ideology and to their spirit. For these particularities are knitted together in a rich context of sound evangelicalism, warm fellowship, evangelistic zeal, and deep spiritual devotion.

The problem which the Disciples present to the interpreter arises from the fact that there runs through their history another strand of feeling which is not expressed in the concept of a pattern church to which the ecumenical church must conform. This other strand has made itself articulate from time to time in the voices of individuals who regarded the pattern concept as too mechanical and dogmatic to express the real genius of the denomination. In our time, this feeling has spread rapidly and widely. It emphasizes pre-eminently the plea for unity, and is accompanied by an increasingly clear recognition that the pattern of the united church will not be dictated by a single denomination, but must be sought and found within the framework of the ecumenical movement in the fraternal and open-minded consideration of differences. The Disciples have participated in all phases of this movement from the beginning. It is now realized that some of the features included in their pattern church are outdated by the changes that have taken place in the general Christian community, some are of dubious validity, but the conviction persists that there remain important elements which may eventually be recognized as a positive contribution to the emerging Church of Christ.

Between these two conceptions a tension has persisted throughout the Disciples' history. To interpret this tension it is necessary to understand the circumstances of their origin. They began as a separatist group in Western Pennsylvania, in 1809, under the leadership of Thomas Campbell who was disciplined by his Seceder Presbyterian Church for receiving members of other denominations to the Lord's Supper and for other ecclesiastical irregularities. Reluctant to create another denomination, his followers adopted the name "Christian Association" in the hope of becoming a "movement" in the general church for the advocacy and practice of Christian unity. A statement of principles was drawn up by Campbell called "A Declaration and Address," which began with this proposition: "The Church of Christ on earth is essentially, intentionally and constitutionally one." The separation of Christians in rival denominations was deplored as unchristian. Human creeds and unscriptural practices were responsible for these divisions. Only by following the simple procedures of the New Testament church could Christian unity be attained.

Thomas Campbells's son, Alexander, arriving from the University of Glasgow, heartily joined his father in the new undertaking. The "Christian Association" soon assumed the form of a local church. On the birth of Alexander's first child the question of infant baptism arose and the practice was ruled out as unscriptural. Further study of the New Testament led to the adoption of immersion as the true form of baptism. It was evident that the group was moving toward the Baptist position. Unwilling that the Brush Run church should be the beginning of another denomination, they turned to the Baptists who received the congregation and its leaders into the Redstone Association. For two decades the Campbells and their followers maintained an unassimilable fellowship with the Baptists.

Meanwhile, the younger Campbell had become the ablest

preacher and theologian in all that region and had been winning converts in his own and neighboring associations to his views which proved to be in sharp conflict with the prevailing Calvinism. The points at issue involved especially the conversion experience, the place of baptism in salvation, and the work of the Holy Spirit. By 1830, several entire associations were so thoroughly permeated with Campbell's teaching that they were dissolved as Baptist associations and their churches were openly committed to the Campbellian leadership. This marks the beginning of the separate existence of the Disciples as a distinct denomination. Shortly thereafter, a similar development in Kentucky, Presbyterian in origin, led by Barton W. Stone, united with the Disciples. From this time forward the original vague idea of being a "movement" instead of a denomination had to be abandoned in fact, though the verbal distinction has persisted down to our own day and, strange as it may seem, has been a cause of actual, though not too serious, tension in the body.

As in the case of every restorationist denomination, the marks of its origin in separatism persist in the ethos of the Disciples as an inhibition upon their united and wholehearted response to the ecumenical ideal. But in the case of the Disciples, this is particularly difficult for others to understand, inasmuch as the ideal of Christian unity was the prompting cause of their origin and has been the predominant theme of their preaching through their entire history. As the editor of their leading newspaper recently stated it, "The Disciples were ecumenical from the beginning." But their witness to the ecumenical ideal has been eclipsed by the restorationism with which it was coupled. The spirit of the one is in irreconcilable conflict with the spirit of the other. How much of this restorationism is traceable to the sojourn of the Disciples with the Baptists whose restorationism lacked any mitigating counterbalance such as the Disciples took with them into the Baptist fellowship, is a purely speculative question. It is well to remember, however, that when Thomas Campbell made the great statement on the unity of the church, which we quoted above, he was speaking out of his Presbyterian heritage. It can also be said that it was while Alexander Campbell, the Baptist, was defending the Baptist position on some points and ruthlessly attacking it on others, his own conception of the restoration of the primitive church was frozen into the stereotype which, until the turn of the present century, eclipsed the greater ideal. By subordinating the "plea for unity" to the illusory assumption that the Disciples had already found in the New Testament the true basis of a united church, their own sectarian consciousness was intensified and the influence of their ecumenical testimony was circumscribed.

The progress made by the Disciples in the past half century in emancipating their thinking from the sectarian feeling produced by this assumption has been rapid to the point of phenomenal. And yet the drag of their restorationism, reinforced by the psychology of separatism and uniqueness, strongly suggests the necessity for the ecumenical movement to address itself to the problem presented by the restorationist denominations more explicitly than it has yet done.

A Monumental Absurdity

It would be unprofitable to extend our consideration to other denominations in the restorationist category. The four whose origin in separatism we have discussed are representative of the great majority of the Protestant bodies that have originated on American soil. Of the 50 denominations whose membership is above 50,000 each, and whose total membership accounts for 92 per cent of American Protestantism, at least thirty originated in, and each justifies its separate existence upon, the conviction that it is a restoration of the New Testament church. Of the remaining 161 of the gross total of denominations, no less than 146 separated from a parent body each in the solemn conviction that it was starting a new church on the true biblical basis.

Obviously we have here a monumental absurdity! What kind of book is our Bible that it could yield 176 different conceptions of the Church of Christ, each deemed of such importance that it required a separate church to be founded upon it? If the absurdity to which Protestantism has been reduced is not in the Bible, it must be in the misuse or gross misunderstanding of the nature of the Bible by those who cherish it as the sacred Scripture of the Christian community.

All these restorationist denominations are the spiritual descendents of the Anabaptists, including under that name the multiplicity of sects which arose in that period characterized by Adolph Harnack as "the flowering period of sectarianism." The Baptists are mistaken in their notion that they have a monopoly of this ancestry! The proliferation of sects since the early seventeenth century would have begun in the early sixteenth century had the Anabaptist restorationism been embraced by the Reformation. Each of the three tributaries of the Reformation would have been split into a congeries of impotent sects which the Roman church could easily have overcome. The wisdom of the Reformers in steering clear of these sectaries, however sincere and, in some points, however more advanced than the great Reformers, is thus vindicated by history. Protestant denominationalism is thus not the true child of the Reformation but the offspring of the biblicistic restorationism which the Reformation rejected.

That the Christian faith requires the restoration of the details of the primitive church is a belief without any foundation cither in the spirit or the letter of the New Testament. Those denominations which imagine that they have restored it have only created a stereotype composed of a few arbitrarily selected features of the biblical pattern and omitted other far more important features. Especially have they been blind to the overarching ecumenical character of the apostolic church. Thus, instead of restoring the New Testament church, these separatist churches have denied and rejected its most outstanding feature, namely, the fact that the New Testament church was ecumenical. The restorationist heresy has diverted the Christian mind from the path of realism into a blind alley of fantasy. The church of New Testament times was the infant church. Protestantism should be that church grown up.

The ecumenical movement has yet to address itself directly to this root cause of the major portion of Protestant denominationalism. It has been concentrating upon the problems presented by the reformist type of denomination, whose sense of history and of the continuity of the church provides the more ready feeling-response to the ecumenical appeal. But this appeal is touching all too superficially the restorationist denominations whose conscious

historical background hardly extends beyond their founding as
separate churches. If the united church is to emerge from the Babel
of restorationist tongues, each crying, Lo here is the New Testament basis of unity! the ecumenical movement must candidly deal
with this delusion which has been the radical source of militant
sectarianism. We shall discuss this matter more fully in Chapter
VIII.

VII

Surmounting Three Major Obstacles
to Unity

IT IS DOUBTFUL that the major obstacles to Christian unity are
to be found in the realm of theological theory. More likely they
exist in the ethos of the denominations—their disposition,
attitude, sentiment attaching to their particular traditions, and the
human feeling for the familiarities of procedure, nomenclature
and special fellowship. This is not to say that the conceptual
differences can be ruled out or disregarded. The ethos of a denomination carries with it the sense of uniqueness derived from the
original reasons upon which it justified its separate existence.
These reasons were, in most cases, as we have seen in the previous
chapter, derived from the Bible, and have become stereotyped by
usage as slogans for maintaining the morale of the denomination.

It is not easy for a denomination to segregate the original biblical sanctions for its separate existence from the tissue of its total
ethos and re-examine them to see just how distinctive they may be.
But this is precisely what is being done under the influence of the
ecumenical spirit that is now abroad, with the result that the denominations increasingly recognize how thin and virtually non-
existent is the doctrinal wall which separates them from other
Christians. Few are the denominations in our inclusive list of
fifty which, if they were not already in existence, would feel any
theological or biblical compulsion to start their denomination over
again. This is only a way of saying that the major obstacles to
Christian unity are not doctrinal, but are found in the inertia and
momentum of the denomination as a going concern. If, therefore,

the ecumenical goal were so envisaged as not to require the summary dissolution of the denominational fellowships, but only the dissolution of their churchism, we can well believe that the chief inhibition upon their wholehearted response to the ecumenical movement would be appreciably relaxed.

Nevertheless, there are certain ecclesiastical features of our denominations which present really stubborn problems and require constructive adjustment, if not a change of mind, as prerequisite to an inclusive unity of Protestantism. Unlike our theological differences which we have insisted must be welcomed and embraced in a united church, these involve action or practice as well as theory and conscientious conviction. And the practices are such that they cannot be taken into a united church without patient re-examination with a view to the attainment of either conceptual agreement or a practical *modus vivendi*. These problems center in three salient features of our denominations. They are (1) the historic episcopate, (2) immersion-baptism and (3) congregationalism as a theory of church polity. We shall examine these in that order.

THE HISTORIC EPISCOPATE

The problem here is that of providing the united church with a ministry competent to function throughout the whole church. Obviously, there can be no real union if the ministry of a part of the church is unacceptable in other parts of the church. It is a fact, of course, that the ministry of the various denominations is now acceptable in many other denominations without reordination. One of the signs of growing unity is the frequency and facility with which ministers are crossing denominational lines and being received as true ministers without raising any question concerning the full validity of their ordination. This generous practice, however, transcends denominationalism. No denomination may demand or even assume that its ministers shall be accepted by other denominations. If they are so received, it is because the Christian spirit has triumphed over the ecclesiastical logic of sectarianism. A ministry acceptable and responsible to the whole church can be realized only when the whole church is competent to create a ministry for itself.

What stands in the way of this achievement is, most notably, the attitude of the Protestant Episcopal Church which recognizes only those ministers as truly ordained who have been ordained within the succession of the historic episcopate. There are other churches which have their own reasons for recognizing only their own ordination. But the problem they present will more easily yield to the ecumenical spirit. In the case of the Episopalians, however, it is no lack of the ecumenical spirit that creates the problem. The entire Anglican communion with its branches throughout the world, including the Episcopal Church in America, is oriented both in feeling and in ideology toward the ecumenical goal, in the sense that it yearns for the whole body of Christ to reassume the unitive functions of which sectarianism has robbed it.[1] The leadership of the Anglican church in the ecumenical movement is a natural and profoundly sincere expression of this yearning.

Yet in the eyes of other churches, this church presents itself as a paradox. Desiring unity with a deep Christian passion, it nevertheless seems to be the most formidable obstacle to its attainment. In practice, it follows a policy of the most extreme exclusiveness, refusing, in particular, to accept as valid an ordination performed by other Protestant denominations and insisting that only a minister ordained in its way of ordaining shall be admitted to a functioning place at its altars. Inevitably, this ultrasectarian exclusiveness becomes the subject of impatient and sometimes cynical comment by other Christians. Probably no other Protestant church experiences an inner tension of conflicting impulses comparable to that of the Anglican communion in its relation to other churches.

It is important that the problem be not oversimplified in our thought. Other Christians would do well to try to understand the peculiar predicament in which the schismatic state of Protestantism has placed this particular church. Its predicament is created by the fact that its profound desire for unity with the whole of Protestantism is thwarted by its unique possession of something *which it cannot let go*. This is the historic episcopate. The Reformation in England, as we have seen, was less radical than on the Continent. It not only maintained continuity with the medieval

[1] These unitive functions were listed and considered in Chapter III.

church as did Lutheranism and Presbyterianism, but it conserved unbroken the historic succession of the episcopacy which other sections of the Reformation disregarded and allowed to lapse.

What value inheres in the continuity of this succession is no part of our present interest to consider. The predicament of the Episcopal Church lies in the fact that it cannot gain its consent either to compromise it or to surrender it. Whether its value be great or little, its nature is such that it must be maintained in its historical purity or lost altogether. Besides, if we view it on the lower level of the psychology of those who stand within it, it is too much to expect of human nature that they will voluntarily relinquish the dignity with which it invests their status. Even those Episcopalians who hold a "low" conception of the episcopate still cling to it with a kind of mystical feeling that something important for the Christian Church would be lost if the historical succession were impaired or abandoned. The conception is deeply rooted that the Anglican communion has been entrusted by historical circumstances with an institution which belongs to the unity of the Christian Church, and that it must guard this treasure until the rest of the church is willing to receive it.

The problem is further complicated by the dogma of the apostolic succession. This in its extreme form is the theory that the episcopate was instituted by the apostles under direct authority from Christ himself. The Roman Catholic sacerdotal hierarchy rests upon this dogma. A minority of Anglicans, the Anglo-catholic party, adhere to it while rejecting the papacy. The majority of Anglicans both in England and the United States recognize the entire lack of historical evidence for such a dogma and accept the episcopate as a divinely guided development in the ancient church and inherently venerable for its long history. We can see this more plainly in American Episcopalianism where the church is not entangled with the state, as in England. Here, its bishops and ministers are democratically selected by the churches and are responsible to the churches. The act of ordination does nothing to modify this democratic relation more than it is modified by Presbyterian or Methodist or Congregational ordination. In its famous "Quadrilateral" proposal for church union, renewed again and again, the Anglican church asks for the acceptance only of the historic episcopate, not for the acceptance of the apostolic succession. It asks for the ministry of the united church to be ordained within this ancient succession, with the implication that respect for it, but no particular *theory about it,* is required.

What is the attitude of the nonepiscopal denominations to the historic episcopate so conceived? Some regard it with suspicion as the carrier of the sacerdotal principle, than which nothing is more repugnant to Protestantism as a whole. Others, taking counsel of Anglican history and contemporary character and practice, believe that the historic episcopate could be maintained in a united church without danger of sacerdotalism. This belief is reinforced by the consideration that the united church, possessing the episcopate, would be composed of so great a body of antisacerdotal conviction (the non-Episcopalian portion outnumbering the Episcopalian by much more than 10 to 1) that the fear of sacerdotalism is fantastic.

Still other nonepiscopalians assume an attitude of indifference with respect to the importance of the historic episcopate. They do not see wherein the effectiveness of the ministry would be enhanced or the spiritual life of the church enriched by a ministry ordained in this venerable succession. On the other hand, they are unable to point out wherein any vital principle of Christian faith or practice would be compromised by its adoption. This third class probably represents the largest body of feeling in the nonepiscopal churches. In the situation of Anglicanism *vis-à-vis* the rest of Protestantism, we thus have an inviolable sense of trusteeship on one side, and a body of favorable open-mindedness plus a larger body of virtual indifference on the other. It would seem, therefore, that the problem of providing a ministry for the united church competent to exercise its vocation throughout the church as a whole is not to be summarily written off as insoluble.[2]

If the nonepiscopal ministries were carefully examined, and without the illusions of difference arising from the use of dissimilar vocabularies, it would be evident that, in principle, these ministries

---

[2] From this point on, I am following, with only slight variations, the concluding paragraphs on this subject in my book, *What is Christianity?* pp. 296-99.

present characteristics which approach more closely to the epis-copal pattern than is generally recognized. The simple fact is that each of these denominations has a neat little historic episcopate of its own! True, their histories do not go back as far as that of the Anglican communion, but they go back to the beginning of each denomination. True, also, they have not been so scrupulously safeguarded as the Anglicans safeguard theirs, and there may be a few missing links in the succession; but even so, there cannot have been many, not enough to impair the succession, and certainly not enough to impair the principle upon which each denomination provides itself with a ministry.

Virtually all our ministers are ordained in the succession of ministers, that is, they are ordained by other ministers who were themselves ordained by other ministers and they, in turn, by others, all the way back to the time when the denomination split off from some other denomination. Few ministers would feel that they had been properly set apart to the ministry unless some other minister or ministers participated in their ordination. This holds true even of those denominations with a congregational polity—Baptists, Disciples and Congregationalists—as well as the more orderly bodies such as the Lutherans, the Presbyterians and the Methodists. There are differences in theory, no doubt, but these do not touch the objective fact, namely, that these ministries are carried on in a historical succession.

We shall be reminded at once that the historic episcopate in Anglicanism is something more than succession by ordination: it is succession by *episcopal* ordination, that is, ordination by bishops. But here also the difference, while real, has been greatly exaggerated. This is due to the illusion that bishops have no counterpart in nonepicsopal Protestantism. The fact is, however, that virtually all Protestant denominations have bishops, whether they are called by that name or some other. American Methodism and certain other denominations frankly designate them as "bish-ops," though they maintain a dubious theoretical distinction be-tween their bishops and those of Anglicanism. Other denomina-tions call their bishops "supervisors" or "superintendents" or even "secretaries." Upon them devolves the care of all the churches in a given district or region—which is the distinguishing function of a bishop. Wherein these office-bearers differ from the Anglican conception of a bishop, the advantage would seem to lie with the Anglican conception which is more consonant with the spiritual character of a Christian bishop as shepherd of souls, rather than as mere admininstrator of church organization.

The bishop's part in ordination would require of other denominations the surrender of no cherished principle but would add two elements of value which many of these bodies lack. Considered quite apart from the New Testament doctrine of grace imparted in the laying on of hands, the bishop's part in the act represents (1) the key office whereby ordination is rightly held as a function of the whole church, and (2) it also symbolizes the competence and acceptability of the minister so ordained to exercise his vocation throughout the whole church on behalf of the church as a whole. It is thus both a democratic and an ecumenical function. The acceptance of the historic episcopate by other Protestant churches would involve a much less radical departure from their present practice than is generally assumed, and would require the surrender of no vital principle. It would have the effect of unifying the sectarian successions which now exist in Protestantism by a succession which goes back, not necessarily to the apostles, but at least as far back as historical knowledge can trace the development of church organization.

But the considerations we have brought forward will meet only a cold response from those who accept the denominational system with undisturbed complacency. No effective reason can be given to such minds for even bothering with the subject we are discussing. The motivation for a serious interest in it can spring only from a profound desire to restore to Christ the church of his living body. As the call to unity increases in urgency and the response to its imperative becomes more positive and wholehearted, the indifference with which nonepiscopal Protestantism has always regarded the historic episcopate will be quickened into a willingness to consider it with an open mind. Then, we may believe, the problem of providing a ministry for the whole church will present itself in a new light.

On the other side, the ecumenical movement confronts the Anglican church with an acid test of the sincerity and depth of its ecumenical protestations. It too must make adjustments. If Protestantism cannot ask Anglicanism to surrender the historic episcopate, neither can Anglicanism ask Protestant ministries to accept reordination. Conscience is involved on both sides. Some way must be found by which episcopacy may be shared with the whole church without either reordination or the impairment of the historical succession.

Such a way has been found in South India where episcopal and nonepiscopal churches have become one church. The details of this development are known throughout the Christian world. In a word, an organic unity has been attained with the complete and unprejudiced acceptance of the ministry of all the uniting churches and the provision that, for a period of thirty years, all new candidates for the ministry shall be ordained within the historic episcopate. If the principle involved in this inspiring achievement were extended to the whole of Protestantism the impasse caused by the rigorous absolutism of both sides would be broken through without violation of conscience on either side. The attitude of the bishops at Lambeth in 1948, in failing to grant intercommunion with the South India church because of the intransigence of the Anglo-catholic minority, is regretted, we can believe, no less by the main body of Anglicanism than by the whole of nonepiscopal Protestantism. Unless the Anglican church is willing to make practical adjustments involving no sacrifice of the institution which it holds in trust for the whole church, its activity and leadership in the ecumenical movement can hardly be regarded as sincere.

IMMERSION-BAPTISM

The problem which baptism presents to a united church arises from the fact that the divergent opinions concerning it lead to separatist and exclusive practices. If differences on this subject were only matters of opinion or conviction, they would naturally fall into the category of those diversities in theological opinion and biblical interpretation which would be welcomed and embraced in the ecumenical fellowship. Baptism is the corporate action of the church by which it receives new members into its fellowship. In many denominations the manner of administering baptism is optional—both affusion and immersion are practiced according to the desire of the candidate. But those who identify baptism with immersion in water cannot gain their conscientious consent either to practice any other mode or to sanction its practice by belonging to a church that practices it. They invest immersion with the high importance not only of New Testament authority but of an explicit command of Christ. Obviously we have here a really difficult problem as we strive to envisage a united church. It is a different kind of problem from that presented by diversity in the realm of theological opinion. The immersionist denominations are in much the same position as the Episcopal Church in respect to the historic episcopate. The analogy is precise. The immersionist bodies—Baptists, Disciples and numerous others— have traditionally thought of themselves as holding in trust for the whole church the practice of immersion, as the Episcopalians similarly feel that they hold in trust for the whole church their historic Episcopate. The approach of the ecumenical movement to both groups meets with hardly more promising response in one than in the other.

The analogy extends even further. The rest of Protestantism reacts to the special claim of each of these groups in an identical manner. It regards each with virtual indifference. The rest of Protestantism (including the Episcopalians) regards the immersionist claim as an unwarranted inference from New Testament writings and spurns with repugnance the idea that Christ commanded the physical act of immersion in water as a condition of fellowship in his church. Likewise, the rest of Protestantism (including Baptists, Disciples and other immersionists) holds the historic episcopate as a nonessential, though venerable, institution and considers its own manner of ordination as fully valid.

But the whole of Protestantism regards both the practice of immersion and the historic episcopate with complete respect— the one as valid baptism, the other as valid ordination. No opposition to either exists throughout Protestantism. On the contrary, all denominations accept baptism by immersion as true baptism, and most of them practice it as an optional mode. Likewise, no denomination would demand reordination of a minister who had been ordained within the historic episcopate. But this optional acceptance satisfies neither the immersionists nor the Episcopalians. They could be satisfied with it only if they were comfortably complacent in being a sectarian church, in which case each denomination could go right on practicing its particular mode—of ordination or immersion—and leave the rest of Protestantism out of account.

But this sectarian complacency is now impossible, not only because the ecumenical movement has quickened throughout Protestantism a profound disillusionment with respect to the sectarian system and a yearning for the unity of the Church of Christ, but because the immersionist denominations and the Episcopalians alike avow that each holds its particular practice in trust for the whole church, that is, for the united church. (In the previous section we discussed the Episcopal side of this predicament and can therefore drop the analogy at this point.) This avowal of trusteeship by the immersionist denominations is itself a tribute to the ecumenical ideal. Their attention should be sharply drawn to its implications. Especially should its implications be clearly felt by certain of the Baptist denominations among whom the ecumenical movement meets with less explicit favor than among any of our larger Protestant bodies. It is impossible to believe otherwise than that Baptists do hold their immersionist practice under the conception of such a trust on behalf of the whole church. This being so, they are thereby committed to the ideal of a united church, and their frequent asseverations of indifference to the ecumenical movement belie their deepest feeling.

In somewhat different terms the same considerations apply to the Disciples of Christ. The terms are different because the Disciples, like the Episcopalians, and unlike the Baptists, are highly articulate on the subject of Christian unity. As we saw in the previous chapter, the Disciples originated as, in a true sense, an ecumenical movement. But their thinking later congealed into a sectarian pattern of the New Testament church which must be restored as the true basis of a united church. The exclusive practice of immersion became, not necessarily the most important, but certainly the most conspicuous feature of this pattern church. Therefore, with respect to the mode of baptism, the Disciples seem to be in virtually the same position, *vis-à-vis* a united church, as the Baptists. Instead of being a movement for church union they became one of the major problems to its attainment.

But this statement must be qualified by a recognition of the contemporary re-emergence among the Disciples of their original motivation. The effect of this is to reverse the priority as between their pattern of the primitive church and the ecumenical imperative by subordinating the former to the latter. This does not mean an abandonment of the traditional pattern which, Disciples still maintain, includes elements which they earnestly hope to contribute to a united church. It means, however, that the sectarian spirit in which these convictions had come to be held and were put forward as the only basis of union, is giving way to their open-minded reconsideration in the fraternal fellowship of the ecumenical procedure. With respect to immersion-baptism, Disciples churches in increasing numbers are accepting unimmersed members of other churches without rebaptism. The motive for this is not proselytism, but the desire to "practice Christian union" within their own fellowship without pressing their exclusive practice of immersion to the point of a sectarian dogma.

The churches of the American Baptist Convention (Northern) are moving in the same direction, though they lack the special motivation in a traditional commitment to Christian unity which gives a more potent imperative to the Disciples for the more fraternal practice. A distinguished Baptist leader, coming out of a conference on the union of his denomination with the Disciples, made this significant explanation of the problems they had been discussing: "We Baptists are at a disadvantage with the Disciples because they have been thinking about Christian unity through all their history, and we have only recently begun to think about it." Few Disciples will allow such a generous remark to flatter their self-esteem as they remember their own intransigency through most of their history.

The Southern Baptists present the problem of immersion-baptism in its most stubborn form. Unimpressed by the ecumenical imperative, this great denomination insulates itself from vital contact not only with its neighbor denominations but with its sister denomination north of Mason and Dixon's line. The sectarian stereotype, including the immersion dogma, in which the concept of its mission is rigidly fixed, is so completely protected against the possibility of modification by contact with the spirit of modern evangelical scholarship, that any adjustment with other Christians is likely to be slower than in the case of the Northern body. We have previously expressed some hope for the Southern Baptists derived from the presence among them of many scattered churches and ministers whose vision and feeling transcend the self-sufficiency of their denomination.

In our discussion of this subject it is unnecessary to give extended consideration to infant baptism, because this problem tends, in the United States, to solve itself. As we pointed out in Chapter VI, in this country where church and state are separate, the rite of infant baptism does not entail the social and political consequences which it carries in England and on the Continent. There, where the established church, or the tradition associated with establishment, still exists, infant baptism is practiced almost indiscriminately by most people, Christian or pagan. It is expected that the infant will be baptized just as he is expected to be vaccinated, and a good deal of superstition attaches to the rite. Certain privileges are denied to one who cannot produce a certificate of baptism—for example, marriage in church or burial in the church yard. In our country, the rite of infant baptism as practiced among Protestants is a recognition that the child of believing parents belongs in a true sense to the Christian community. The practice of pedobaptist churches really divides the baptismal function into two acts, the consummative act being confirmation. Among immersionist bodies, there is a strong trend to make the same distinction by practicing some form by which the church recognizes that the child of Christian parents belongs in a true sense to the Christian community which shares with the parents in the responsibility for his upbringing "in the nurture and admonition of the Lord." This rite is sometimes called "dedication" or "consecration," and is an act in which both the church and the parents share. The term "baptism" is reserved for use where pedobaptist bodies use "confirmation." The long controversy over infant baptism thus tends more and more to become a matter of words.

How, in a constructive and hopeful spirit, can the ecumenical movement deal with this problem of immersion-baptism? In the first place, it is well to remember that the membership of immersionist bodies constitutes a little less than one-half of American Protestantism—seven times larger than, for example, the Protestant Episcopal Church. The problem which they present must therefore be taken seriously. Second, the progress toward unity on the part of those churches which recognize one another's ministries and sacraments should not be impeded by the difficulty inherent in the baptism problem. Third, the immersionist problem should not be set aside as hopeless. If its difficulty seems insurmountable at the moment, it must be constantly kept in mind that profound changes are taking place in the thought and temper of the whole of Protestantism. The possibility of change in the area where this problem exists is not an unreasonable expectation. Fourth, it must be recognized that the problem of immersion-baptism is not more difficult than that of the historic episcopate upon which, together with its implications concerning ordination and the administration of the sacraments, the ecumenical movement has already devoted so many years of yet unexhausted patience and hope. A similar attention to the baptism problem might yield even more substantial results and in less time. This is a gentle reminder of our earlier criticism of the ecumenical movement for its neglect of the restorationist denominations in its approach to Protestantism.

The place to begin such an approach to the immersionist denominations would seem to be at that point where they avow the trusteeship principle as the justification of their rigorous exclusivist position. We have seen that this is the principle upon which the Anglican church stands in its unyielding attitude with respect to the episcopate. Yet this has not deterred that church nor the ecumenical movement from long and intensive labor in the area of faith and order in the hope of surmounting this obstacle to unity. No more should the conscientious conviction of the immersionist churches that they hold their mode of baptism in trust for the whole church deter them or the Faith and Order side of the ecumenical movement from engaging in similar labor on the baptism question. If the immersionist denominations, many of whom are included in the World Council of Churches, feel that they are not really on the inside of the discussions on faith and order, they should be reassured by a serious recognition of the special problem which they bring into it. They deserve such recognition on the ground that they hold their particular exclusivist practice as a trust for the ecumenical church. Such an approach to this large body of Christians would invest the ecumenical movement in American Protestantism with a realism it has not yet developed.

What this approach would lead to in terms of specific results is, of course, unpredictable. But the immersionist bodies would be confronted at the outset with this challenging question: How shall this trust which we hold on behalf of the whole church best be discharged? This is the question which the ecumenical ideal raises in the conscience of every denomination. The immersionist bodies have not yet been realistically confronted by it. Instead, they have been proceeding on the unchallenged assumption that a particular brand of theology or of biblical interpretation requires a separate denomination for its conservation and propagation. The ecumenical approach to the immersionist bodies will challenge this assumption with respect to baptism. Or better, it will move them to challenge it for themselves.

Once this relation is established between the ecumenical movement and these denominations we may expect three possible procedures to be considered. The first will be to continue the inflexible sectarian exclusiveness in the hope of converting the rest of Protestantism to the exclusive practice of immersion. This might well be called the way of sectarian imperialism. In all candor, we must say that such a hope, if it is cherished by any denomination, is, if not utterly fatuous, at least highly unrealistic and unpromising. The history of denominationalism is a demonstration of the fact that a sure way to sterilize a Christian truth or a biblical interpretation is to build a sectarian wall around it.

A second procedure that will insist on being explored is the possibility of some adjustment that will free the exclusive practice of immersion from its present stark sectarianism without doing violence to the immersionist conscience. This, we believe, is the motivation of those Baptist and Disciples churches which receive Christians from other churches without rebaptism, while they continue unmodified their own practice of baptism exclusively by immersion. It is conceivable that this unsectarian practice could be carried over into a united church. Thus freed from the prejudice with which immersion is regarded when offered by a sectarian propagandist, it would make its appeal on its own inherent merits to Christian intelligence. No doubt other suggestions of adjustment would arise once the immersionist bodies entertained the possibility that their trusteeship of immersion could be discharged in other ways as well as, or better than, by isolating it in a separate denomination.

Third, a more earnest consideration of the immersionist churches by the ecumenical movement would surely open up the whole question of baptism for restudy in the light of our greatly enriched knowledge of the apostolic church. When one considers the volume and significance of this new knowledge, brought to us by New Testament scholarship in the past generation, it is pathetic to contemplate the musty reasoning on both sides of the baptismal controversy. The simple truth is that this new knowledge has set baptism in a distinctly new context which renders most of the traditional polemic obsolete. The churches which practice optional forms are, of course, less concerned with a question which they have long since relegated to the limbo of indifference. But their leaders would be no less wise than their immersionist brethren to free themselves from the delusion that the immersionist position can be honestly withstood in terms of yesteryear's knowledge of the primitive church. The full pathos of the situation, however, appears when one contemplates the aggressive argumentation of immersionist leaders on grounds which are no longer tenable.

This knowledge, common to scholars, must be brought to bear

upon the baptismal issue. How can this be done except by the procedure followed by the ecumenical movement in its intensive study of the historic episcopate and the doctrines and practices which it subtends? Representatives of all the denominations share in this study, with meager results, it is true, in terms of solution, but with great results in terms of spreading widely an understanding which may lead to a solution. Why should not the ecumenical movement take the immersionist problem with equal seriousness? Deliberate and extended conferences including officially appointed representative scholars from Baptist, Disciples and other immersionist bodies, and from what we may call the "optionalist" bodies, could issue from time to time reports of their findings, their agreements and disagreements, that would bring the question home to the whole of Protestantism as the urgent issue it really is for the ecumenical movement.

CONGREGATIONALISM

The term "congregationalism" is used, not to refer to a particular denomination, but to a theory of church polity or organization which Congregationalists share with Baptists, Disciples and numerous other bodies. It is the theory that regards the local church as invested with complete independence and autonomy and that rejects every form of connexionalism which involves an ecclesiastical bond or union between local congregations and the church as a whole. This is a statement of the abstract principle or theory of congregationalism. As we shall see, the main denominations which carry this theory in their tradition and emphasize it as a structural—or perhaps we should say, structureless—principle of church polity do not exemplify it in their practice. But since it is the theory that inhibits these denominations from a candid recognition of the contrary theory, we shall have to devote some attention to it as a general principle.

But first it should be made clear why this absolute congregational principle is an obstacle that must be surmounted in preparation for a united church. It is obvious that a united church, emerging from the dissolution of the churchism of the denominations, must itself assume a structure or form of its own. It need not and should not be an elaborate form. But it should provide those orderly procedures that will enable the church to enjoy an integrated ecclesiastical fellowship and to act as a whole in those matters which are the true functions of the whole church. That this is possible without restricting local autonomy in those matters which are the true functions of the local congregation is universally recognized by all who participate in the ecumenical movement. But all parts of the church must be integrated on the broad principle of their ecclesiastical obligation to the whole church. It is quite unthinkable that any part of the church should set itself up as absolutely independent and autonomous. Least of all could local congregations so consider themselves. Nor can the whole church consider itself superior to or independent of the local churches, for, as we have seen in Chapter V, the ultimate responsibility of any united church which Protestants are able to conceive or willing to enter must ultimately rest upon the democratic consent of the local churches.

Thus it should be plain why the theory of unqualified congregational independence and autonomy is incompatible with the ecumenical ideal. This principle cannot be carried as a theory into a united church. Union requires that it give way explicitly to its opposite, namely, the interdependence and mutual responsibility of the local churches to one another and to the church as a whole. If this obstacle to Christian unity is to be surmounted, it is necessary to consider the abstract principle in detachment from the inconsistent practice of the denominations which profess their adherence to it. In a word, we have to consider whether it is a sound principle of the Christian faith. Our conclusion may be stated in advance. We shall find that, strictly as a theory, it is a thoroughly unsound principle, and, as a matter of fact, belied in practice by those denominations which profess to be founded upon it.

It is maintained by these denominations that their theoretical position is derived from the New Testament: (1) that the New Testament knows no other empirical church except the local congregation; (2) that these congregations were independent and autonomous, there being no organized or recognized churchly interdependence among them; (3) that the emergence of organization (assumed to be some time after the New Testament period) represented an apostasy from the order established at the beginning; and (4) that this New Testament pattern is normative and mandatory upon the church for all time.

It will be impossible in a brief space to utilize the ample New Testament evidence in opposition to this congregational theory, nor shall we attempt it. But the theory must be rejected at all points. We shall take them in reverse order, beginning with the one last mentioned.

There is not a word or suggestion in the New Testament to warrant the assumption that the formal pattern of the primitive church is normative and mandatory for all time. This is a sheer dogma held sincerely by many Christians, not all of whom belong to denominations of the congregational persuasion. This view takes no account of the fact that the New Testament church was the infant church. It assumes that the church came into existence at Pentecost fully implemented with a fixed order which could not be expanded as the church "grew up." Many other things changed —from the Jewish messianism of Peter at Pentecost, to the universalism of Paul's Letters, to the mysticism of the Fourth Gospel. The New Testament is rich in the variety and diversity of its interpretations of the gospel, none of which, let us hasten to say, changed the gospel. We are bound to believe, are we not, that these varieties of interpretation were manifestations of the guiding presence of the Holy Spirit, and we would dishonor the Spirit were we to fix our attention upon the earliest of these interpretations to the exclusion of the later ones.

If, then, we allow for change and variety to appear at the very center of the Christian faith, on what grounds can we take the embryonic structure—or lack of structure—of the infant church as definitive and mandatory for all time? If the Holy Spirit was manifested in the developing interpretations of the gospel itself, why may there not have been development in the structure of the church under the guidance of the same Holy Spirit? As a matter of fact, there are clear indications in the New Testament that there was such a development even in New Testament times.

Those who insist upon the pattern of the primitive church as normative and mandatory for all time should just as logically insist upon the Old Testament as the sole Bible of the church for all time. The primitive church had no other Bible save the Old Testament. The New Testament was itself a slow growth and was not available as Scripture until well on into the second century. The earliest writings in our New Testament (the only ones contributed by an apostle) are Paul's letters, composed twenty-five and thirty-five years after Pentecost. These were followed by the Gospels of Mark and Matthew at the time of Paul's death, about A. D. 65. But Paul's Letters had been the possession of the several churches to whom they were addressed, and were not collected for general use until sixty years after Pentecost, at about which time Luke wrote his Gospel and the Acts. The latest of our "books" were the Fourth Gospel, the three Johns (or four, including the Apocalypse), the two Peters, James, the two Timothys, Titus, Hebrews, and Jude.

Some of these later books contain allusions which presuppose the existence of a formalized interdependent connexionalism among the churches, including even a bishop of the churches in a particular area.[3] How early this development of polity began is not known, but its existence was evidently taken for granted by the later New Testament writers, not one of whom conveys the slightest hint that it represented an apostasy.

During all this time—roughly a full century—the church had no Bible save the Old Testament. Yet all Christians believe that the development of the New Testament was guided by the Holy Spirit. Why should it not be equally believed that the developing organization of the church was guided by the same Holy Spirit. And if the Spirit through the bishops of the middle second century gave us the canon of our New Testament, why must we go back to the infancy of the church when there was as yet no integrated

[3] I suggest some books for the reader who would pursue this subject further: R. R. Williams, *Authority in the Apostolic Age* (London: S. C. M. Press, 1950); Clarence T. Craig, *The One Church* (New York and Nashville: Abingdon-Cokesbury, 1951); E. J. Goodspeed, *The Formation of the New Testament* (Chicago: University of Chicago Press, 1926); Daniel Jenkins, *The Nature of Catholicity* (Landon: Faber & Faber, 1949).

organization of the rapidly proliferating units of an ecstatic spiritual movement to find the normative organizational pattern of the church for all time? Christianity did not begin as an organization; it began as a religion of the Spirit—hardly less than explosive in its emergence—and assumed organs and a structure as need arose for them.

But this is not all that must be said. We are not concerned here with what particular structure and organs are really normative— for example, whether the threefold ministry of bishops, elders and deacons is normative. Our sole concern is whether the local churches of the primitive church were independent and autonomous. That they did not so conceive themselves, even before they had an organization, is plainly indicated in the New Testament itself. Professor Craig has pointed out two distinctly recognized limitations on the local churches: one, the authority of the Apostles, the other the special position of the mother church in Jerusalem. Neither of these represented the authority of ecclesiastical status, but rather what Professor Williams, the Anglican scholar, has finely described as moral or spiritual authority. In the case of the apostles, it was the personal and moral authority of those who alone could bear firsthand witness to the revelation of God in Christ Jesus. In the case of the Jerusalem church, it was a parental solicitude for the churches to which it had given birth and which recognized in love the mother's right to guide her own children. The point here, however, is not as to the kind of "authority" that was exercised, but the fact that *it was recognized by the local congregations.*

That is to say, even in the earliest period of Christianity, no local church claimed independence and autonomy. Such a claim would have been repugnant to the churches themselves. They had as yet no ecclesiastical organs through which to express their interdependence and unity, but they were one church, the veritable body of Christ, and were being guided by the Holy Spirit toward the attainment of a structure and organs through which their unity could be given empirical manifestation and guarded against dispersion into an atomistic multitude. In a word, the Christian Church was ecumenical from the beginning. As an abstract theory, congregationalism must, therefore, be regarded as a heresy. Its espousal as an absolute principle of church polity cannot be expected to figure as a factor in determining the form of the united church.

Happily, however, all the so-called congregational denominations which are in the orbit of hopeful or possible inclusion in the ecumenical movement, are only theoretically committed to this principle. In actual practice, none of them is truly congregational. They have an organized unity of their local churches for which there is no pattern in the primitive church. The body that comes nearest to the actual practice of the independence and autonomy of the local church is the group known as Churches of Christ, an offshoot of the Disciples of Christ. They live under the illusion that they have actually restored the primitive church, and they are quite untouched by the ecumenical movement. The Disciples themselves, however, and the Baptists and Congregationalists whom we have chosen for convenience as representative of congregationalism, differ from the connexional denominations —Methodists, Presbyterians, Lutherans, Episcopalians, and so on—in this respect only in degree, despite the exaggerated claim of the former group to differ radically.

The favorite term with which the former group describe themselves is to say that they are the "Free Churches." This term deserves examination. In England, it has a legitimate meaning as over against the established church which is not free. (It should be parenthetically noted that these "free churches" are not really free, and cannot be, in a society where one church is established by the state. They exist only under "toleration," however benevolently it is administered.) Historically, the term "free churches" was properly applied to the Baptists and Congregationalists at their origin in England by virtue of their separation from state control. But in the United States where church and state have been constitutionally separate for a century and a half, the term "free church" has lost its historical meaning. All churches are truly free in this country, in this original sense.

Yet the term persists. It is adopted by those denominations which claim to be congregational in polity as marking the contrast between themselves and the churches of the second group mentioned above. Thus Baptists, Congregationalists and Disciples speak of themselves as "free churches," with the implication that the local churches of Presbyterian, Lutheran, Episcopalian and Methodist denominations are, in some sense, not free. Closely allied with this concept is the claim that they are "democratic" churches in contrast with those of the other group. Both of these ideas carry invidious implications. In the interest of the ecumenical movement, they deserve some attention in the present context.

It is not too clear precisely what is intended by the designation "free churches" in the United States. Its most probable meaning is that the local churches of one set of denominations are both free and democratic in some sense that those of the other set are not free and democratic. This claim will hardly bear examination. The local churches of the connexionalist group will reject the implication that they are not free. True, there are certain respects in which they do not act independently and autonomusly—their property is usually held in trust for the whole denomination, not in fee simple; in the call of their ministers, they recognize that the church at large has a spiritual and moral stake in the pastoral leadership of every local church, and this principle is implemented by presbytery or diocese or bishop. Such limitation of autonomy is *freely accepted* by the local churches as not only an essential of unity, but as a moral obligation inherent in the Christian fellowship. For the other group of churches to claim to be more free, because, forsooth, they do not recognize such moral obligations, only betrays their lack of insight into the nature of the Christian Church.

As for the claim to be more democratic, the advantage would seem to lie with the connexional group rather than the congregational. The difference between them in actual practice is one of degree instead of principle. That is to say, in one group the democratic process is provided with more orderly and dependable procedures than in the other. This difference appears in the ecclesiastical functioning of the denomination as a whole. Both types of denomination have the same kind of agencies—missionary, educational, evangelistic, philanthropic, public relations, ministerial pensions, social action and the rest. These agencies are functions of the unity of the denomination. They represent the interdependent integration of its local churches.

One would expect, in the case of a denomination which makes high claim for the autonomy and independence of the local church, that its local churches would desire and assert their democratic right to participate effectively in directing the operations of these agencies. It does not appear that they have such a desire. At any rate, they allow a great mass meeting, consisting of those members of their churches who wish to attend (and usually, pay their own expenses), to hear reports of the agencies and approve decisions made by *ad hoc* committees or by the agencies themselves. Only a small fraction of the local churches are "represented" in these mass meetings which are always overloaded by those from the churches in the immediate region where the convention is held. This loose and relatively irresponsible procedure is the basis on which the claim of superior democracy is made. But it is not truly democratic. It results inevitably in the concentration of responsibility in the hands of those who are interested in exercising it. Not infrequently, this has resulted in the virtual control of the policies of the whole denomination by an elite group. Sometimes a single newspaper which has attained a kind of papal authority over the officiary of the agencies dictates the policies of the denomination.

To claim that its churches are free in such a system is an affront to democratic intelligence. They can be truly free only in a system in which the delegated or representative principle inherent in democracy is provided by a polity that evokes from the grass roots of the local churches their advice and consent. This the denominations of the connexionalist type grant to their local churches in an orderly procedure through presbyteries and synods (the particular name is immaterial) in which each local church is represented. For this reason, it must be claimed on behalf of the Presbyterians, Lutherans, Episcopalians and Methodists that they are more democratic than their congregational neighbors.

In this discussion we have made no distinction among the three denominations that were chosen to represent congregationalism. It would have been awkward to carry such a distinction through the various phases of the argument. To let our discussion stand without making such a distinction would be manifestly unfair. Though they all lay claim to the abstract principle of congregationalism, and use it as a rallying slogan to maintain denominational self-consciousness, there is a distinct gradation among them in terms of actual practice. We may say that the Congregationalists are the least congregational of this group. Their "associations" are recognized by the local churches as having a legitimate interest in the ordination of a minister, in calling him to a parish church and installing him in it. Their General Council is as fairly representative of the associations and local churches as is the General Assembly of the Presbyterian Church. But the loyalty of its membership is easily vitiated by long indoctrination in the abstract principle of local autonomy. This principle seems to lie around where it can be handily picked up and used on occasion to frustrate, or at least confuse, the will of the great majority of the denomination. This has recently been illustrated in the unhappy litigation over the union of the Congregational denomination with the Evangelical and Reformed Church.

Probably the American (formerly the Northern) Baptists should be ranked next to the Congregationalists, though considerably behind them. Their "associations" in some parts of the country are genuine presbyteries, without the name. Their American Baptist Convention is a representative body, in theory. But it lacks the intermediate structure by which all the local churches could representatively participate in its deliberations. The spirit of this denomination, in defense against subversive influences, was indicated not so long ago by the adoption of a rule which required that only those churches could send delegates which gave at least 25 per cent of their missionary and benevolent budget to the agencies of the convention. This action certainly could not be justified by New Testament precedent! But, it is just another evidence of the inconsistency between theory and practice in this "congregational" denomination.

It is difficult to say whether the Disciples or the Southern Baptists should rank next in order. If we look at their actual practice, there seems to be little basis to distinguish them in respect to their congregationalism. But it is probably fair to say that the Disciples are further on the way out of their extreme congregationalism than their Southern neighbor. Both transact their denominational affairs in great popular mass meetings of their members who attend as individuals, though, in each case, an informal gesture is made toward the idea that each person "represents" his local church. The Disciples, however, a generation ago, supplemented this mass convention with a "Committee on Recommendations," consisting of more than two hundred persons appointed on a proportional basis by the state conventions. This committee sits continuously throughout the entire period of the convention in special quarters provided for it. To it all reports of agencies, all resolutions and matters of business are referred and brought back to the main convention with recommendations. Rarely are these recommendations voted down, though they may be. At this point, the Disciples have substantially modified their extreme congregationalism by recognizing the state conventions as responsible intermediaries between the churches and the General Convention. It should also be added that the long-time practice of ordination by a local church, acting independently, is coming to be seen by the Disciples as a usurpation of a function which belongs to the church as a whole, represented by the participation of neighboring local churches. However, the neighboring churches have not been organized into "associations" as formally as among Baptists and Congregationalists.

The Southern Baptists represent an extreme form of the ideology of congregationalism. Like the other bodies in this category, they cherish the illusion that they have restored the primitive church of the New Testament. On this subject they are more vocal than the Northern Baptists and perhaps more even than the Disciples; certainly more than the Congregationalists. Nevertheless, the Southern Baptists have agencies and conventions and superintendents or supervisors and executive committees and much else that was totally unknown in the New Testament church! These integrate their local churches in a loose ecclesiastical system, though, like the Disciples, they affect to despise such a system

by calling it "ecclesiasticism." Also, like their fellow congregationalists, they evade the truth about themselves by emphasizing
the "voluntary" nature of their local church participation in these
super-New Testament organized activities, with the implication
that the denominations in the connexional category are under
coercion of some sort. But their conventions are sufficiently "ecclesiastical" to justify the rejection of a heretical or obstreperous
minister or congregation from participation in their deliberations.
And their agencies make plans for the united action of the whole
denomination.

All this is a far cry from the infant church of the New Testament
which congregationalism theoretically claims to "restore." But it
is not a far cry from those denominations—Presbyterian, Methodist, Episcopalian and Lutheran—which frankly avow the principle that every local church is an organic part of the whole church,
with responsibilities which transcend its independence and autonomy. The difference between the two groups of denominations,
we are insisting, is a matter of degree and of orderliness and of
true democracy, rather than of some sacrosanct principle.

Thus, if the several congregational denominations in whose
mentality an illusory, unbiblical and unchristian notion of congregational independence and autonomy has become ingrained,
would only look realistically at their own practices, they would
see how narrow is the cleft that must be closed when once they
make a wholehearted response to the ecumenical ideal.

It is not beyond reasonable expectation that, in the united
church, provision may be made for what may be called a "mixed
polity" with respect to certain functions of local churches. By this
is meant that some local churches within the framework of the
united church may retain, for example, their present title to local
church property, their independence in calling and dismissing a
pastor, and his independence in accepting a call to another parish;
while other local churches would prefer to hold their property in
trust for the united church, accept as its pastor one appointed by
bishop or presbytery, and his integration in such a system. The
two procedures are not necessarily incompatible or divisive. If a
plan for including them both in the united church can be devised

it should facilitate union by surmounting this much exaggerated obstacle to Christian unity. The ecumenical movement should earnestly devote itself to an exploration of this possibility and the formulation of such a *modus vivendi*.

We close this chapter with an observation that is somewhat detached from the main line of our discussion, but which belongs in this connection. The whole problem of church polity has been confused by a bad nomenclature: the use of such legalistic terms as "authority," "power," "government," "law," "legislation," "courts," and so on, by the connexionalist denominations. This has prejudiced the mind of the congregationalist denominations against the orderly democracy which connexionalism represents. Such terms have no place in the vocabulary of the Christian faith. Their use in the Presbyterian Church, for example, belies both the spirit and practice of that church. A new vocabulary is called for, a vocabulary growing out of the fundamental concept of *responsibility* rather than authority. No Christian church should invest any man or set of men with authority or power. The language of authority is alien to the Christian faith. It should be eliminated not only from the formal actions of church bodies and from all church documents, but from the informal conversation of all Protestant churchmen. The Christian Church can delegate responsibility, which it actually possesses, but it cannot delegate authority,which it does not possess. This is, in reality, what the connexionalist denominations do, all of them—Presbyterian, Lutheran, Episcopalian, Methodist. The conception of ecclesiastical functions in terms of responsibility must be made explicit in the polity of the ecumenical church if the illusory prejudice of congregational denominations against connexionalism is to be overcome. In the Church of Christ, he alone, as we shall maintain in the following chapter, possesses authority.

VIII

Loyalty and Freedom in a United Church

CHRISTIAN UNITY requires an answer to this fundamental question: Upon what principles of cohesion may the united church depend for the maintenance of its unity? It should be said at once that no infallible guarantee is conceivable. The Christian Church has always lived and always will live precariously. Because human nature shares with divine grace in its composition, error and intransigency must be expected to appear in its ongoing life. This will be true of the united church, as it is true of all our denominational churches. But the ecumenical movement presupposes that the united church will have freed itself from the major causes that have produced Protestant divisions in an endless series of chain reactions. If this presupposition is unsound, the ecumenical ideal is an illusion. Therefore the idea of a united church must be clarified with respect to its greater promise of cohesion than the methods which have notoriously failed to maintain the unity even of our independent and autonomous denominations.

It is obvious that the principle of coercive authoritarianism must be rejected. It has already been rejected by the denominations themselves. The whole of American Protestantism, without exception, as we have repeatedly pointed out, is organized in its separate denominations on the democratic principle. They all operate in structures which rest upon "the consent of the governed." Some are loosely integrated; others are provided with more orderly procedures. Some follow the pattern of a modified New England "town meeting"; others, adopting the representative principle which is inherent in democracy, provide more orderly procedures with checks and balances to assure against the unwisdom of precipitate action. But all, by intention, are democratic. It is therefore inconceivable that a united church in which these denominations would lose their identity as churches, would consent to mantain its unity on any other than a democratic basis.

The problem that we have set for our consideration is to conceive a united church which embodies the principle of democracy and, without recourse to the sanctions exercised by political democracy, is nevertheless able to maintain its organic life in a truly Christian unity. We shall identify and attempt to clarify two principles of unity which, if they are held together, will provide a united church with the maximum promise of its continuing cohesive solidarity. These are (1) the principle of loyalty and (2) the principle of freedom. As abstract principles they will not take us far. We shall, therefore, have to show the respective places of their concrete embodiment in the structure of the church. Our conclusion may be stated at the outset. The principle of loyalty must be given its place in the *constitution* of the church, and the principle of freedom in the *fellowship* of the church. The constitution is the focus of loyalty; the fellowship is the locus of freedom.

We shall maintain that the basic cause of sectarian divisions in Protestantism lies, historically, in the failure to make a clear distinction between the constitution and the fellowship, and between the principles of loyalty and freedom which properly belong to each area, respectively. By the same token, it will be maintained that, in clearly making these distinctions and consciously providing for their recognition in the united church, lies the hope of maintaining its unity.

It should be strongly emphasized that the united church must provide for *both* loyalty and freedom—for these are the cohesive bond of unity only if they are held together. They are not antithetical, though they are often so conceived. They are supplementary, and require to be held together in any form of democratic union. Loyalty without freedom tends toward static uniformity and opens the way to autocracy. Freedom without loyalty breeds anarchy. But when the two co-exist in the same body they are creative and cohesive, and, as such, they protect and foster the unity of the body.

How shall we conceive a united church which embodies both principles? In search for an answer to this question, let us examine our denominations themselves. Looking at them historically they will guide us away from the wrong answer. But if we observe them as they are operating today, they will, perhaps to our surprise, tell us something strongly suggestive of the right answer. A brief glance at their history will disclose the fact that the successive secessions which we now deplore as the scandal of Protestantism occurred as the result of constitutional restraint upon the freedom of the Christian fellowship. After the Reformers of the sixteenth century were compelled by historical conditions (described in Chapter I) to relinquish their hope of uniting the three tributaries of the Reformation, the free spirit of Protestantism was congealed in an orthodoxy of belief to which faith itself was virtually made subordinate.

The multitude of divisions which have occurred through the centuries have been caused by deviations from the standards of orthodoxy. Beginning with the Puritan secessions from the Anglican church at the turn of the seventeenth century, each new denomination established its own standards of orthodoxy. They were used as tests of an applicant's qualification for membership and as tests of the loyalty of both ministers and members. The apologetic which each denomination put forward to justify its break with a parent body, and its separate existence in contrast with other denominations, was formulated in terms of sound doctrine or strict conformity to a pattern of church organization believed to be divinely authorized.

Thus each denomination erected an orthodoxy of its own which, in good conscience, it applied as a restriction upon the fellowship of the church. Each imagined that by forcing or allowing division it was preserving its unity, and the seceding group put its trust in a new orthodoxy as the conservator of its unity. Now and then a denomination even seriously thought that its orthodoxy, being the veritable truth of the gospel, would ultimately prove acceptable to the whole church as the basis of ecumenical unity! So this fissiparous process went on until, by the close of the nineteenth century, the folly and sin of it all began, though dimly, to be recognized. This history is instructive because it gives the obviously wrong answer to the problem of loyalty and freedom in a united church, and warns the ecumenical movement not to adopt it.

THE ENLARGING FREEDOM

But if we observe our contemporary denominations, they will tell a different story. A great change has come over the whole of Protestantism in the past half century. The unity of our denominations is now maintained by a large increase of freedom and a distinct shift of loyalty. A significant clue to the nature of this change is seen in the virtual passing of the heretic. The last great heresy trials were held at the end of the nineteenth century. They taught the churches concerned, and all other churches, a lesson which was seriously taken to heart. They made it clear that the churches must provide in their fellowship a much wider area of freedom for their members, ministers and scholars. The hunting down of heretics proved to be vastly unpopular and the churches came to see it as scandalously unchristian. Plainly, a new spirit was emerging in most Protestant churches. It found voice in the demand that the creeds be radically revised, or replaced by new ones, or laid on the shelf as ancient symbols no longer applicable by ecclesiastical authority to the faith of modern Christians. Some revisions were made in response to this demand. In the case of the Presbyterian Church, a "Restatement" of the Reformed Faith was completed in 1902 and its noble and catholic formulation was unanimously adopted by the General Assembly. Since that time the spirit of the heresy hunter has cropped out only sporadically, and has been dealt with, for the most part, by other processes than formal ecclesiastical action.

The intense Fundamentalist excitement of the 1920's produced some defections. There was, it must be admitted, real gound for disquiet but, as it has proved, none for defection. Many leaders of the churches had become fascinated with a form of liberalism which seemed to threaten the evangelical character of the gospel. But the outcome, as we are now able to see, is proof that it would have been far better had the dissenters remained in their churches and trusted the principle of free discussion within the fellowship to resolve the issues. For the liberalism of that period, against which they reacted, is now being displaced by a sound evangelicalism which, had the dissenters remained, would give no cause today for a break in the fellowship. Besides, had they remained, they would have shared in the deeper understanding of the gospel which the churches are now experiencing. Instead, by defection, the partisan opinions of Fundamentalism, formed in bitter controversy, have been frozen in the crudest form of orthodoxy known in Protestant history.

It is important also to note that contemporary religious thought cuts across the lines of all denominations and is changing the ideological orientation of most of them. The inculcation of specifically denominational doctrines is a diminishing discipline. The challenging questions confronted by the Christian mind of today are no longer denominational, but ecumenical. They are not the kind of questions that can be expressed in terms of the standards of one denomination over against those of other denominations. They concern and enlist the attention of all the churches. Their impact upon denominational mentality tends to undermine the constitutive status of the traditional standards of faith and to enlarge the freedom of the fellowship to embrace wide diversities in both theological and social thought.

This widening freedom in the fellowship often makes room for differences which go to the root of a denomination's most cherished traditions. While causing tension, the unity of the fellowship is maintained by the new spirit of which we are speaking— the spirit of confidence that Christian truth can take care of itself in freedom, under Christ, without resort to ecclesiastical apparatus. We shall find this illustrated if we look into almost any of our denominations. In the Episcopal Church, there is wide diversity of opinion on the episcopate, the sacraments and the ministry. The premises upon which the so-called "catholic" conception of these matters is based are challenged by large sections of this communion, including some of the most outstanding scholars and ecclesiastics, among them not a few bishops. All Presbyterians do not interpret their standards in the same way, and there is wide diversity of theological and social opinion. Within their own fellowship there is probably more divergence of doctrinal opinion than that which used to obtain between Presbyterian and other churches. This denomination, like many others, has discovered a deeper ground for its fellowship than that provided by a uniform body of belief.

Nor do all Baptists and all Disciples of Christ see alike on immersion-baptism. This is a subject that has long bulked large in the evangelism and apologetic of both denominations. It is true that the divergence of opinion on baptism is the cause of tension which sometimes becomes serious, but this difference has existed for a long time without open rupture of the fellowship. And of course the schools of thought commonly labeled as "conservative" and "liberal" are also registered in each of these bodies. Yet the principle of the freedom of mind and conscience, under Christ, provides a hope of maintaining unity which any formal ecclesiastical measure would surely defeat. Similarly, Congregationalists, Baptists and Disciples embrace in each fellowship strong differences on the autonomy of the local church. In the previous chapter we have dealt sufficiently with these varieties of opinion to make further comment unnecessary, except to say that these differences on a subject which once was held to be definitively settled are being increasingly taken up by the fellowship for free and tolerant re-examination.

There is no need to extend the discussion to include examination of other denominations. Some of these would add to the evidence of widening freedom, though ambiguous evidence would also appear. But by and large it must surely be clear that the denominations themselves have found that litigious or coercive ecclesiastical measures in dealing with doctrinal deviation are provocative of greater evils and are essentially unchristian. When, therefore, we speak of freedom as a cohesive principle in the united church, we are proposing nothing new and dangerous, but only recognizing the considerable degree in which this principle is modifying the feeling and practice of the denominations themselves.

How shall we account for this enlarging freedom in respect to doctrinal, ethical and ecclesiastical opinions in our present churches? There are, of course, numerous answers. One is that the churches inevitably partake of the spirit of the time in which they live. Our time is characterized by a greater flexibility of mind due to the enormous increase of knowledge brought to us by modern scholarship. The world and life are not so simple as in earlier periods, and therefore the dogmatic spirit inherent in orthodoxy is not too comfortable in our time. This has bred a less brittle temper, a more tolerant mood which inevitably would be reflected in some degree in the churches by a loosening of the dogmatic spirit of orthodoxy.

A second answer is found in the influence of Christian scholarship upon much of the subject matter of orthodoxy itself. The mind of all the churches has been more or less penetrated by the new understanding of the Bible which has resulted from historical research into the origins of its various writings. A generation ago there was widespread disquiet over the effects of the so-called "higher criticism" upon evangelical Christianity. Indeed, the great heresy trials to which we have referred revolved largely around this subject. But after these trials the churches began to come to their senses and accepted their scholars as Christian and honest men. With the result that what was once regarded as "destructive" criticism now actually underlies the work of the foremost champions of evangelical Christianity in the Christian world. Instead of being destructive, our scholars have rendered an inestimable service to the Christian Church. Once called heretics, we now see that their labors prepared the way for a more profound understanding of our holy relegion than a literalistic method of dealing with a level Bible could possibly provide.

THE SHIFT OF LOYALTY

But such considerations as we have just mentioned only partially and indirectly explain the enlarging freedom in all sections of Protestantism. A more positive and adequate explanation will appear if we extend our observation of the denominations still further. We shall discover that the broadening of the area of their freedom has been accompanied by a distinct shift in the focus of their loyalty; and that this is the radical explanation of the increase of their freedom. We have said that the united church requires for the maintenance of its unity that its freedom must be joined with loyalty. But the focus of loyalty must be consistent with freedom and the freedom must not only be consistent with loyalty but derived from it. Thus the shift of loyalty in the denominations may throw still further light upon our conception of the united church.

Through all the years since the end of the sixteenth century, the denominations of Protestantism have elevated orthodoxy to the supreme position of authority in their churches. Each new sect, following the example of its predecessors, felt it necessary to define for itself a standard of belief by which to determine the qualifications of applicants for membership and the loyalty of its ministers and leaders. By this standard, also, the denomination was to be distinguished among the multiplicity of existing denominations. In some, this standard of belief was more elaborate, in others less so. In still others, it was not committed to a formal instrument at all, but was expressed in the writings of founders and leaders which became the standardized ideology and practice, and was no less effective in its application than if it had been formally declared. We have already seen how these standards were used to protect the original beliefs of the denomination against change or innovation. In trials for heresy, no consideration was given to the faith or the Christian character of the alleged innovator. His fate was determined solely by his doctrinal loyalty or disloyalty to the standard of orthodoxy as formulated in the creed. Those denominations which made a point of their "creedlessness" had their own subtler ways of dealing with anyone who was out of step.

As we observe these denominations today, we find that their standards of sound doctrine are, if not disintegrating, little used as tests of loyalty. We do not wish to exaggerate the change, for the old allegiance to formalized orthodoxy dies hard. Many in the churches regard with some anxiety the recession of these standards into the background and are reassured by the fact that they are still there and available if necessary! The fear has not been wholly allayed that the ark of God might actually tumble unless steadied by the hand of those who are sure that they know what sound doctrine is. We can understand this feeling, however, if we consider how long the denominations have been putting their trust in, and giving their devotion to, this doctrinal idol of their own making. Their psychology has been deeply ingrained with the feeling that Christian truth cannot be trusted to take care of itself. Nevertheless, despite this lingering hesitation, orthodoxy has been steadily losing its status as a test and focus of loyalty. The movement for the emancipation of the Christian faith goes steadily forward in all denominations. It goes forward because another loyalty is emerging which transcends orthodoxy.

What is this transcendent loyalty? It is the response of Christian faith to a new vision of Jesus Christ whose authority in his church has been emerging from a long eclipse behind the multifarious orthodoxies, mistakenly designed to reveal him, but which concealed him by actually usurping his place. Whether the denominations are generally aware of it or not, the change in their attitude toward these ancient standards is the direct result of a new loyalty which the living presence of Christ has evoked in the souls of modern Christians. They definitely feel that there is an incongruity between their trust in doctrinal standards and their trust in Jesus Christ. And it is the transfer of their loyalty from the authority of their standards to the authority of Christ which accounts for the enlarging catholicity of their fellowship. The realm hitherto monopolized by the creeds is coming under the authority of Christ, and the subject matter of the creeds, stripped of their authority, are finding their true place in the freedom of the Christian fellowship. We are not saying, and must not be understood as saying, that Christ has not been present in his church through all the centuries, and devoutly recognized as present. But in using their orthodoxies as tests of loyalty to him, the denominations, besides dividing his church into many fragments, have cast a veil over his countenance and impeded the full flow of his grace.

Today, the figure of Christ is seen more clearly than at any time since the last apostle died. Fellowship with him and with his church has tended, silently but irresistibly, to transcend all our distinctive sectarian orthodoxies. This movement of the Spirit is creating in the denominations themselves the beginning of an ecumenical consciousness, which increasingly weakens the appeal to the orthodoxies on which the denominations were founded. It is now felt to be incongruous with the mind of Christ to confront an applicant for church membership with any test of fellowship in terms of his acceptance of the standards of the denomination. It is sufficient that he confess his faith in Christ and declare his purpose to lead a Christian life. Even in the ordination of a minister, the test of his qualification has less and less to do with his conformity to the doctrinal standard than with his personal devotion to Christ and the church.

We have here the mark of a great change in the spirit of the churches. We have called it the ecumenical spirit—an ecumenical spirit in the sectarian churches themselves! It is the spirit of Phillips Brooks, inspiring prophet of this new day, who declared: "To me, the gospel is just one great Figure standing with outstretched arms." It is the spirit of Martin Luther who, in his earlier years, desired the Reformation to rest upon no other foundation than "the forgiving love of God in Jesus Christ." This new ecumenical spirit cannot be long contained in the ecclesiastical forms of the denominational system. It is new wine and is already bursting the old bottles of our dogmatic and exclusive orthodoxies. It demands a new ecclesiastical order of inclusiveness and comprehension; in other words, a church which embraces all who in their love of Christ acknowledge him as divine Lord and Savior and whom, as the churches themselves now gladly confess, he has received into fellowship with himself.

The line we have been pursuing in this discussion has been intended to make it clear that the contemporary spirit and practice of the denominations in this crucial matter of the relation of loyalty and freedom is nothing less than a foreshadowing of the spirit and practice that must be embodied in the united church. Not only so, but it is intended to disclose how short, or perhaps we should say only how logical, is the step that the churches must take in order to be one church. We have no desire to minimize the obstacles that must be surmounted. But it seems clear that if the denominations project their growing practice of catholicity in the same direction in which it has been moving they will inevitably come out on ecumenical ground.

THE CONSTITUTION AND THE FELLOWSHIP

We began our discussion by asking this question: How shall we conceive a united church which embodies both freedom and loyalty? We have found the beginning of an answer in the profound change which the denominations have been undergoing by the enlargement of their area of freedom under the inspiring imperative of a higher loyalty. It remains, however, to translate this development into terms of ecclesiastical structure. This is necessary in order to bring out its full relevancy to the conception of a united church. So far, the denominations have not been consciously aware that their experience of this development has produced a profound, though incomplete, modification of their ecclesiastical structure. We must now show that the character of this structural modification points distinctly in the ecumenical direction.

When we think of the structure of the church we have to think of two structures. One is external, the other internal. The external structure is concerned with such matters as polity, episcopacy, baptism, the officiary (bishops, presbyters and deacons), and with the organic relation of the parts of the church to the whole body. These matters have received attention in their proper places in previous chapters. To call them external is not to derogate from their importance. They involve the whole possibility of the empirical existence of the church. But their particularites can hardly be claimed to be determinative of the character of the church. Rather, they are determined by the church's character. (We are purposely avoiding the conventional distinction between the *esse* and the *bene esse* of the church, because the external organs of the church are more integral to its "being" than is indicated by the term "well-being.")

But there is another structure within this external structure, and it is here that the very character of the church is determined.

This inmost structure consists of two parts: (1) the constitution of the church, and (2) its fellowship. The constitution is the locus of authority and therefore the focus of loyalty, the fellowship is the locus of freedom. All ecumenical thinking about the united church must carefully distinguish these two areas and assign to each what, and only what, belongs to each. Failure to think clearly at this crucial point causes endless irrelevant controversy and beclouds our conception of the ecumenical goal.

The constitution of the church is forever determined by Christ himself. In him alone and in his Lordship the church has its sole constitutive authority. His authority has never been abrogated, or modified or delegated. It has not been delegated to any hierarchy or pontifical vicar to be exercised on his behalf, as in Roman Catholicism. Nor has he committed any authority to any office-bearers in Protestantism, be they called bishops, presbyters or deacons; nor to any ecclesiastical administrative or legislative body, however democratically its members may have been chosen. Nor yet has he delegated his authority to the church as a whole; its democracy is not self-government. It too, like all its parts and all its ordained and appointed representatives, is responsible to Christ who is its living head and whose Holy Spirit is his empirical interpreter.

Here we must repeat an observation more sharply stated in Chapter VII. The concept of authority has bedeviled the Christian Church throughout its history. It is alien and repugnant to the Christian faith when applied otherwise than to Christ. Except for this proper usage, the very word should be thrust out of the vocabulary of Christian conversation. Its use in Protestant ecclesiology is a remnant of Roman Catholicism which thinks of Christ as having ascended to the right hand of God where he remains *in absentia,* having committed his authority to a vicegerent with power to exercise it until he returns. Protestantism cannot think of Christ in this manner. For us the "right hand of God" is no faraway place in space where Christ dwells apart. He is a living presence, the sole head of his living church which is permeated by his Spirit and rests always under his judgment. Protestant office-bearers, representative bodies and local churches should speak of themselves in terms, not of authority or autonomy or power, but in terms of responsibility. Their responsibility is, of course, proximately to the church, but ultimately to Christ alone.

Coming closer to the matter that now concerns us, we are ready to say that the fundamental error of Protestant denominationalism has been its usurpation of the authority of Christ. Each denomination presumed to determine for itself the constitution of the church by assigning to it matters that he has left to the fellowship. In giving constitutional status to matters which he has not made constitutional, each denomination has invaded his jurisdiction and, unwittingly, taken his authority into its own hand. And because Christians did not ask Christ to rule on what should go into the constitution, each group put its own ideas into it, thus dividing the church into a multiplicty of churches and consigning the Church of Christ to invisibility and impotence. The matters which the denominations erroneously placed in the constitution of the church may be listed as follows: (1) a standardized body of belief, (2) special interpretations of the Bible and (3) the Bible itself.

A STANDARDIZED BODY OF BELIEF

After what has been previously said about the standards of orthodoxy in relation to the principles of loyalty and freedom, it will be unnecessary to go over that ground again. It should now be apparent that the denomination, by standardizing a body of belief as a test of fellowship and loyalty, transcended the authority of Christ and determined for itself the constitution of the church. But we have observed in the contemporary practice of the churches a strong trend toward catholicity in their fellowship—that is, a fellowship as broad as the Church of Christ itself. It is increasingly recognized that Christ, in counting the sheep of his fold, totally disregards their attitude toward these standards of orthodoxy. The incongruity of maintaining a fellowship that is narrower than the fellowship of Christ's own church is increasingly felt as an affront to his authority.

What we wish now to note in this connection is the effect of this broadening fellowship upon the interior structure of the denominations. It is radically modifying their interior structure, albeit without a too conscious awareness that any such change is taking place. Their spirit and practice are considerably in advance of their ecclesiology! But the fact is that the traditional standards, as the result of their practical disuse, are now being gently pushed out of denominational constitutions. Does this mean that the evangelical faith which they embodied is being weakened? By no means. Insofar as these standards are no longer explicitly used as the focus of loyalty, the creedal subject matter which they formerly standardized is finding its true place and proving its inherent strength in the fellowship of the church which is the locus of freedom.

What is the effect of this change upon (1) the standards themselves, (2) the integrity of the evangelical faith and (3) the unity of the denomination? The standards, as such, are plainly on the way out, whether their disappearance is formally recognized or not. The evangelical faith is proving that it can stand on its own feet in the freedom of an open fellowship, without the support of any constitutional restraint. The unity of the denomination, instead of being broken by diversity, as the Fathers would have expected, is more securely protected against heresy and schism than in the old days under strict construction.

Our purpose in directing attention to the modification which the interior structure of the denominations is now undergoing is not merely descriptive. It is of special interest because of its bearing upon the interior structure of the united church which the ecumenical movement is striving to envisage. The overarching ideal of this movement is to bring together into one church from our many churches those whom Christ has received into fellowship with himself. It is a far-flung ideal, and must, of course, be achieved in many stages and in many particular areas one at a time. In this book we are taking American Protestantism as such an area. Our present thesis is that the inmost structure of the united church can have no formal standards of loyalty save the authority inherent in the Lordship of Christ, and that the entire subject matter of the sectarian standards must be given its place in the freedom of its fellowship. Some profess to fear for the integrity of the Christian faith if it is not authoritatively stand-ardized in the constitution of the united church. That this fear is groundless is the lesson to be derived from the contemporary experience of the denominations themselves. In the interest of their own unity and the integrity of the Christian faith they are progressively modifying their inmost structure by withdrawing the creedal subject matter of these standards from their consti-tutions and committing it, under Christ, to the freedom of their fellowship.

Yet it is doubtful that the leadership of the ecumenical move-ment has become fully aware of the negative lesson which the history of denominationalism so plainly teaches, or of the positive lesson implied in the contemporary experience of the denomi-nations. The major concern of this movement appears to be to find a doctrinal consensus upon which the united church, once it is achieved, may hope to maintain its unity. Under the auspices of the World Council of Churches, numerous commissions of outstanding scholars from all denominations have for years been studying together the various fields of theological problems with the aim of attaining such a consensus. It is to be feared that there is danger of repeating over again the fallacious procedure of the centuries past which has brought, not unity, but division.

There is one question which the ecumenical mind has not yet fairly considered: What shall be done with such a consensus of belief, or even with a viable adjustment of differences, if and when it is achieved? Shall it be written into the constitution of the united church, or shall it find its place in the fellowship? If it is stand--ardized in the constitution it will afford no basis for a permanent unity. Instead, it will be a standing invitation and provocation to heresy and schism, precisely as this same procedure by the denomi-nations has always been. A consensus for today may, conceivably, be attained, but it is unrealistic to imagine that such a consensus can be legislated for tomorrow. In short, a united church, so con-stituted, would be only another, albeit a vastly larger, denomi-nation, beset by the same perils that have dogged Protestant his-tory through the centuries. It is a fortunate fact by which the ecumenical movement may now be wisely guided, namely, that the denominations themselves are emerging, slowly but unmistakably, from their long-time delusion that Christian truth can be permanently enshrined in a static constitution of the church.

It is far from our intention to derogate in any degree from the great importance of the work in which the ecumenical commissions are engaged. They have already made substantial progress in ironing out the differences of doctrine that exist among the denominations. Historically, these differences have been unduly magnified by the fact that they have been long maintained by our walled-in sectarian churches which, until our time, precluded the free circulation of Christian truth. The interdenominational composition of the commissions opens up channels of understanding which have not formerly been available. Besides, their labors mark the beginning of a process that will continue always in the fellowship of the united church when it comes into existence. New differences will always be emerging. If they emerge in the fellowship instead of the constitution, they will be resolved in the same spirit that characterizes the conferences of the various commissions on faith and order of the ecumenical movement. Thus, the united church itself, with its open forum of theological fellowship, can be conceived as a continuing and unending ecumenical conference.

INTERPRETATIONS OF THE BIBLE

The ultimate justification given by all the denominations for their standards of belief and practice is that they are "based upon the Bible," that they are indeed a sort of epitome of biblical truth. Thus the denomination imagines that it is absolved of the offense of establishing a merely human body of opinion in the constitution of the church. The authority for the constitutional standard is thus thrown back upon the Bible. This presupposes that the Bible is constitutive of the church, a concept that we shall consider in the subdivision following. For the present we are concerned with the question whether the standardized beliefs upon which the denominations were founded and which still survive, though, as we have seen, with lessening emphasis, are indeed the truth of the Bible or human interpretations of it.

The high degree of assurance with which each denomination has held to the belief that its distinctive understanding of the Bible is absolutely true, is indicated by the fact that it was willing to build a church upon its interpretation. No denomination has been content to claim merely that its interpretation of the Bible was true only for itself, and that the interpretaions of others might be as true as its own. A sectarian church would long ago have lost the loyalty of its members if it had even mildly hinted that its interpretation did not literally and absolutely conform to the teaching of Holy Scripture. "This," said each denomination, pointing to its standard, "is what the Bible teaches!" It will not be stretching the truth to say that most denominations conceived of their interpretations as, in effect, the divinely ordained basis of Christian unity. Many propagandized them as such, and still do. Others, less aggressive, were content to cherish their biblical belief with an ardent hope that it would, in the end, be accepted by all Christians. A few small sects, despairing of the church and of the world itself, withdrew into clannish settlements where they have lived in social isolation and maintained their biblical doctrines and practices in expectation of a divine intervention, tho hope of which was also derived from the Bible.

One takes no pride in cluttering the pages of one's book with specific samples of the weird interpretations that have been digged with solemn ingenuity out of the Bible and actually elevated to a constitutional status in the churches of Protestantism. But let us note a few of them: Anti-instrumental music in worship, anti-organization for missionary work, exclusive psalm singing, speaking with "tongues," pre- or postmillennialism, fixing the time and even the exact date for the Second Coming, perfectionism, foot washing, Saturday versus Sunday, the holy kiss, trine immersion, hooks and eyes versus buttons, beards, two seed in the spirit Calvinism—these are only samples of the innumerable progeny of sanctified interpretations of the Bible which have been spawned on the margins of Protestantism.

But none of the greater and more "respectable" denominations may throw a scornful stone at those who have founded churches upon such quaint trivialities. For they, too, live in glass houses.

The diversities which distinguish our leading denominations from one another, and which have attracted our attention throughout these pages, are all "based upon the Bible." When looked at objectively, they are hardly less trivial than those listed above. It is only time and their present respectable context that sanctifies them. The actual differences among their creeds, whether written or unwritten, ancient or modern, are trivial when one contemplates the use to which they have been put in the constitution of separate churches. Yet this narrow margin of difference has been defended by each denomination as a veritable requirement of the Word of God. Similarly, their differing polities, their conflicting views of the ministry, of baptism, of the Lord's Supper and many other doctrines and practices, are alleged to rest upon Scriptural authority. They are all unworthy of the respectability they have attained.

What kind of book is this Bible of ours which lends itself to so many conflicting but infallible interpretations and breeds so many churches? A detached onlooker is bound, wonderingly or cynically, to ask precisely this question. Ought not Christians also to ask it in amazement and soul-searching? Is it possible to get Protestant intelligence out of its sectarian huddles long enough to face the truth that its divisive interpretations of the Bible are nothing more than human opinions, and that it is these human opinions, not the Bible, which they have written into the constitutions of their churches? The mind of the churches may have become so embedded in a certain conception of the Bible that it cannot be opened to a larger and more profound conception. But if so, should not the absurd consequences of its method of dealing with the Bible at least excite the amazed expostulation: Something must be wrong here! Are all others wrong, and we alone right? How can we be so sure that the Bible says what we believe it says when innumerable other groups equally intelligent and devout fail altogether to find our kind of church in its pages? Can a book that says so many different and contradictory things to so many equally devout readers be the inspired Word of God?

It is not irreverent to ask such a question, for it is none other than Christ himself who demands not only that we ask it but that, in loyalty to him, we answer it. His authority is involved. His headship of the church is involved. The very character of our Christian faith is involved. The failure of the churches long ago to perceive the absurdity into which their human interpretations of the Bible was leading them has had tragic consequences. It has allowed an unspeakable indignity to be perpetrated upon the Bible by making it responsible for the petty ideas and the obvious absurdity of the endless proliferation of churches whose separate, trivial and conflicting constitutions all claimed to be the veritable teaching of the Word of God. We are thus brought to the final section of this chapter.

THE BIBLE ITSELF

How, then, shall we conceive the true place of the Bible in the united church? It will be agreed that it belongs in the interior structure of the church, not in its exterior structure. Next to Christ, the Bible is the most precious possession of the Christian community. But though it belongs in the inmost structure of the church, it does not belong in the constitution. Unless the ecumenical movement sees this clearly, it will have great difficulty in convincing the Christian community that a united church is a realistic poossibility. The Bible is not the true focus of the church's loyalty —Christ himself claims its undivided allegiance. The Bible, then, belongs in the fellowship of the church which is the locus of freedom.

To say this should not be acounted as heresy. For Protestantism from the beginning has included among its cardinal principles "the right of private interpretation." The freedom of the Christian man to read the Holy Scripture for himself, without the imposition of any ecclesiastical restraint upon his mind, has been historically included in the same bracket with "justification by faith" and "the priesthood of all believers." But while the latter two principles have been consistently maintained throughout Protestantism, the former has been seriously tampered with and practically nullified. The right of private interpretation came to mean *the right to establish separatist churches upon the private interpretation.* The exercise of this "right" involved the presupposition that the Bible itself belonged to the constitution of the church. Each new denomination, on the assumption that its private interpretation was the veritable truth of the Bible, justified its existence as a separate church because it was "based on the Bible." Thus the whole tragic history of denominationalism is to be explained by the adoption of the fundamental error that the Christian Church is founded on the Bible. "The Bible and the Bible alone," said Chillingworth in the seventeenth century, "is the religion of Protestants." This statement has been oft-quoted, and rarely, if ever, challenged.

It must now be challenged by those who long for and believe in the possibility of a united church. There can be no unity of Christ's people so long as the Bible is given a place beside Christ in the constitution of his church. To invest it with such authority results inevitably in the obscuration of Christ's own authority, and also in the continued multiplication of sectarian churches. The Bible, so used, is the great divider of the church.

Protestantism must be called back to first principles, among which none is more important than the right of private interpretation. This clearly means a right to be exercised within the *fellowship* of the church. It means the right to hold diversities of interpretation in a community which refuses to standardize any interpretation because it refuses to standardize the Bible itself as the constitutive principle of the church. These diversities of interpretation would thus take their true place as human opinion in a realm in which Christ has left his church free, a realm whose rules are tolerance, argument, persuasion and example, but not authority. Relieved of the false authority long attributed to the Bible, it would become a living book instead of the static book which its standardization as the authoritative blueprint for the organization of the church has made of it. In the fellowship of the church, the Bible would undergo a transvaluation of its values. The petty, trivial notions, like those that have been digged out of it and elevated to a status of the constitution of a particular denomination, would have a chance to be consumed in the fellowship of free discussion, informed as it would be by the consciousness that no issue involving our fundamental loyalty to Christ hung upon the outcome. The encrusted surface of a level Bible which the eyes of the literalist, blinded by his sectarian stereotype, cannot now penetrate, would break open and let the mighty ideas which lie at the depth of the Bible come through and consume the letter that kills by the spirit that giveth life.

That the Bible and its interpretation do not belong in the constitution of the church, but in its fellowship, is proved historically by the fact that the New Testament (which is the portion of the Bible that is relevant to our problem) was itself a product of the fellowship of the early church. The primitive Christian community lived for nearly a hundred years without benefit of the New Testament as we have it. It lived for a quarter of a century before the earliest writings of the New Testament, the letters of Paul, began to appear; for more than thirty years before Mark, the earliest of our Four Gospels, was written; and for from forty to seventy years before the other Gospels and Epistles were written. The process of collecting these scattered writings into a single volume began in the early decades of the second century and was recognized as virtually complete by the middle of that century. Prior to that period, it would have occurred to no one that these writings were constitutive of the church. It was within the living church that each precious piece of writing had been produced, and it was the church itself, through its bishops, which had canonized the whole as Scripture.

During all this period the church used the Old Testament in its worship. This was supplemented by scattered fragments of memorabilia of the doings and teachings of Jesus, some pieces possessed by some churches, others by others. These were used not only in worship but for instruction. It was from these scattered fragments that the writers of our Four Gospels gathered their materials. The Letters of Paul were the possession of the particular congregations to which they were addressed, and were given general circulation among the churches only after they had been collected as a unit at about A. D. 90. That there are differences among scholars as to this or that date does not affect the general picture which shows that the church was prior to the New Testament, that the New Testament was the product of the church's own life and that the church recognized no authority save that of the Lord-ship of the risen Christ whose empirical interpreter was the Holy Spirit.

It is beside the mark to say that the early church had the apostles, that the apostles had the authority and that their author-ity passed to the New Testament. No apostle save Paul wrote any part of the New Testament, and Paul was a convert, not an original disciple who had seen Jesus in the flesh. But more impor-tant, no apostle ever claimed to be an authority in place of Christ. Paul incontinently disclaimed it in his first letter to the Corin-thians. And every apostle would have disclaimed it as blasphemy. They called themselves "witnesses," not authorities. They testified to the things they had seen and heard and to the meaning which they saw in the events which they had experienced. In the nature of the case, they would have precedence over all other disciples and would be accorded unique honor in the young church. This precedence naturally invested them with the responsibility of leadership in the administration of the church's affairs, in the guidance of its faith and the spread of its mission. But their "authority" was not conceived as a legalistic right to exercise power; it was the kind of authority which inhered in their prestige as firsthand witnesses or, to use the term of R. R. Williams, the authority of "moral weightiness." The early Christians knew but one authority, namely, that of their crucified and risen Lord. They had no New Testament, but they had *him*. Those, therefore, who would restore the New Testament church should begin by restor-ing the New Testament itself to the place it held in primitive Christianity. Plainly its place was not in the constitution of the church.

As this picture becomes clear in the thinking of modern Chris-tians we shall have a firm foundation in the New Testament itself upon which to build the ecumenical case for the transfer of the Bible from its false position as a competitor of Christ in the con-stitution of the church to its true place in the church's fellowship. So long as it remains in the constitution it will always proliferate sectarian divisions.

THE SOURCE OF DOGMATIC BIBLICISM

We must now inquire how the Bible came to be regarded by the larger portion of Protestantism as, in effect, superior to Christ in determining the constitution of the church. Such an inquiry will take us back to the period of the Reformation. This dogmatic biblicism represents the re-emergence in historical Protestantism of the principles of the Anabaptists. As we have seen in Chapter VI, they had opposed the Reformation because it was not radical enough. They demanded a clean break with the historical church by the restoration of the primitive church, instead of the reform of the existing church. They found the pattern of the primitive church in the pages of the New Testament and proceeded to establish churches on the basis of this New Testament pattern. They found many dissimilar patterns, and therefore divided into innumerable sects. This result has followed the whole history of this attempt to found the church on the Bible.

It is not necessary to repeat here what was said at greater length previously. But attention must be directed specifically to the radical difference in the use of the Bible by the Anabaptists and the main body of the Reformation. Luther, in particular, held sternly to the undivided Lordship of Christ as the constitutive authority in the church. He would not let the Bible compete with Christ. In 1535 he wrote: "When our opponents [the Anabaptists] urge the Scriptures against Christ, we urge Christ against the Scriptures." This laconic declaration was, no doubt, ambiguous and open to misunderstanding. But taken as Luther intended it, it draws the destination sharply where it should be drawn. He affirmed that "Scripture must not be understood *against* Christ, but *for* Christ; therefore the Scripture must be referred to Christ (that is, for his judgment or approval) or one cannot claim it as true Scripture." Summing up his view, he said: "I urge (insist upon) Christ, the Lord, who is Lord (*Rex*) also of the Scriptures."[1] Thus, the "right of private interpretation" in the use of the Bible is to be exercised, not autonomously, but under the approval or correction of the mind of Christ.

[1] *Martin Luther's Works* (Weimas Ed.), Vol. 39, I, *Disputations,* p. 47.

We shall not understand Luther's position unless we clearly grasp his conception of Christ himself as the *Word of God*. The Bible, as a book, is not the Word of God. The Word of God is that supreme Person whom the Scripture unveils to the devout reader of its pages. And Christ then, in turn, becomes the judge and interpreter of the Scriptures. The Bible discloses him, unveils him, and at the same time releases him into his own sovereign, self-authenticating supremacy over the heart of man, over the church and over the Bible itself.

This was a conception which the Anabaptists could not grasp. And their successors, the restorationist denominations, beginning with the Puritan separatists at the turn of the seventeenth century, failed to grasp it. "The Bible and the Bible alone," to quote Chillingworth again, became "the religion of Protestants." Christ was subordinate to it, pendant to it, governed by it. Anything, however trivial or fantastic or commonplace, that one could dig out of the Bible by however ingenious a manipulation of its texts and words was claimed to be authorized by Christ, and was made constitutive of a church "founded on the Bible." This false conception spread throughout the whole of Protestantism and is held uncritically even by the reformist denominations—Presbyterian, Lutheran and, in less degree, Episcopalian—with whose earliest tradition this literalistic, legalistic biblicism is inconsistent. It has only recently occurred to any Protestant church to look at itself through the eyes of Christ, to let *him* judge whether its distinctive doctrines and practices derived from the Bible do in truth belong in the constitution of his church. All our denominations freely confess that they know what his judgment is.

Any use of the Bible which divides Christ's body is *ipso facto* false to him. The notion that he delegated his authority to a book, or to the writers of a book, for the legalistic regulation of his church has no basis in fact. Its result is to dethrone Christ. One who has been fairly confronted by him in the pages of the Bible can hardly imagine that he who swept all traditional literalisms and ecclesiastical legalisms into the discard, thereafter invested a book with his authority to set them up again. His authority deals with more profound and vaster issues than those upon which this misuse of the Bible has divided the church. Of all these churches "founded on the Bible" he would say, he does say, that none is his church. He cares not at all for their special claims of scriptural authority, but finds his church in the community of all who have received him and whom he has received into fellowship with himself. To bring this hidden church into empirical existence the Bible must be removed from its static and divisive position as constitutive of the church so that Christ may reign unchallenged as himself the only true interpreter of the Bible and the sole head of his church.

ENCOURAGING SIGNS

It will be difficult for some to believe that the task we are setting before the ecumenical movement is other than an unrealizable ideal. It will be said that the mind of the churches has so long been accustomed to and molded by the conception of the Bible as the ground of the church that it will seem hopeless to dislodge it from its constitutional status and set it free, under Christ, in the fellowship of the church. We do not believe that the case is so hopeless as it might seem. For our encouragement, let us direct our attention to three actual developments in our contemporary church life which point in the same direction toward which our thought has been moving. These should invest our discussion with an appreciable degree of realism and promise.

1. *The Historical Understanding of the Bible*. The ice was broken for a reconception of the Bible by Christian scholars who, in the later decades of the nineteenth century, devoted themselves to its study in terms of the historical origin of its various parts. Their work on the Old Testament was well completed in the early twentieth century. On the New Testament the work has gone on into our own time. This new discipline at first evoked in the churches violent reaction and resentment. Its scholars were regarded as heretics, and the famous heresy trials revolved about the issues which it raised. Instinctively, the churches felt that it was an atttack upon both the use and the place of the Bible—its use as the inspired Word of God and its place as the norm for the constitution of the church. The second half-century is opening

with the results of the historical criticism accepted widely by the scholarship and the trained ministry of all the churches. Few indeed are the theological seminaries in which the results of these researches are not accepted and used as the basis of instruction in the meaning of the Scriptures. Even in some seminaries founded especially to counteract the spread of this new knowledge, it has become impossible to resist it.

The effect has been to make obsolete the older conception of the Bible as a level book whose parts are all of equal value and whose words and statements can be reconciled in complete consistency. This has lifted a great burden from Christian intelligence which is now able to read the Bible under a conception of its divine inspiration without having to hold divinity accountable for trivialities, inconsistencies and contradictions.

Of the numerous consequences that have resulted from this historical reorientation of the Scriptures, the one most relevant to our present interest is that it has brought the Bible back into the fellowship of the church from its false position in the constitution. We do not mean to say that it has done so as an accomplished fact, for the churches are slow to see the bearing of their fuller knowledge of the Bible upon the interior structure of the church. What is meant is that this is the *potential* result of the changed understanding of the Bible. Only a static Bible, a level Bible, a *verbally* inspired Bible, could ever have been thought of and used as constitutive of the church. The kind of authority which had been attributed to the Bible and used as the justification for the creation of each new denomination was a mechanical authority whose language could permit of only one meaning. Of course, each denomination had found the one and only true meaning! Only its blindness to the fact that other denominations did not find this meaning, but found other meanings, prevented it from challenging its own presupposition that the Bible was the constitutive authority.

This new knowledge percolates all too slowly into the thinking of church people and their leaders. But it does percolate! Its implications are gradually being discerned. We may confidently expect that the churches will be led by their scholars to see the

Bible as a dynamic book rather than as a static one. In its profound ideas of God, the world and man, of life, of time and eternity, rather than in its supposed infallible language, they will sense the essence and secret of its divine inspiration. As this insight increases in vividness, the use of the Scriptures as normative for the constitutional structure of the church will be felt as petty and as incongruous with its spiritual and moral grandeur. In this assured development, the ecumenical hope of restoring the Bible to its true place in the fellowship of a united church may not prove so remote and unrealistic as, at first blush, it may seem.

2. *The Growing Ecumenical Character of Christian Thought.*
A remarkable phenomenon, crossing denominational lines, has accompanied the changing conception of the Bible which we have just discussed. It is the emergence of a more profound understanding of the Christian faith itself, produced by theologians and biblical scholars representing all denominations, but working together without the slightest restraint by the standards of their denominational constitutions. For the modern Christian scholar, these standards have practically ceased to exist *as standards*. The doctrines which they contained have been dissociated from constitutional authority and stand or fall according to their merits. The Christian theologian of today carries on his work, not in an academic huddle of his fellow sectaries, but in an ecumenical fellowship of his peers. This anticipates one aspect of the fellowship of the ecumenical church itself. In books, in periodical literature, in formal commissions and informal conferences, even in theological seminaries, the minds of Christian scholars, representing all schools of thought from all parts of the Christian world, are meeting in cross currents of free discussion dealing with the faith of the Christian gospel. Underlying all their agreements and disagreements is the common acceptance of the profounder meanings of the Bible which historical research has brought to light.

The results of their labors find hospitable acceptance and stimulate similar free discussion in all the denominations. Over a wide range of the parish ministry there is complete awareness of and actual collaboration in this movement of Christian thought. It is a movement away from loyalty to static standards into the faith that Christian truth, given freedom, under Christ, will be able to take care of itself. It is doubtful that there is a single scholar in all this fellowship who would desire to have his thought or his school of thought standardized in the constitution of his church. The meaning of this development for the thesis we are striving to clarify, namely, that the possibility of a united church constituted neither by the Bible nor by theological doctrines, but only by the Lordship of Christ, is not so unrealistic as it might seem, or so remote. This, however, brings us to the final consideration.

3. *The Actual Trend in Protestant Churches.* The churches, we have maintained, are nearer the ecumenical goal than they themselves realize. We have shown that their creedal standards are being progressively detached from their constitutions and entrusted to the freedom of their several fellowships. This is distinctly a movement within the denominations toward ecumenical ground. It now remains to point out that the churches are also farther along than they realize in emancipating the Bible from its static bondage in their constitutions. In most of the denominations ample room is now made for the Protestant "right of private interpretation." Divergence from a standardized interpretation hardly creates a ripple in the fellowship. The results of historical study, discussed above, are gradually flowing down from the level of specialized scholarship into the thinking of the laity.

The Bible is being read with a more flexible mind which is not bothered either by a standardized interpretation or by the dogmatic assumption that every word is divinely dictated. The enlightened layman is now able to hold in abeyance his interpretation of a difficult passage of Scripture until he asks: Who wrote it? When and under what circumstances was it written? To whom was it addressed? What was the author's purpose in writing it? These are the identical questions which biblical scholarship asks. By the answers which this scholarship offers, the lay reader is able to penetrate many an otherwise opaque verbalism and enjoy a true spiritual communion with each inspired writer. He is thus freed from bondage to "the letter that killeth" into the liberty of "the Spirit that giveth life." How far this process has gone may be indicated by two or three observations of the trend in modern church life.

Take the Methodist Church for one example. In 1944, the official publishing house of this great denomination issued a series of twelve manuals entitled, *Know Your Bible,* written by the distinguished editor of Methodism's national newspaper, Dr. Roy L. Smith, for use in church school classes and other church groups. This series has enjoyed an enormous circulation throughout Methodism and in many other denominations. It deals with all the books of both Testaments in terms of their historical origin and setting and utilizes the results of modern biblical scholarship in a way that lifts the whole body of Scripture out of its encrusted literalism into the dimension of a living, inspired and dynamic book of faith and life.

The point here is that the use of this series of texts by millions of Christians is one evidence of the degree in which the emancipating results of biblical scholarship are permeating the churches and thus tending strongly to dissolve the conception of the Bible as the authoritative constitution of the church. It is impossible to use such a Bible to sanction the stereotyped trivialities and fantastic interpretations which sectarian usage has derived from it. If Dr. Smith's books had been written at the beginning of this century he would have been declared a heretic, and his church would not for a moment have countenanced their publication.

Another encouraging sign may be found among the Presbyterians. The liberalism of a generation ago had drawn premature and shallow inferences from the new biblical knowledge. A great deal of the graded literature of religious education used by the churches had distinctly subordinated the biblical material to the teaching of what was called "religious values." Reacting against this type of teaching, the Presbyterian Church U.S.A., authorized a commission to prepare a new body of literature in which the Bible would be given its unique place in Christian education. The significant aspect of this action, in our present context, is the fact that this new body of literature did not return to the traditional level Bible, but based its new curriculum upon the living Bible as it had been released to Christian intelligence and devotion by modern scholarship. Its editors rejected the shallow inferences prematurely drawn by liberalism from historical biblical research, and they found that the evangelical Christian gospel was more clearly disclosed in the Bible of Protestant scholarship than in the Bible of Protestant sectarianism. This literature is now being used not only by thousands of Presbyterian churches, but by many other denominations.

One more observation. The International Religious Education Association (now a division of the National Council of Churches) was distinctly influenced for a period by the concept of "religious values." Its editorial leadership has now returned to the biblical concept while definitely rejecting the legalistic conception of the Bible which has lent itself so long to sectarian exploitation.

Other evidences of the leavening of the churchly mind with this more profound and ecumenical conception of the Bible could be brought forward. Those we have mentioned are typical. Similar evidence exists in all our denominations in varying degrees. It is easily discernible even in our most conservative churches. All this indicates that the churches are more ready for ecumenical action than is generally recognized. The Bible is being progressively removed from its sectarian position in their constitutions and finding its true place in their fellowship. We thus have substantial ground for believing that this most formidable bulwark of sectarianism is in progress of yielding to the authority of Christ.

We are identifying as a single movement (1) the release of the Bible from its captivity in the constitution of the church, and (2) the advance of a critically intelligent understanding of the Bible in the thinking of the churches. These are not two movements, but one. The knowledge which modern scholarship has brought to us has shown that the Bible cannot be a competitor of Christ who, as Luther said, is "Lord also of the Scriptures." Had this conception of the supreme and sole authority of Christ in his church been grasped and held after the Reformation, it is hard to believe that the sectarian churchism "based on the Bible" could have wrought the havoc in Protestantism which the ecumenical movement is now out to overcome.

We are now ready to say, plainly, that Protestantism, in making the Bible constitutive of the church, has not only obscured the authority of Christ but has demoted the Bible itself to a status below its inherent dignity. It is not a statutory norm for a constitution; it is a book of life, a living book, from whose inspired pages unsuspected new truth is evermore breaking forth. To standardize it in a static constitution is to freeze the springs of its vitality and to inhibit the free flow of its profounder meanings into the hearts and minds of the faithful. It becomes thereby the victim of innumerable stereotypes of private interpretation which inevitably lead to sectarian divisions. Only if this legalistic indignity which Protestantism has perpetrated upon the Bible gives way to the freedom of its interpretation in the self-corrective fellowship of the church may we hope to provide a united church with a cohesion that promises to maintain its unity under the single, unqualified authority of Christ.

In conclusion, it seems necessary to add that the thesis of this chapter has not been expounded in the interest of latitudinarianism. Instead, it has been motivated by the faith that evangelical Christian truth can and will take care of itself, under loyalty to Christ, in the free fellowship of the church, without the artificial support of fixed standards of belief or standardized stereotypes of biblical interpretation. There are two great delusions under which Protestantism has been operating. One is the delusion that the Christian faith requires for the maintenance of its evangelical purity that some test of its purity be standardized in the constitution of the church. This, we have sufficiently argued, is the mother concept of sectarianism. The other delusion is that it is these standards, "based on the Bible," that are to be credited with the maintenance of the evangelical Christian faith, and that, without such support, it would have slumped into latitudinarianism. This we must now say is indeed a delusion.

Where, then, if not in constitutional control, is the explanation of the invincible strength, the dynamic, the power of perennial renewal, of evangelical Christianity? The explanation is found in the inherent genius of evangelical Christianity itself. It can be trusted to take care of itself, under Christ, in the freedom of the church's fellowship. Given this freedom, the Christian faith is self-corrective. If the Bible is interpreted in terms of triviality, its interpretation will be met by another which opens up the deep meanings of the Bible. Innovating ideas will be winnowed in this process of fellowship interaction. Most of them will likely prove crude and innocuous. Some may have validity and may work their way into the ethos of the faith, thus clarifying and enriching it. The fear that heresy will creep in and dilute or debilitate the faith is grounded in unbelief in Christ's sovereign rule in his church.

This freedom from authoritarian standards, as we have previously shown in this chapter, is no new thing, but is the actual practice of our denominational churches, despite the delusion that their standards are the bulwark of their evangelicalism. In a united church where sectarian walls no longer isolate a stereotyped way of looking at the Bible and of conceiving the Christian faith, we may expect the process of fellowship interpenetration to produce an ethos of the faith far more solid and formidable than our divided Protestantism has ever known.

IX

Epilogue

W̲E HAVE ENDEAVORED to clarify the *idea* of a united church, that is, to bring the goal of the ecumenical movement within a more realistic *conceptual* grasp than has yet become explicit in the general literature of the movement. Up to the present time it has seemed to be the deliberate intention to avoid a too explicit discussion of the nature of a united church as the concrete achievement toward which our striving is directed. Perhaps this has been, tactically, a wise restraint. There were other things to be done preliminary to any attempt to conceptualize the end in view. For one thing, it seemed necessary to consolidate the co-operation of as many churches as possible under the principle of a federal union. The structure of such a federation has now been achieved on both a national and a world scale.

But the spirit of unity accepts these inspiring achievements with no illusion as to their finality. They register grateful progress on the way to a more integral fulfillment of the divine imperative for the unity of the Church of Christ. Instead of resting in these accomplishments and relaxing its energies, the ecumenical spirit has been quickened and emboldened by them to present the divine imperative with more urgency and greater explicitness than ever before. This is notably manifested in the World Council itself whose faith and order branch is actively engaged in exploring the problems and possibilities of achieving the true ecumenical goal. It is also manifested in American Protestantism. Many of our denominations, acting spontaneously, as we saw in Chapter I, are merging, and negotiating other mergers, in a movement that is informed with the true ecumenical spirit. Both of these activities,

218

however, stand in need of a conceptual projection of the ecumenical goal. We shall have a further word to say on each of these movements presently.

The writing of this book, has been conceived as a contribution to the clarification of the ecumenical goal. The task has not been conceived in terms of devising a "plan of union," in the sense of a detailed blueprint. That would be not only premature but presumptuous. Instead, we have sought to bring together in one picture an exposition of certain principles and actualities by which a united church may be hopefully brought within a fairly realistic conceptual grasp.

If we now take a backward look over the way we have come, it will appear that, in our undertaking to clarify the *idea* of a united church, our thought has moved within an octagonal framework of eight presuppositions, or axioms, or guiding principles. As these principles have been constantly present in the author's mind, it may prove helpful to the reader if they are gathered up and re-expressed in a final statement. This we wish now to do. It should be kept in mind that the entire text of the book has been delimited in its constructive parts to American Protestantism for whose unity it is both a plea and a rationale. A word in justification of this delimitation will be found in the preface. Our guiding principles have been as follows:

1. The true Church of Christ already exists and is in our midst, but hidden behind the denominational system which denies it any empirical manifestation and denies to Christians any experienceable relations with it. Protestantism knows, and our denominations confess, that the true church exists in the mind of Christ, and that Christ recognizes none of our denominations as his church, but embraces all who acknowledge his divine Lordship and whom he has received into fellowship with himself.

2. The ecumenical movement, in its most fundamental and essential genius, is the dedicated endeavor of Christ's people, under his leadership, to bring this now hidden church into visible, potent and empirical realization as one body, consisting of all Christ's people, which church alone can claim him as its living head. This is the ecumenical goal. The united church, when it is

attained, will not be a new church, but will be the identical church which now exists but is hidden by our man-made denominational churches.

3. The attainment of the ecumenical goal is possible only by the dissolution of the denominational churches, *as churches,* thus releasing the true church of Christ's people from its bondage to the apostate denominational system, and restoring to the now hidden Church of Christ its freedom to be what it really is, namely, one body of which alone he is the living head. This goal cannot be achieved by any mechanical contriving or adjustment among denominational churches, nor by the attainment of a consensus of theological belief, though such efforts are proper and helpful concomitants of its pursuit. But they must not be allowed to obscure the necessity of removing the radical cause of Protestant sectarianism which is the denominational system itself.

4. The radical source of the denominational system does not lie in our theological differences, but in the presumptuous assertion of the right to erect and maintain separate churches on the basis of variant interpretations of certain aspects of the Christian faith. It is the assertion of such a right that has broken the body of Christ into sectarian fragments. This is the sin of Protestantism. The churchism of the denomination is utterly and absolutely unassimilable in the true Church of Christ. It is the only characteristic of the denomination that is, *in principle,* unassimilable in a united church. Diversities of theological belief, familarities of practical procedure, variety in forms of worship, treasures of particular traditions, and warmth of special fellowships—these all are, in principle, assimilable in a united church. Even some differences in polity, as was suggested in Chapter VII, may not, in principle, be unassimilable. In the area of these unlikenesses there can be adjustment and a *modus vivendi.* It is *being a separate church* that is alone, in principle and in reality, unassimilable in the united Church of Christ. In this area there can be no adjustment, nor compromise, nor *modus vivendi.*

5. The primary task of the ecumenical movement is to evoke from the denominations a willingness to abdicate their churchism and to restore to the now amorphous and empirically hidden

Church of Christ the churchly organs and functions which they have sinfully usurped. Thus, reinvested with its own organs, the true church will become manifest as an empirically functioning entity. The perception of this as an essential task will provide the ecumenical movement with a methodology which it now seriously lacks. This will save the movement from much random activity involving misplaced emphasis on subordinate or irrelevant matters. It will also conserve the ardent interest which the ecumenical movement has awakened among the churches but which it is in danger of losing by the vagueness of its present procedure.

6. The ecumenical movement is the resurgence in Protestantism of the spirit and the rationale of the Reformation of the sixteenth century. The radical and inspiring intention of the great Reformers was to release the hidden and submerged Church of Christ's people from the apostasy into which it had been led captive by a sacerdotal hierarchy which had usurped the functions of the true church. Despite the heroic efforts of the Reformers to complete their work, they were compelled to leave to us an Unfinished Reformation. The denominational system is the Protestant counterpart of the Roman hierarchy. The ecumenical movement in our time is engaged in releasing the same Church of Christ's people from a Protestant apostasy into which it has been led by the evil spirit of sectarianism.

7. The *form* of the united church must be conceived under the admonition of humility, in recognition of the truth that it will be, primarily and finally, the work of God who may overrule many of the plans of men. But it is not presumptuous to affirm that the errors which led Protestantism into the apostasy of sectarianism shall be strictly guarded against in the structure of a united church. The fundamental error which led Protestantism into the sin of its churchism was its failure to distinguish between the constitution of the church and its fellowship. In the interest of its own stability and permanence, the united church must make this distinction clear (1) by recognizing no constitutional authority save the sovereign authority of Christ, and (2) by providing in its fellowship a place for all whom, with all their differences, he has received into fellowship with himself and who constitute his now

hidden church. This means that creedal formulations must be abandoned as constitutional standards, and that the truth of the Christian faith shall be entrusted to the fellowship of Christ's people. It means that the interpretation of the Bible, and the Bible itself, shall be given their true place, which is not in the constitution of the church where Christ alone is sovereign, but in its fellowship, that Christ may be all and in all.

8. The prime motivation of the ecumenical movement is found in the will of God manifested in Jesus Christ and made articulate in his prayer that all who believe on him may be one, that the world might believe. Our denominational churches, long separated from one another, and deeply involved in the habits of sectarianism, may feel that they lack a sufficient endowment of divine grace to respond realistically to so ultimate a motivation. Confronted by its appeal, they may turn away in despair of ever attaining so loftly an ideal. But their eyes should then be opened to an inspiring fact. They should be made aware that, without their conscious effort, the Spirit of Christ has been drawing them together over a period of many years, and under many influences, until they are nearer the goal of a united church than they realize, and much nearer than the generation before them could have imagined as a possibility. This should invest the ultimate divine imperative with a realism which could hardly have been conceived in an earlier day. Throughout these pages we have endeavored to keep this contemporary fact in view, namely, that in all save a very few of the churches the ecumenical spirit has been steadily permeating their life and practice like a hidden leaven. The churches have been hardly aware that it was the ecumenical spirit, for it has not been so labeled. It has been called brotherliness, co-operation, understanding, mutual recognition and other precious names drawn from the vocabulary of the Holy Spirit. These spiritual resources must now be identified as the gift of the ecumenical spirit and capitalized as a realistic reinforcement of the divine imperative.

Perhaps it is merely a fanciful notion to conceive these eight guiding principles as an octagonal enclosure within whose boundaries the thesis of this book has been controlled. The reader is not asked to make any use of this geometrical imagery unless it appeals to him. In drawing our discussion to a close, we must re-emphasize the importance of achieving a conscious *method* by which the activities of the ecumenical movement can be guided and saved from undue entanglement in random or remote interests, legitimate in themselves, but deferable until more essential and realistic matters are boldly confronted. There is no way by which such a method can be achieved except by a more concrete conceptualization of the end in view.

The united church, up to now, has been chiefly referred to, positively, in terms of the divine imperative and, negatively, in acknowledgment of the sin of our divisions. But these terms represent its spiritual dynamic and provide no conceptual goal by which the course of the movement can be steered. The term "organic union" is increasingly used. This marks an advance in objectivity. But until this term has been conceptually implemented, it will cause as much confusion as enlightenment.

Consequently, there is a growing feeling that the ecumenical movement does not know where it is going, and that it is in danger of losing its orientation in dealing with the mass of theological details involved in the subjects assigned to the various commissions of the World Council of Churches.

It is difficult to describe this feeling without seeming to minimize the importance of the theological approach. We would not for a moment encourage a depreciative appraisal of the work of these commissions. On the contrary, their work is indispensable and must go on. But it would go forward with surer footing if its selection and treatment of subjects were controlled by a more concrete conception of the ecumenical end in view. Without such a conception of the united church, the theological approach is likely to become entangled in many theoretical problems that should be left for the united church itself to resolve. A distinguished bishop, coming out of a forenoon's session of one of the sections of the Amsterdam assembly, was asked: "What did you do in your section this morning?" With a gesture of impatience, he replied, wryly: "We spent the whole morning debating the question whether or not the Christian Church is the New Israel!"

The ecumenical movement should be carrying on, parallel with its consideration of theological and ecclesiological problems, and on an equally broad front, a discussion of the way in which the united church should be conceptually envisaged. One conception of its goal may require a decision on the subject of the New Israel and countless other questions. Another conception may wisely leave such questions to what we have called the "perennial ecumenical conference" which the united church itself will be.

It is important that the united church shall be conceived as a continuing spiritual and theological fellowship as well as an organizational event. So conceived, a principle of selection becomes available by which the theological approach may be substantially simplified.

A further reason why the ecumenical goal should be brought more distinctly into view is that only so can the movement evoke an intelligent response from the rank and file of the people in our churches. The widespread popular interest aroused in anticipation of the great ecumenical conferences, such as that at Amsterdam, was notably disappointed by the intangible nature of the results achieved. This could be, and probably was, in a fashion, explained.

But the disappointment extended also to the paucity of subject matter which the event produced for the lay mind to work upon. The laity are more deeply concerned with church union than is generally recognized by their leaders. But thus far they have been presented with no major issues in the solution of which they could participate. Anyone who has attempted to interpret to local churches the results of a conference such as that at Amsterdam has been made aware that his effort produced a certain bewilderment mixed with disappointment because the subject matter seemed to be beyond the reach of the average person. The movement seems to "move" on a plane of highly specialized theological knowledge. It is doubtful that the initial ardor of the laity for Christian unity can be sustained unless they are presented with an aspect of the total undertaking which invites their participation.

By releasing the present inhibitions on the discussion of the ecumenical goal, the laity will have something to take hold of, something conceptually concrete, down on the ground, albeit still in the realm of the unattained. The paralled discussion of the concrete nature of a united church—on a front equally as wide and as active as that now engaged in the theological approach— would bring the total ecumenical problem home to the people in the churches. We are not suggesting that this teleological—if we dare to use the word—aspect of the total problem can be considered without reference to the aspects now preoccupying ecumenical attention. Nor do we suggest that the lay mind would make its contribution in a theological and historical vacuum. Such a notion would be not only naïve, but thoroughly inconsistent with the whole text of this book. Our suggestion points in the opposite direction.

By opening up the problem of conceptualizing the end in view the enlightened laity of the churches would find themselves cooperating with the scholarly leadership of the churches. They would discover and come to understand why many of the issues whose relevancy to church union is not now clear, must be faced. And, not less important, the dynamic of their actual participation in defining and redefining the ecumenical goal might save the scholars from the danger of endless entanglement in academic discussion of issues that can, both practically and logically, be reserved for consideration in the fellowship of an achieved united church.

The foregoing comments apply to the ecumenical movement in general. They may have semed to take us beyond the scope of this book which has been delimited to the scene of American Protestantism and the achievement of its unity. It can hardly be said that ecumenical activity among American churches is slowed down by preoccupation with remote and unnecessary theological issues. But, as we shall see presently, what has just been said has a bearing on the ecumenical awakening in the United States. Here the spirit of unity has already developed considerable practice in conceptualizing the goal and, indeed, in achieving at least some fragments of it. In the various mergers of denominations that have taken place over the past generation, and in those now in negotiation, the drafting of plans of union has stimulated—one might say educated—the mind of the churches to think about the possible basis upon which the union of the whole of Protestantism might be achieved. This occurs even in the uniting of two denominations where it is found that pragmatic difficulties far outweigh the theological differences.

And when the number of denominations concerned is multiple, as in the case of the so-called Greenwich movement for the union of eight or nine denominations which "recognize one another's ministries and sacraments," it turns out that the plan of union assumes hardly less than ecumenical proportions. That is to say, the union of that many denominations involves most of the problems and principles that would be involved in a union of Protestantism as a whole. Thus every partial achievement of union becomes an example and an earnest of the more ultimate consummation. And it is an interesting discovery that the theological problems involved in these more inclusive mergers are few and, relatively, easily disposed of. This is in large part due to the fact that the undertaking to conceptualize, or think out, the framework of a proposed union is automatically selective of only those matters which are actually relevant to the end in view. A distinction is thus clarified between those things that are necessary for agreement as a preliminary to union, and those that may be left for solution in the fellowship of an achieved united church.

Now, the ecumenical movement on the world scale must not be allowed to inhibit or becloud this more promising procedure by involving the American churches in the endless academic discussion of matters that are not at issue in the union of American Protestantism. While the movement in our country is pendent to the world movement, it is not dependent upon it—certainly not dependent for its own rate of progress. Indeed, the reverse may be true: the world movement is more likely to be dependent for its rate of progress upon the actual progress made in the United States. As the Methodist bishops declared in their episcopal address to the General Conference of 1948: "The union of American Christianity would electrify the world and accelerate the trends toward union in every continent."

The churchmen who return from the great ecumenical conferences and go among the American churches to report and interpret their experience would do well to clarify in their own minds the distinction we are now making. They are easily tempted by the sheer magnitude and the glamour of these great gatherings to unload the excess baggage of world-wide ecumenicity upon our churches, with the implication that the world problem and the problem of American Protestantism are the same. This is not the case. The result is to confuse the awakened mind of the churches and appreciably to quench their ardor for the more realistic possibilities of union by cluttering the way to it with unrealities and unnecessary impediments. Some concern exists lest the World Council Assembly which is to meet in this country in 1954 may, for the same reason, have a repressive rather than an inspiring effect upon the ecumenical spirit now so eager to welcome this great convocation. The leadership of the World Council will be well advised in projecting its program to guard against the possibility that its effect upon the American churches will prove to be disillusioning.

It is inevitable that any earnest mind dedicated to the ecumenical ideal will tend to think with constructive imagination about the *form* of the united church. This tendency should no longer be discouraged or repressed. The ecumenical movement will die of inanition if it postpones too long the opening up of a forthright consideration of the end in view. The only restraint on such free expression should be the admonition to a humility which recognizes that our conceptions of the end in view must be held tentatively, as working hypotheses, subject to change and discard as the total movement of God's Spirit in the ecumenical awakening more fully unveils his own, the only true ideal, for the unity of his church.

There are two ways in which the task of the ecumenical movement can be conceived. They may be stated in the form of two questions. First: How can Christ's people be brought together in spirit and in thought so that they can live together in one ecclesiastical fellowship? This is a proper statement of one aspect of the ecumenical problem. There are real differences and many illusions of difference that must be reconciled before Christ's people, long habituated to their separate existence, can be expected to envisage the possibility of living together with other Christians in the fellowship of the one true church. But, as we have repeated until the reader may have become wearied with its reiteration, the differences that divide Christ's people now are fewer and far less formidable than in any period since the Reformation. Nevertheless, such as they are, they require mutual interpretation and reconciliation.

But this first question needs to be supplemented and balanced by another: How can a united church be conceived in which Christ's people can live together in one ecclesiastical fellowship so that they can *grow together* in spirit, in thought, in action and in solidarity? This second question is no whit less important than the first. The two must be asked and answered together—the one to gain a consenting response to the divine imperative, the other to open the way for the Spirit of God to do for Christ's people what can be done only in a united church.

In this book, the author has undertaken to contribute his answers to both questions, with special consideration to the second, because it has lain too long unasked.

Index

Acts of the Apostles, 150, 177
American Baptist Convention, 10,
146, 148, 149, 170
not congregational, 182
American mind, 34 f., 192
Amsterdam Assembly, xi, 1, 32, 48,
54, 64-65, 66-67, 82, 224
Anabaptists, 20, 21, 131-33, 134,
141, 145-48 passim, 157, 208
209
Anglicanism, Anglicans, 16, 18, 21,
97, 137, 139
and historic episcopate, 161 ff.
See also Episcopalians
Anglo-catholics, 137, 140, 162, 166
Apollos, 95, 96
Apostles' Creed, 95
apostles, the, 110, 111
authority of, 178, 207
apostolic succession, 44, 162-63
See also historic episcopate
Archbishop of Canterbury (1910),
31
See also Temple, William
Arminianism, 149
Asbury, Francis, 152
Assembly of God, 4
Augsburg Confession, 139
authority of Christ
See Lordship of Christ
authority vs. responsibility, 128 f.,
185, 197-98

"Babylonian captivity," 72, 130, 140
Bainton, Roland A., 14
baptism, 44, 52, 55, 57-58, 133, 136,
137, 145
believer's, 147, 153, 191
immersion, 147, 150, 153, 154,
160, 166-74
infant, 147-48, 154, 170-71
scholarship's views of, 148, 173

Baptists, 4, 44, 52, 58, 63, 77, 134,
141, 142, 145, 146-49, 154, 155,
157, 179, 191
and baptism, 168 ff. passim, 173
statistics on, 146
See also American Baptist Convention
Southern Baptist Con-
vention
Barth, Karl, 148
Baxter, Richard, 15
Bible, the
as authority, 7, 201 ff.
character of, 203 f.
false use of, 209
historical criticism of, 210-12
interpretation of, 198, 201 ff.,222
Methodist manuals on, 214
new understanding of, 192, 210-12,
213 ff.
place of, in united church, 204 f.
private interpretation of, 204 ff.
passim, 208, 213
weird interpretations of, 202
See also New Testament
biblicism, 139, 145, 208 ff.
produces 176 ideas of Church of
Christ, 156
bishops, counterpart of, in nonepiscopal denominations, 164-65
Blakemore, W. Barnette, xvi
Blanshard, Paul, 125
Boston, 37
parishes and churches in, 143
Brooks, Phillips, 195
Brunner, Emil, 148
Bucer, Martin, 16
Buddhism, 114
Buffalo, N.Y., 37
Bullinger, Heinrich, 16
Bushnell, Horace, 144

229

Set in Linotype Times Roman
Format by David Rosenberg
Manufactured by The Haddon Craftsmen, Inc.
Published by HARPER & BROTHERS, *New York*